Senses of the Empire

The Roman empire afforded a kaleidoscope of sensations. Through a series of multisensory case studies centred on people, places, buildings and artefacts, and on specific aspects of human behaviour, this volume develops ground-breaking methods and approaches for sensory studies in Roman archaeology and ancient history. Authors explore questions such as: what it felt like, and symbolised, to be showered with saffron at the amphitheatre; why the shape of a dancer's body made him immediately recognisable as a social outcast; how the dramatic gestures, loud noises and unforgettable smells of a funeral would have different meanings for members of the family and for bystanders; and why feeling the weight of a signet ring on his finger contributed to a man's sense of identity. A multisensory approach is taken throughout, with each chapter exploring at least two of the senses of sight, hearing, smell, taste and touch. The contributors' individual approaches vary, reflecting the possibilities and the wide application of sensory studies to the ancient world. Underlying all chapters is a conviction that taking a multisensory approach enriches our understanding of the Roman empire, but also an awareness of the methodological problems encountered when reconstructing past experiences.

Eleanor Betts is Baron Thyssen Lecturer in Classical Studies at the Open University. Her research focuses on the multisensory interrelationships of the human body, material culture and archaeological landscapes. Her particular areas of interest are Roman urbanism and religion in Roman and Iron Age Italy (primarily Picenum, modern Marche), with an emphasis on concepts and use of space.

Senses of the Empire

Multisensory Approaches to Roman Culture

**Edited by
Eleanor Betts**

Routledge
Taylor & Francis Group

LONDON AND NEW YORK

First published 2017
by Routledge
2 Park Square, Milton Park, Abingdon, Oxon OX14 4RN

and by Routledge
605 Third Avenue, New York, NY 10017

First issued in paperback 2021

Routledge is an imprint of the Taylor & Francis Group, an informa business

Publisher's Note
The publisher has gone to great lengths to ensure the quality of this reprint but points out that some imperfections in the original copies may be apparent.

British Library Cataloguing-in-Publication Data
A catalogue record for this book is available from the British Library

Library of Congress Cataloging-in-Publication Data
Names: Betts, Eleanor, 1973– editor of compilation.
Title: Senses of the empire : multisensory approaches to
    Roman culture / edited by Eleanor Betts.
Description: Milton Park, Abingdon, Oxon ; New York, NY :
    Routledge, 2017. | Includes bibliographical references and index.
Identifiers: LCCN 2016040967| ISBN 9781472446299
    (hardback : alkaline paper) | ISBN 9781315608358 (ebook)
Subjects: LCSH: Rome—Antiquities. | Rome—Social life and customs. |
    Senses and sensation—Social aspects—Rome—History. |
    Social archaeology—Rome. | Social archaeology—Methodology.
Classification: LCC DG78 .S37 2017 | DDC 937—dc23
LC record available at https://lccn.loc.gov/2016040967

ISBN 13: 978–1–03–224225–5 (pbk)
ISBN 13: 978–1–4724–4629–9 (hbk)

DOI: 10.4324/9781315608358

Typeset in Bembo
by Apex CoVantage, LLC

Contents

Figures

Tables

Colour Plates

Contributors

Eleanor Betts

Baron Thyssen Lecturer in Classical Studies, The Open University

Eleanor Betts is Lecturer in Classical Studies at the Open University. Her research focuses on the multisensory interrelationships of the human body, material culture and archaeological landscapes. Her particular areas of interest are Roman urbanism and religion in Roman and Iron Age Italy (primarily Picenum, modern Marche), with an emphasis on concepts and use of space.

Jo Day

Lecturer in Greek Archaeology and Curator of the Classical Museum at University College Dublin (UCD)

Jo Day is Lecturer in Greek Archaeology and Curator of the Classical Museum at University College Dublin (UCD). She edited the 2013 volume *Making Senses of the Past: Toward a Sensory Archaeology* (Carbondale). Apart from multisensory approaches to archaeology, her research focuses on early ceramic technology, human–plant interaction in the past and Aegean Bronze Age iconography. She co-directs excavations at the multi-period site of Priniatikos Pyrgos in east Crete.

Thomas J. Derrick

School of Archaeology and Ancient History, University of Leicester

Thomas J. Derrick is interested in Roman perfumes and medicines, and in particular, the role that glass played in their consumption. By extension this interest extends to wider material culture-oriented studies of the Roman world, and particularly to those in provincial contexts. His work on perfume and glass has in turn led to a wider interest in sensory archaeology and the perceptions of these evocative materials in antiquity but also to wider applications, including the role that urban environments played in structuring sensory and social space.

Miko Flohr

Lecturer in Ancient History, Leiden University, the Netherlands

Miko Flohr is Lecturer at the Institute for History of Leiden University, the Netherlands, formerly Assistant Director of the Oxford Roman Economy

Project. His research interests include urbanism, urban economic life and textile production in the Roman world. His monograph, *The World of the Fullo*, was published with OUP in 2013, and he is currently writing a monograph on the history of the Roman *taberna*.

Emma-Jayne Graham
Senior Lecturer in Classical Studies, The Open University

Emma-Jayne Graham is Senior Lecturer in Classical Studies. She is interested in the archaeology of Roman Italy, especially how bodily experiences of the material world gave meaning to people's sense of self and how the treatment of the body and its representation in material culture served as a locus for the construction and expression of that sense of self. This includes work on mortuary practices and the treatment of the human body in death, infant health and death including swaddled infant votives, as well as anatomical votives and the materiality of religion. Recent publications include *Bodies of Evidence: Ancient Anatomical Votives Past, Present and Future* (Routledge 2017).

Valerie M. Hope
Senior Lecturer in Classical Studies, The Open University

Dr Valerie Hope is Senior Lecturer in Classical Studies at the Open University, and has published widely on Roman funerary customs, death rituals and commemoration, including commemorative practices of key social groups such as freed slaves, gladiators and soldiers. She is currently researching mourning rituals in the Roman world and co-editing a book on *War as Spectacle*. Recent publications include *Roman Death: The Dying and the Dead in Ancient Rome* (Continuum 2009) and *Memory and Mourning: Studies on Roman Death* (Oxbow 2011).

Ray Laurence
Professor of Roman History and Archaeology, University of Kent

Ray Laurence is Professor of Roman History and Archaeology at the University of Kent (the UK's European University). His book *Roman Pompeii: Space and Society* (1994) provided the disciplines of Ancient History and Archaeology with a fully developed analysis of streets and public space. Over the last two decades, he has sought to develop the study of space in Roman Italy and has published extensively on the subject. Publications include a second edition of *Roman Pompeii: Space and Society* (2007), *Rome, Ostia, Pompeii: Movement and Space* (2011), *The City in the Roman West* (2011) and *Written Space in the Latin West* (2013). In addition to this, he has worked on the role of movement in the development of the Roman landscape, exemplified by his book *The Roads of Roman Italy: Mobility and Cultural Change* (1999). His work based in Archaeology, History and Classics is characterised by a cross-disciplinary aspect that causes it to be accessible to architects, landscape historians, geographers and urbanists.

Ian J. Marshman
School of Archaeology and Ancient History, University of Leicester, Alumnus
Ian J. Marshman was awarded his PhD by the School of Archaeology and Ancient History at the University of Leicester, and is Education and Outreach Officer at the Heritage Trust of Lincolnshire. His thesis considered the use of signet rings and intaglios in Roman Britain, and their role in the construction and presentation of identity within the province. His research interests focus on Roman material culture, especially small finds and the minor arts, as well as public and community archaeology.

Helen Slaney
University of Roehampton
Helen's primary research interest is the embodied phenomenology of classical reception. She recently completed a British Academy Postdoctoral Fellowship at St Hilda's College, investigating first encounters with ancient material culture in the late eighteenth century. A particular area of interest is how the sense of touch was involved in generating ideas about the ancient world. Helen completed a DPhil on the performance history of Senecan tragedy in 2012. Supported by the Randall McIver JRF, she went on to study the intersection of emotion and human movement in ancient dance. In 2013, Helen set up the TORCH network 'Ancient Dance in Modern Dancers', an interdisciplinary research project established in conjunction with the Institute of Social and Cultural Anthropology.

Jeffrey Veitch
Classical and Archaeological Studies, University of Kent
Jeff completed a PhD in Classical and Archaeological Studies at University of Kent, Canterbury. Prior to starting his PhD, Jeff worked in live sound production before completing Master's degrees in Biblical Studies and Classical Art and Archaeology. His PhD project explored forms of knowledge and experience in urban and religious space at Ostia in the second to fourth century CE.

Alexandre Vincent
Université de Poitiers
Alexandre Vincent is maître de conférences at the Université de Poitiers (France). After a PhD on the social and political role of the professional musicians in the Roman Empire mostly grounded on the analysis of Roman inscriptions, he focused his researches on the social history of sounds and sonic perception in the Roman antiquity. Former member of the Ecole française de Rome, he is currently co-leader of a transperiodical research program called *Soundscapes and Urban Spaces of the Ancient Mediterranean (Egypt, Greece, Rome)*.

Candace Weddle
South Carolina School of the Arts, Anderson University
Candace Weddle is Assistant Professor of Art History at the South Carolina School of the Arts at Anderson University; she received her PhD from the

University of Southern California. Candace's current research explores the sensory experience of ancient life, particularly the sights, sounds, smells, tastes and other sensations experienced by worshipers during ancient Greek and Roman religious ceremonies. Her most recent publications include chapters in the edited volumes *Making Senses of the Past: Toward a Sensory Archaeology* (ed. J. Day, Center for Archaeological Investigations) and *Archaeology and Anthropology: Past, Present and Future* (co-authored with R. Irvine and N. Hanks; ed. D. Shankland, Berg).

Acknowledgements

My warmest thanks go to Michael Greenwood for his unwavering support and infinite patience as this book has taken shape and to all the authors who have contributed with such enthusiasm. I must also extend my gratitude to the anonymous reviewers of the book proposal and manuscript, and to Marc du Rey for his speedy translation; also to Sarah Butler for assistance with the bibliography. Thanks also to Stefania Falchi, Anna Rita Neroni and Elvira Angeloni at the Archivio Fotografico Sede di Ostia Antica for permission for the cover image, which I hope captures the essence of the volume.

The catalyst for this book was a conference held at The Open University Regional Centre in Camden in November 2013. I would like to thank all the speakers for a range of interesting and thought-provoking papers, especially those who wrote chapters which had to be omitted from the volume. Many people remarked afterwards on the congenial nature of the conference and I would like to extend my gratitude to everyone who attended and participated for creating a positive environment and engaging in such stimulating discussions. Especial thanks must of course go to my co-organiser Emma-Jayne Graham, who brought so much to the conference and who remains a valued colleague. Thanks also to Katy Soar, Yvonne Bartley and colleagues in the London Regional Office in Camden who helped everything run smoothly.

This volume is much more than the proceedings of that conference and I am indebted to everyone who has inspired and conspired with me since. In particular, I would like to thank Jeff Veitch for helping me launch the Sensory Studies in Antiquity network (https://sensorystudiesinantiquity.com), Mark Bradley for his invitation to present in his *Smelling Rome* panel at the Classical Association Annual Conference (Bristol), Anna Foka for her invitation to *Challenge the Past/ Diversify the Future* (Gothenburg) and Alessandra Abbattista for co-organising *Multitudo* (Roehampton). I would also like to acknowledge the many colleagues who are taking forward sensory studies in classical studies, as well as those from other disciplines who have inspired us.

Eleanor Betts
The Open University

Introduction

Senses of empire

Eleanor Betts

A sensual revolution or a 'sensory turn'?

The title of this book pays homage to David Howes' *Empire of the Senses*, the introductory volume of Berg's *Sensory Formations* series which, by collecting the senses together, led 'a revolution in the representation and analysis of culture' (Howes, 2005b, p. 14). The year 2015 marked the tenth anniversary of this 'sensual revolution' (Howes, 2005b, p. 1), or 'sensory turn', which has only recently impacted classical studies. Mark Bradley and Shane Butler's emerging *Senses in Antiquity* series and Jerry Toner's (2014a) edited volume *A Cultural History of the Senses in Antiquity* (itself part of Howes and Classen's new series) offer a rich array of literary, philosophical and social historical studies of the senses in the Graeco-Roman world. Taken together these recent and forthcoming volumes demonstrate some of the insights that can be gained if we pay attention to the senses, and they offer a new and exciting direction for all areas of classical studies. The current volume has as its focus the application of new methods and theoretical approaches to the Roman empire's material culture and historical sources, which are influenced by the socio-anthropological approaches in Howes' series and by sensory archaeologies (see for example Tilley, 1994; Hamilton and Whitehouse, 2006; Skeates, 2010; Fahlander and Kjellström, 2010a; Day, 2013a; Hamilakis, 2014).[1] The contributors to this volume follow Howes' premise that:

> Sensory studies involves a cultural approach to the study of the senses and a sensory approach to the study of culture. It challenges the monopoly that the discipline of psychology has long exercised over the study of the senses and sense perception by foregrounding the sociality of sensation. History and anthropology are the foundational disciplines of this field. However, sensory studies also encompasses many other disciplines as scholars from across the humanities and social sciences have, over the past few decades, successively turned their attention on the sensorium.
>
> (Howes, 2013)

Sensory archaeologies have their roots in the philosophies developed by Heidegger and Merleau-Ponty (Husserl is largely forgotten; though see Ihde, 2007, pp. 17–24), and despite its shortcomings Christopher Tilley's *A*

Phenomenology of Landscape inspired a generation of archaeologists, notably pre-historians, to bring studies of human experience into their work:[2]

> The key issue in any phenomenological approach is the manner in which people *experience* and *understand* the world. Phenomenology involves the *understanding* and *description* of things as they are experienced by a subject. It is about the relationship between Being and Being-in-the-world. Being-in-the-world resides in a process of objectification in which people objectify the world by setting themselves apart from it. This results in the creation of a gap, a distance in space. To be human is both to create this distance between the self and that which is beyond and to attempt to bridge this distance through a variety of means – through *perception* (seeing, hearing, touching), *bodily actions* and *movements*, and *intentionality, emotion* and *awareness* residing in systems of belief and decision-making, remembrance and evaluation.
>
> (Tilley, 1994, pp. 11–12; my emphasis)

Multisensory phenomenological approaches have been undertaken in fieldwork projects and in (re)interpretation of existing sites and material (see for example Whitehouse, 2001; Betts, 2003; Hamilton and Whitehouse, 2006, forthcoming; Till, 2015). Catalysed by Howes' *Sensory Formations* series, associated CONSERT project and the Centre for Sensory Studies, the last decade has seen a sea change, with phenomenological approaches in archaeology becoming more refined and linked to other theoretical models which have developed concurrently. Amongst these are 'embodiment', which 'describes the manner in which people experience the world through their bodies, a world of which they are always a part, and points us in the direction of the sensory qualities of places and things' (Robb and Harris, 2013, p. 17), and 'archaeologies of the senses' (Hamilakis, 2011). These are broad, but often interrelated, approaches which recognise the diversity of human bodies and experiences, collective as well as individual identities, and the significance of the body in habituated spaces (often taking an insider rather than an outsider perspective) (see for example Hamilakis, Pluciennik and Tarlow, 2002; Borić and Robb, 2008; Skeates, 2010; Fahlander and Kjellström, 2010b; Hamilakis, 2011, 2013, 2014; Robb and Harris, 2013, p. 17 – all with further bibliography). At the same time, the 'importance of attending to the multiple sensory dimensions of objects, architectures and landscapes is quickly becoming a central tenet of material culture theory' (Howes, 2006, p. 161). The multisensory agency, not only of the human body but also of animals, objects, architecture, spaces, places and landscapes, is being recognised and explored (see for example Ingold, 2000, p. 195; Gosden, 2005; Knappett, 2005; Hoskins, 2006). It has taken twenty years for all these ideas and approaches to coalesce. Some aspects of this thriving field have been tied directly into a sensory agenda, whilst others are linked to broader debates, particularly those concerned with the body as the locus of identity, experience and memory, and the meaning of space and place, which has a particular focus on movement (kinaesthesia).

Sensory archaeologies, and sensory studies more generally, are not a theoretical approach, nor a subfield of archaeology or ancient history, but a way of broadening our perspective on the past by recognising that by focusing on the visual we have neglected a vast body of data and interpretative tools for understanding ancient societies (Zardini, 2005, p. 22; Hamilakis, 2011, p. 220, 2013, p. 409, 2014, p. 10). Fahlander and Kjellström note that '[t]here is no "ready-made" theory and method available especially designated for an "archaeology of the senses". Undoubtedly, such an apparatus would be a strange creation of little use' (2010b, p. 10). Consequently, the chapters in this volume are each unique in the way that their authors explore the impact that reconstructing sensory experience has on our perceptions of life in the Roman empire.

The rule of three: Person–object–place

To date the focus of sensory studies within classical studies has been on human perception of sensory stimuli and, like Alexandre Vincent, I suggest that this is an unnecessary limitation of the approaches it is possible to take. Sensory Roman histories and archaeologies must include the evidence afforded by textual sources, material culture and embodied spaces, ideally beginning with the recording of sensory data through experimentation (whether that is in the field or via modelling) in order to understand the affordances of the material (on affordances, see Gibson, 1986; Knappett, 2004, 2005). Only then can the personal experience and cultural meaning of these data be explored.

Where should we begin an analysis of the impact of sensory experience on everyday life and extraordinary events in the Roman empire? A person, object or place each makes a suitable starting point, but all three interrelate and impact sensorially on one another to construct what Hamilakis refers to as a 'sensorial assemblage' (2014, pp. 126–8). One element is the human body: here the person is the perceiver of sensory stimuli. Whether or not we accept Merleau-Ponty's concept of the physiological body as the 'universal measurement' (1968, p. 268), there are sufficient parallels between the modern and Roman body to investigate how particular sensory stimuli may have been physiologically, and perhaps emotionally, perceived, something which cognitive neuroscience may enable us to explore further. Physiological functions operated the same way in ancient bodies as they do in ourselves, but the cultural context in which they were activated determined how they were experienced. This premise is at the heart of phenomenology and continues to be valid in sensory archaeologies (Tilley, 2010, p. 487; Hamilakis, 2013, p. 410). Cultural discrepancies will inevitably make it impossible to appreciate fully how people in the past perceived their sensory experiences (see also Hamilakis, 2011, 2013, 2014; Day, 2013b, p. 6), but physiological commonality is a touchstone to the past. As Korsmeyer (2005, p. 3) puts it:

> [A]ll sense experience occurs within a perceiving subject, and we know from experience that not all people see or hear or feel or smell exactly alike (although it is important not to exaggerate differences either; if we did not on the whole share sensory worlds that overlap to some extent, life would be constant blundering).

This approach therefore comes with significant caveats which must be taken into consideration: (i) all bodies are subtly different according to gender, age, physical fitness and so forth; (ii) cultural specificity makes the stimuli and the experience different at both an individual and community level (Howes and Classen, 2014, pp. 1–14); and (iii) sensory stimuli prompt and produce memories. It is possible to recover glimpses of memories from the authors of Roman literature and epigraphy, but for the most part we rarely know exactly how someone emotionally experienced a particular sensory phenomenon, nor the meaning it had for them. If we follow Merleau-Ponty's premise we find that it is possible to reconstruct physiological perceptions of sensory stimuli, and are able then to hypothesise some particular individual and collective emotional, intellectual and social responses to them. As Candace Weddle and Valerie Hope show in their chapters, literary and visual sources give us some insight into cultural perceptions and can contribute to our piecing together of certain sensorial assemblages. In pursuing these lines of enquiry it is vital to pay attention to the nuances of sensory perception and experience created by different bodies, cultural norms and memory.

Emma-Jayne Graham notes in the introduction to her chapter that 'a range of sometimes conflicting sensory affordances and embodied memories can be associated with any artefact' and Jo Day considers how the smell of saffron might have prompted memories. Ian Marshman explores the idea that a signet ring acted as a mnemonic for a person and their reputation (a 'sensory artefact' because the object was an extension of the person as a result of its sensory properties and its symbolic meaning; Betts, this volume). Graham takes the idea of multisensoriality a stage further, citing David Howes' concept of multi-directionality and exploring the *conflicting* sensory data that material culture, in this case terracotta votives of swaddled infants, can produce in the perceiver. Each of these examples illustrates that whilst memories cannot be recaptured they leave material traces and echoes which can aid our interpretation of the sensorial relationship between human perceivers and the objects with which they interact, as Hamilakis puts it, 'creating complex and rather messy sensory stratigraphies' (2013, p. 413).

The second element is the emitter of sensory data, which may be an animate or inanimate object and includes humans, animals and material culture, all of which have the capacity to stimulate the senses of the human perceiver. We might add to this the notion that the human body can be objectified, as in the case of the mutable body of a *pantomimos* (Slaney, this volume). Objects and architecture have agency, acting upon and influencing human perception, experience, behaviour and memory, since they have particular, measurable physical properties (Gosden, 2005; Knappett, 2005; Hoskins, 2006). The function of an object does not necessarily follow its form, but form provides some empirical data. For example, a Dressel 20 amphora has a quantifiable weight, shape, size, capacity, texture and colour. Each of these aspects can be explored in order to understand something about the way the amphora could be picked up, transported, stored and used. If we know what was kept in it (olive oil in this example) we can rediscover, and even replicate, the tastes, smells, sounds, visual and haptic affordances which were associated with its use, which can in turn inform us about its function in commercial and everyday life. This combination of the material and sensory affordances of an object may be termed a 'sensory artefact' (Betts). If we utilise scientific approaches in our analyses we can garner quantitative data such as ascertaining contents from residue analysis or provenance via petrography. The acoustic, haptic, visual and gusto-olfactory properties of an object and its contents (where applicable) can be measured empirically, or else imagined, enabling us to draw a little closer to understanding the meaning or significance it had when in use. The limitations of this approach are: (i) absence of evidence of residues, which may be a result of a lack of sufficient data or analysis, either due to the early excavation date of the object or insufficient funds to carry out the analysis; (ii) removal of the object from its context (often along with poor recording of that context); and (iii) lack of cultural context.

Two of the chapters in this book explore the embodied experience of interacting with a specific type of artefact (signet rings and swaddled baby *ex-votos*). Ian Marshman considers a signet ring as both a personal object worn upon the body and also a very public symbol of its wearer's status, entwined with their identity and sense of self. He considers how a sensory approach to studying these objects can offer a deeper understanding of their function in society, and what they meant to the individuals who owned them. For instance, gemstones were believed to possess different magical properties depending on their colour and translucency. The gleam of precious metals and the sparkle of different gemstones would also have had an important role in how visible they were when worn. Beyond vision, we can consider the different haptic sensations of wearing an iron or a gold ring, and even taste played a part in the use of these objects. Their role in sealing meant that signet rings also had the ability to extend a wearer's authority and sense of self beyond the reaches of their senses, wherever they impressed their seal in the world around them. Emma-Jayne Graham presents a case study of the votives of newborn infants which were dedicated at sanctuaries in central Italy during the Roman Republic and explores what the implications might be when the senses do not agree with one another, or when individual senses offer internally conflicting information. Based on her first-hand experience of holding swaddled baby *ex-votos* when she was granted museum access to them, she considers how sensory dissonance may have contributed to the attribution of multiple possible meanings to an object, and the consequences for the activities in which these sensorially ambiguous types of object were implicated (see also Foster, 2013, pp. 372–5).

For these two authors in particular it is the interaction between the human body and artefact that is key; and their focus is very much on possible variables in the sensory perceptions an individual may have had when interacting with a particular object. The agency of the artefact is an underlying thread in their analyses and is present also in the chapters by Eleanor Betts, Miko Flohr, Jeffrey Veitch, Thomas Derrick and Alexandre Vincent, who focus on artefacts and architecture as emitters of measurable sensory data, the stimuli which cause sensory experience in the human body. Material has specific properties which produce measurable physical effects, and many of these properties can be retrieved from ancient contexts. If we see material culture as producers of sensory data we can begin to collect and collate those data in a meaningful way and in so doing gain some insight into the affectiveness of artefacts, assemblages and architecture.

Like objects, places have physical properties which may be measured and recorded, so the third element is to focus on a place and movement around the spaces which make that place meaningful, as exemplified in the chapters by Ray Laurence, Eleanor Betts, Miko Flohr, Jeffrey Veitch and Thomas Derrick. The senses have been present in spatial studies for some time (see for example Howes, 2005a; Lefebvre, 2014) and one premise of these chapters is that each of the senses – or different sensory stimuli and responses to them – affects the way that spaces and places are perceived. Like people and objects, places are embodied and have agency. The visual cues, textures and other haptic affordances, sounds, smells and tastes (whether permanent or transient) present in spaces help to characterise them as places, and consequently give them affective properties, many of which can be reconstructed for the Roman world (see also Betts, 2011). This is with the caveat that they have been manipulated over time (reconstructed elements of Rome, Ostia and Pompeii are cases in point). Eleanor Betts, Miko Flohr, Jeffrey Veitch and Thomas Derrick consider the relationship between internal and external spaces, their analyses being pertinent for the exploration of insider/outsider, place/space, active participation/casual observation perspectives in their selected examples of shops and workshops on the streets of Rome, Pompeii and Ostia, and the fort of Vindolanda. Betts takes a multisensory approach, whilst Flohr focuses predominantly on kinaesthesia and the effects of light, but also considers sound and smell; Derrick's study is of a smellscape, Veitch's sound. These are important studies because they draw attention to the different perspectives and experiences engendered by places as emitters of sensory data.

Thomas Derrick bases his discussion on the material evidence from Vindolanda, taking as his case study an archaeologically rich and well recorded site, which provides him with a strong data set with which to analyse the site's olfactory geography, whilst noting that imagination plays a part in any archaeologist's interpretation of the past and attempts to reconstruct human activity at the site. He argues that odours – savoury, fragrant, malodorous or neutral – would have been a by-product of many of the activities that occurred in Roman forts. The positioning of certain members of the military community within this smellscape would have informed the way in which they saw themselves and others saw them. Derrick argues that it is no coincidence that the *praetorium* was often located centrally, away from many of the sources of malodour, or that the most cramped accommodation within the fort (and the extramural *vicus*) was often located near the smoke of the bathhouse, the bread ovens and the refuse dumps. He presents evidence for a strong smellscape which reflected the business of everyday life at the fort.

Miko Flohr uses a series of focused case studies of *fullonicae* in Ostia and Pompeii to explore the sensory affordances of those locales and the people and material culture within them. He considers the perspectives of those engaged in the fulling industry, its clients and passers-by, taking both an insider and outsider point of view and evaluating the literary, visual and material evidence accordingly. The chapter examines evidence for the sensory impact of the fulling process in each of its key phases, the ways in which the fulleries' spatial layout conditioned the perceptions of what was going on in these workshops and, briefly, explores the sensescape of the *fullonicae* in relation to other industries in Ostia and Pompeii. Jeffrey Veitch also explores insider/outsider perspectives, with specific reference to the soundscape, or aural architecture, of part of the *cardo maximus* in Ostia. Beginning with the spatial context of a room's measurements, construction and decoration, he applies the physics of sound to discrete architectural spaces and examines the production and physiological perception of sounds in this second-century CE built environment. Following Amphoux (2001), he explores the temporal nature of soundscapes and the way in which the urban soundscape of Ostia reflected the everyday rhythms of the city. Ray Laurence takes a different approach to Roman soundscapes, combining a study of literary sources with an autoethnographical approach so as to create a series of real and imagined soundscapes in the city of Rome and its environs. Like Veitch, he places sounds in their spatial contexts, but in this case the focus is on literary evidence rather than acoustic architecture.

Eleanor Betts also combines a study of literature, material culture and architectural space to present a methodology for the reconstruction of multisensory landscapes, choosing first century CE Rome as her case study. She achieves this via an exploration of sensory artefacts, which are embodied people, objects and places whose material and sensory affordances combine into a whole and which have multivalency, varying according to the temporal and spatial conditions in which they existed and the individual(s) who experienced them. An individual's response to a sensory artefact would be affected by several factors, including their cultural context, degree of sensory sensitivity or deprivation (perhaps caused by disability or ageing), the extent to which s/he had normalised the artefact's sensory stimuli and seasonal variation.

Approaches to Roman sensory studies

Recapturing sensory data is difficult since '[t]he senses seldom leave a direct imprint in the archaeological record and more typically must be implicitly inferred' (Fahlander and Kjellström, 2010b, p. 6), but the Roman empire has left us with a wealth of evidence with which to infer that data. The qualitative and quantitative both have places in this volume. Most of the contributors take an embodied and qualitative approach, considering what it might have been like to experience specific events (Hope, Weddle, Slaney, Day) or to interact with particular objects (Graham, Marshman, Vincent), buildings (Flohr) and landscapes (Laurence, Betts, Derrick). These contributions contrast with the quantitative methodological approaches which can be taken, as illustrated by Jeffrey Veitch. In both qualitative discourses and quantitative analyses, the evidence from textual and visual sources can be combined with archaeology to construct multisensory interpretations of particular aspects of Roman life. Each of the authors of this volume does this, though their particular datasets, fields of study and approaches vary widely.

Ray Laurence brings together a range of textual sources to demonstrate the richness of Roman literature as a database from which to extract references to, and descriptions of, sound, whilst highlighting the subjective nature (and therefore the inherent limitations) of our sources. Alexandre Vincent takes this much further, exploring both the problems and some solutions that we must acknowledge when engaging in sensory studies of past cultures. He uses the example of the *tuba* to demonstrate how text mining can be used in combination with the reconstruction of material artefacts in order to access information about the emission and perception of Roman sounds. Vincent also rightly emphasises the importance of context – not just collocations within the texts, but also the socio-cultural context of the authors of those texts and of the material culture which is (the source of the sounds) being examined. In so doing he presents a methodology which can be adapted for a wide range of sensory studies for Roman and other literary cultures, a methodology which encourages us to question what particular sensory data meant in their specific socio-cultural, or individual, contexts. Jeffrey Veitch presents a lucid explanation of the physics of sound, whilst Helen Slaney invites her readers to use their own kinaesthetic expression to better understand her methods and argument, at the same time reminding us that scrutiny and interpretation of material culture and literary sources are vital to her study.

The aims of this volume are twofold: to begin a collaboration in which scholars of the Roman world develop methodologies for sensory studies; and to demonstrate a variety of approaches which can be taken by classical archaeologists and ancient historians who wish to incorporate sensory studies into their research, following Howes' concept of 'intersensoriality, that is the multi-directional interaction of the senses and of sensory ideologies, whether considered in relation to an individual, a society, or a work' (2005b, p. 9). The authors in this volume apply multisensory approaches to their existing areas of expertise, illustrating Hamilakis' premise that sensory studies (in archaeology) should be part of existing research methods and theoretical approaches rather than being a separate subfield (2014, p. 10). The best illustrations of this are the chapters by Valerie Hope and Miko Flohr, who have introduced a multi-sensory dimension to their respective work on Roman mourning and *fullonicae*, but each author demonstrates in a number of quite different and unique ways how taking a multisensory approach can enrich our understanding of specific aspects of, and places in, the Roman empire. In so doing, they raise – and often answer – new research questions, taking forward not only their own research but the entire discipline. There are some chapters which lean more towards ancient history (Laurence, Betts, Hope, Weddle, Vincent, Slaney, Day), others towards archaeology (Flohr, Veitch, Derrick, Graham, Marshman), but one premise of the book – and a reason for its broad remit of the Roman empire – is that textual and material evidence, in all their forms, are rich sources of data for examining (and potentially for recreating) ancient Roman sensory experience.

Cutting edge methodologies and approaches for undertaking sensory studies of the past are presented in most chapters, and these could also be applied to non-Roman contexts. Alexandre Vincent and Jeffrey Veitch each present new and distinct methodologies for studying ancient sounds and soundscapes. Thomas Derrick explores how smellscapes can be tentatively recreated by combining the data from architectural spaces and places with material culture and environmental evidence, whilst Helen Slaney outlines, and invites you to engage with, kinaesthetic experiences of the pantomime dancers of the Roman theatre. These authors' methodologies illustrate the potential that rigorous sensory studies can have for ancient historians and archaeologists. Emma-Jayne Graham, Ian Marshman and Eleanor Betts evaluate the theories which have developed in relation to sensory studies within and outside the discipline of Roman archaeology, and illustrate how these theoretical frameworks can be developed and applied to specific case studies (terracotta *ex-votos*, signet rings and the streets of Rome). In so doing, they illustrate that it is possible – and indeed advantageous – to develop new theoretical and methodological approaches to sensory studies, which have a wider application than the Roman world. Embodiment and agency (of humans, objects and places) are at the heart of these approaches, and are also present in the less theory-driven chapters.

Alexandre Vincent's premise is that sensory studies of the ancient world must be underpinned by a firm methodology. He argues that the starting point of data collection should be text-based, this lexicographical data then being combined with analysis of material culture. His chapter sets out a methodology for gathering and contextualising the occurrences of Latin words related to sound, such as *strepitus*, *fragor* and *silentium*, in order to gain a better understanding of which words were used by the Romans to describe the specific sounds of the *tuba* and what each sound could have meant for them, using the case study of the Roman *tuba* from Neuilly-en Sullias to test the methodology. He compares the sounds of the replica *tuba* against the lexicographical database to ascertain which words relate to specific sounds and makes every effort to avoid anachronism.

Miko Flohr, Valerie Hope, Candace Weddle and Jo Day demonstrate that incorporating sensory data can enrich specific case studies and lead to a new understanding of sometimes familiar aspects of life in the Roman world. Their subjects are the insider and outside experiences of the *fullonicae* of Ostia and Pompeii, the role of the senses in Roman mourning, the haptic and gustatory experience of animal sacrifice, and the use of saffron in the theatre and amphitheatre. These four authors draw on a range of evidence including literature, epigraphy, reliefs, wall paintings and architecture, demonstrating the richness of our sources of sensory data and the ways that they can be used together to reconstruct a multisensory experience of particular places and events. The result is a more nuanced understanding of the subjects in question, and in each case taking a multisensory approach reveals some of the misconceptions which prevail in Roman scholarship. For example, Miko Flohr argues that fullers and *fullonicae* did not reek of urine, contradicting even the most recent publications on that subject (Aldrete, 2014, p. 53; Toner, 2014b, p. 6; Koloski-Ostrow, 2015, pp. 101–3; Bradley, 2015b, pp. 140–1). He disproves the hypothesis that *fullonicae* were characterised by bad smells, demonstrating the new understanding of the Roman empire that sensory studies can provide, even to specialists on a topic such as Flohr himself.

Valerie Hope's thorough multisensory analysis brings to light the reversal of roles between the living and the dead during the period of mourning following a death (contrast Potter, 2014, pp. 36–44). In the ancient world grief was written onto the bodies of the bereaved. Tear-stained cheeks, dishevelled hair, bloodied breasts and dark clothing transformed the body to give physical representation to the altered emotional state and societal position of the mourner. Hope explores these mourning behaviours, giving special focus to the senses of the bereaved and those who came into contact with them. Funeral rituals were carefully structured performances involving dramatic gestures, loud noises and unforgettable smells. Hope addresses questions such as the extent to which it is possible to recreate the physical, emotional and sensory experiences of the mourners, and how the mourning performance affected the senses of others who were not directly bereaved.

Jo Day brings her expertise in the study of saffron in the ancient world to a topic familiar to any student of the Roman empire: the theatre and amphitheatre. The outcome of her analysis of the synaesthetic relationship between the odour and colour of saffron (and other substances used in acts of public display) is a new perspective which opens further avenues for research into the embodied experience of the Roman spectacle. She argues that, despite the ephemeral nature of smells, it is possible to draw on a vast body of material, both archaeological and textual, that can help make sense of Roman production and consumption of perfumed substances. Her chapter explores the roles of fragrant environments as sensory indicators of munificence and of access to costly spices (compare Wallace-Hadrill, 2014, pp. 70–5). Drawing on the link between olfaction and memory she suggests that the use of perfumes in the theatre and amphitheatre created somatic memories for the participants which connected with other aspects of elite life and practices (compare Betts, this volume).

Candace Weddle's main focus is on two senses which are largely neglected in the study of Graeco-Roman religion: touch and taste (though see Graham, this volume). The result is a closer scrutiny of the experience of sacrifice and spectacle, both a type of performance and both embodying elite power and social codes. Weddle argues that sacrificial rituals were a visceral, aggressively multisensory and vitally important aspect of ancient life which have long been of interest to scholars of Graeco-Roman religion. Using historical and philosophical texts, as well as artworks depicting moments of the sacrificial process, it is shown that the act of touching was carefully controlled at all stages of the proceedings, from preparation of victims to examination of entrails. Improper touch, whether intentional or accidental, could result in negative ritual consequences. The primacy of touch as an essential feature of ritual extended also to the post-sacrificial feasts, where people and deities were understood to partake in a communal meal. At the banqueting table touch and taste reminded worshippers that their physical bodies distinguished them from the immortal gods.

Something these four chapters highlight is the part *all* of the senses played in reinforcing social boundaries, as well as defining public and private spaces and behaviours. The concept of synaesthesia is prevalent in recent publications on the senses (Butler and Purves, 2013; Hamilakis, 2013, p. 413; Toner, 2014b, p. 3), drawing attention to the Graeco-Roman perception of a blurring of the senses and culturally specific sensory perceptions, all of which are in some way haptic.

Where individual senses are the primary focus (Laurence, Veitch, Derrick, Vincent and Slaney), the chapters are largely methodological, each author presenting methods for incorporating specific sensory data into studies of the Roman empire, notably sound (Laurence, Veitch, Vincent), smell (Derrick) and kinaesthesia (Slaney). The significance of haptic space underlies each of these five chapters and they should therefore not be read purely as studies of individual senses. For example, Helen Slaney takes the example of the popular imperial Roman performance genre *tragoedia saltata* to argue that in terms of processing information about one's surrounding environment the brain uses a system of kinaesthetic senses that perceive and regulate motion. These include proprioception, or feedback from the body's interior; the vestibular sense, or balance; and the multisensory assessment of proximity and spatial relationships (Paterson, 2007). Broadly, this category of senses may be defined as haptic, as they are associated with the palpable placement of the body in space, but as this body travels and its coordinates constantly change, their interplay forms an important and often overlooked subset of human experience. One activity which expresses this interplay with particular vitality is dance. Using the terms applied by ancient authors to the choreography of pantomime, Slaney proves that it is possible to develop an impression of its movement vocabulary, and consider how these movements depend upon balance, proximity and kinaesthesia for their execution and effect.

As an overarching principle, this book is structured so as to avoid privileging any one sense over another. The aim is to use the points of similarity to emphasise the diversity of approaches that can be taken in sensory studies. For example, whilst they have been deliberately separated in the organisation of the volume, treating the three chapters on sound (Laurence, Veitch, Vincent) as a suite illustrates particularly well the different directions sensory histories and archaeologies can take, at the same time highlighting the potential benefits of collaboration (as noted by Alexandre Vincent in his chapter). These three authors employ quite different methods, each of them increasing our knowledge and understanding of Roman sounds and soundscapes. Sensory studies can be carried out in various ways, some of which are mutually exclusive and many of which have the potential to be combined.

With its new approaches to a wide range of topics this volume offers an example of how sensory studies can enrich our understanding of the Roman empire, whilst aiming to develop an awareness of the methodological problems encountered when attempting to recover the affectiveness of sensation for culturally and temporally distant people. The Roman empire afforded a kaleidoscope of sensations which interacted and collided with one another. When we begin to consider how the whole sensorium affected human experience, behaviour and memory, we learn to access those sensations and use them to better understand the human past.

Notes

1 Jo Day provides an excellent summary of the development of sensory studies in archaeology in the introduction to her edited volume (2013b; see also Fahlander and Kjellström, 2010b, pp. 1–7).
2 For a concise overview of phenomenology see Thomas, 2006, pp. 43–50. For critique and discussion of Tilley, see Brück, 1998; Day, 2013b, p. 7.

1   The sounds of the city

From noise to silence in ancient Rome

Ray Laurence

We may be able to walk down a Roman street, observe wheel-ruts in the road-way and visually comprehend the parts of buildings that no longer survive; but what would that street have sounded like? Most sensory experiences of the past are lost to us and recreating them tends to be beyond the imagination or our comprehension of Roman space. As a result, the surviving visual remains have always been the focus of attention and vision has become the dominant sense in the study of space in the Roman city. This situation causes our understand-ing of Roman urban space to be, at present, limited and not embracing all the multisensory possibilities of the streets and other public spaces, a situation which several chapters in this volume seek to address (see also Betts, 2011). This chapter takes a step towards a better understanding of the contrasting soundscapes of ancient Rome. Whilst the chapter includes subjective, qualitative descriptions of my personal experiences, the primary approach taken is to identify sounds from a selection of Latin literature and to give a flavour of the extent to which they can contribute to the texture of the cultural soundscape of Rome. In so doing, the chapter aims to draw attention to the richness of sound data that can be obtained from Latin literature and to use it to create a series of vignettes of real and imagined soundscapes in the city of Rome and its environs.

Why sound?

Sound is deliberately privileged in this study to draw out an area of investiga-tion that, when focused on the perceiver rather than the emitter of sound, is associated with subjective rather than objective data (Bull and Back, 2003; see also Vincent, this volume; contrast Veitch, this volume). Sound is chosen for the reason that it adds a dimension to the visual or visualisation of the past. The intention of the chapter is to set out how sound can be used to better under-stand the identities of places within the city of Rome (Smith, 2007, p. 45) whilst recognising that the variation in the intensity of sound from 'disruptive' noise to silence created acoustically textured spaces (Ihde, 2003). The control of this texture was something the elite could architecturally manage in their villas (see Pliny *Letters* 2.17), but the city of Rome presented them with an encounter of sound that was uncontrollable. The noise of slaves at a Saturnalia dinner or of the plebs in the city of Rome was seen by the elite as a negative aspect of their social world, but the very existence of these phenomena help characterise the ancient Roman soundscape. Mapping the representations of sound in literature onto the spaces of ancient Rome allows us to contemplate that city as an acoustic map (Bull and Back, 2003, pp. 12–14 for the concept). The fragmentary nature of our data means that our acoustic map of ancient Rome will not be as comprehensive as that of Bruce Smith (1999) for early modern London, but we still need to consider the intersection of ambient sound, speech and the place of music in the city (see Smith, 2003). However unsatisfactory our evidence for auditory spaces and places in ancient Rome, we need to at least think through how the city may have sounded. I would suggest that this approach is no different from visualisation, such as that found in *Rome Reborn* (Frischer, 2013), which seeks to represent urban environments from the past, including parts of it for which no evidence actually survives. Both visualisation and sound-ification seek to do the same thing; through fragmentary evidence they seek to create knowledge of the experience of the past. At present, we can only look forward to the full development of intersensoriality, in which all the senses can be re-joined to consider how it was to be human in the city of Rome (see Howes, 2005b, pp. 7–12).

Sound is combined in this chapter with another aspect of sensory experience, the kinaesthesia of movement, which is itself an element of haptic experience. This builds on an area of investigation driven forward by David Newsome, where movement is a means to reconceptualise the relationship between people and monuments (Newsome, 2009; papers in Laurence and Newsome, 2011). The combination is a counter to the curation of the visual representation of the past that becomes fixed and is static (Favro, 2014, p. 85). If the city is to be moved through, how do we enrich that movement with an understanding of the body's experience of space and the sensory perception of urbanism that is presented as dirty, smelly, noisy and/or crowded in Latin literature. It is notable that the visual experience of the city is often omitted in the subjective realism of an author such as Martial, who creates urban experiences through the bodily perception of his literary persona. The actual haptic experience of the city was as ephemeral and fleeting as movement. Yet, it would seem from Eleanor Betts' observations on sound in the Forum Romanum that sound can be recoverable through the study of texts linked to the study or experience of sound within the standing remains of archaeological sites (Betts, 2011, pp. 126–9), alongside the representation of crowds in sculpture.

Lost in Roman space

Academic writing on the city of Rome can travel in a number of directions. Most people's knowledge of Rome begins with seven hills and a concept of geographical space based on area; whereas in literature the deployment of the phrase 'the Seven Hills' could mean all of Rome or just the city of Rome as a place (Vout, 2007). Area in any case does not provide us with an experience of the city, which can only be gained through knowledge of routes and spaces. For example, the Via Lata, 'the wide street', a descriptive nomenclature that identifies the other streets as narrower, provides a greater conception of urbanism than knowledge of the distinction of the Palatine from the Aventine, from the Esquiline and so on. Naming, mapping or describing an urban element does not create an urban history for Rome, but instead prevents a history of urbanism from going beyond the knowledge listed alphabetically in a topographical dictionary, or within the linguistic frame of a textual source. The limits to scholarly endeavour need to be understood, so that we may shift forward towards a different academic knowledge base for understanding the Roman city.

Scholars tend to produce a city of Rome that is so situated in Roman history that the history of urbanism is lost on the way and this is particularly true of the non-visual perception of the city. Instead, the structure of this form of writing of the city plays up contact with the Hellenistic cultures of the East through conquest, the transition from Republic to Empire, the shift to Christianity, but there is little actual urban experience here (see, for example, Dyson, 2010, appropriately subtitled 'A Living Portrait'). The visual is emphasised in art history, as seen in Paul Zanker's *The Power of Images in the Age of Augustus*, which combines the textual with the visual representations of monuments and archaeological remains (Zanker, 1988). Alternatively, architectural historians (for example Sear, 2006) tend to collect building types together, such as theatres or circuses or temples and so on, and to write a history of buildings that seem to come into existence and have their form described. These stories of buildings seldom place the structure back into space. To give one example, few students can connect the building of the Theatre of Marcellus with the major access route into the city of Rome associated with the urban extension of the city into Region XIV. The theatre is deliberately placed and becomes a monument as prominent as the future Colosseum was for the Flavian emperors, or the Mausoleum of Augustus was for those entering Rome from the North. Interestingly, Diane Favro had to use the imaginary realism of an adult male leading a child through Strabo's *Geography* (5.3.7–9) to create a sense of the changes associated with the long reign of Augustus to 14 CE (Favro, 1996, pp. 252–80). Her work is much about the image of the city, with the visual perception of, or gaze on, these monuments to the fore. Meanwhile, Simon Malmberg has pioneered the thick description of the urban transect of ancient Rome in his presentation of the urban section of the Via Tiburtina (Malmberg, 2009). Innovators such as Favro and Malmberg are seeking to break the mould that is conditioned by past historiographical and topographical traditions.

Running right through both archaeological topography and the study of Rome in ancient literature is a preoccupation with mapping or visualising texts to comprehend literary journeys across the city; notice the play on sights in Larmour and Spencer's *Sites of Rome* (2007, pp. 6–7). The emphasis on the view of a landscape, rather than on an experience of a landscape, can even cause a waterfall at Tivoli to be described visually, and for its loud soundscape to become lost (Spencer, 2010, p. 108; description of Figure 7). Anyone residing in a hotel next to such a waterfall at Tivoli will quickly discover the soundscape of their balcony overlooking the waterfall becomes intolerably loud after less than five minutes. This real, subjective example demonstrates how our access to sound is experiential and that a waterfall can have no sound if considered from the view of a photograph or a painting reproduced in a book. The link between my experience of the waterfall today and that of the waterfall in antiquity is not precise: changes in the landscape and built environment mean that we cannot actually know that the volume of the sound was the same, and even if it was, it may have been perceived differently. In consequence, we can only begin to hint at the possibilities of reconstructing Roman sound.

The role of sound and, in particular, song and music in the lives of the Roman plebs has been discussed by Nicholas Horsfall in a pioneering study that documented the presence of these phenomena in the city (Horsfall, 2003; also Wiseman, 2014, p. 51). What is far more tricky is for us to associate music with a place or a time in which a place might be transformed by music in the manner of public buildings today inhabited by the music of cultural events (Bull and Back, 2003, pp. 12–14; Filmer, 2003; Kahn, 2003). We can know that Romans danced and played instruments, as well as listening as an audience to musicians, but we do not know where they practised or created the sounds of a novice learning a musical instrument for the first time. The experience of music was recognised as a phenomenon that caused a reaction amongst an audience, such as leading reclining diners to dance (Plutarch *Moralia* 705E–F). Such bodily expression, like many others, was regarded as connected to drunkenness (Cicero *Pro Murena* 13). There was also a sense that sounds had their place and some places in the city should be kept free of some sounds. Singing and dancing in the Forum was seen by Cicero as at odds with civilised behaviour (*De Officiis* 1.145, 3.93); it was also the place in which Julia the daughter of Augustus held her infamous party in 2 BCE (Dio Cassius 55.11.12–16).

Soundscapes in texts

In Latin literature noise was associated mainly with two aspects of citizenship: warfare, and the political processes associated with the Forum and assemblies of the people. The Forum Romanum was a place with a rich acoustic texture (Betts, 2011, pp. 126–9), often associated with noise and the words of anger (Cicero *For Archias* 6 (*strepitus*)), and just stopping short of stone throwing and violence (Livy 2.29). During a speech, however, the Forum would be associated with the silence of the Roman people listening (Cicero *For Rabirius* 6; compare Horace *Art of Poetry* 73). There was a requirement for silence, so its absence was a sign of the resistance of the people to the power of magistrates (Livy 8.33, 3.49). The crowd was seen by Livy to have been able to determine a particular sound to be associated with lictors clearing a way for a magistrate (Livy 8.33). Horace could imagine the loudest noise in the Forum to be three funerals with trumpets and some two hundred carriages (Horace *Satires* 1.6.42–4; see also Hope, this volume). There were also subtler sounds, such as a particular noise of a debtor being pursued by his creditor (Plautus *Pseudolus* 4.7). In all cases, sounds were picked out to be associated with actions taking place in the Forum.

The loudest noises in Latin literature tend to be associated with disorder. Storms are recorded for their sound and linked to the disapproval of the gods (Livy 8.6, 31.12; Cicero *Haruspices* 10), something to be wary of and associated by some with fear (see Suetonius *Gaius* 51.1). There is a sense by which the vanquished, or about to be vanquished, fear noises (Livy 32.24), which crosses over into the realm of the law court and politics with the broken man, Piso, an ex-consul, startled by every noise (Cicero *Against Piso* 41). The Bacchanalia conspiracy of the second century BCE was associated with drums and cymbals, the sounds of which drowned out violence and murder (Livy 39.8). Ultimately, these instances point to the distinction between order and silence, and disorder and noise. In the representation of warfare we find a milieu for ancient authors to recreate the multisensory experience of episodes of military service: sounds not experienced directly, such as battle or even defeat, could be represented to the population of the city in texts, and also in the amphitheatre and theatre. These accounts provide us with a reference point from which to consider how sounds in the city were placed on a scale that features at one end ordered silence and at the other disorder and noise.

Whilst the soundscape of a military camp would have been rather different from that of a city, both had some resonances that were very similar. Approaching a military camp and a Roman city need not have been so different, since in both cases there was an expectation of sounds associated with a higher concentration of population (Livy 9.45). The soldiers in a military camp provide us with an ordered contrast to plebs in the city of Rome, and thus need to be considered here as a reference point for the contrast between that metropolis and other forms of settlement. One of the objections to life in Rome was that sleep was not possible (Juvenal *Satires* 3.234–8). In contrast, the soldiers' camp would have been quiet at night unless they were under attack (Livy 2.62, 4.59). Soldiers could also march silently to represent the ordered nature of their progress (Livy 24.40, 25.23), something that was so different from the crowded streets of the city of Rome associated with noise.

The order of the soldiers silently marching is contrasted with battles in which it is noise that is associated with fear (Livy 10.28; compare Livy 5.37; Tacitus *Agricola* 35). The representation of the battle of Lake Trasimene featured slaughter and the sound of slaughter that was in itself disorientating. It was so loud that it caused a major earthquake to go unnoticed by those at the battle (Livy 22.5). The scale and ferocity of battle was represented, or even measured, by sounds carrying from a battlefield to nonparticipants (Livy 4.41, 9.43); perhaps as far as twelve miles (Livy 44.4). Those hearing the sounds interpreted them not only as an indication of defeat, but also of what followed defeat: a siege of a city (Livy 2.53).

Captured cities also have their soundscape in Livy, with the crowd in panic and the noise of collapsing city walls (Livy 21.14; Alba: Livy 1.29; Veii: Livy 5.21; Sora: Livy 9.24; and Bovianum: Livy 10.42). The capture of the city of Tarentum by Rome during the second Punic war presents a narrative of three soundscapes: the quiet part of the city, the city called to arms and the city captured (Livy 27.15; compare Livy 29.6, 36.22, 38.5).

Thus we can say that sound was incorporated into the historical narratives of Rome's battles. It provided an additional element with which to imagine or create the subjective realism needed to experience an event through a text. Descriptions of battles, like the triumph parading through Rome, brought elements of the experience of war to urban dwellers who never experienced it first-hand. Lucius Norbanus, consul for 19 CE, provides an unusual example with which to comprehend how the imagination of warfare affected the inhabitants of Rome. We are informed that Norbanus had always been devoted to the trumpet (Dio Cassius 57.18.3). He practised regularly and at dawn on 1 January 19 CE, as people were gathering at his house, he played to mark the beginning of his consulship. His visitors did not expect this sound and interpreted it as an omen, or a signal for battle, demonstrating the comprehension of warfare and battle by a population isolated from military service in the early Empire.

For Roman writers, sound provided a means to describe Rome, but if we are going to fully understand the nature of sound in Rome we need to delineate the boundaries of the urban soundscape by comparing it to others. On the one hand, Rome was perceived as noisier than the countryside: Horace (*Odes* 3.29.12) linked noise (*strepitus*) to both the smoke and wealth of the city to present a contrast with the humble man's abode in Tibur (Tivoli). On the other, disorientating noises of battles, and some other soundscapes, were represented as louder than the metropolis. These examples of sounds in texts point to a key fact for understanding Roman urbanism: knowledge of sounds included both those that were physically heard in the city and those that could have been imagined, or were less frequently heard. The point of intersection between imagined and real, Lucius Norbanus playing his trumpet, points to the affectiveness of those imagined sounds. Roman soundscapes should be understood as both the real, situated in the physical spaces of the city, and the imagined, situated in historical narrative and other forms of literature. A sound of battle, a trumpet blast, could have been interpreted as a sound of battle even within Rome of the first century CE, so far from Rome's armies.

Saturday night Pantheon

The discussion so far has used texts to illustrate how a few particular soundscapes were represented by Roman authors. A different approach is to consider how we might understand the role of sound in the ancient city through our own senses and our ability (real or imagined) to inhabit spaces constructed in the Roman period. The aim here is to demonstrate how contemporary qualitative experience of sounds within an extant architectural space in Rome can increase our understanding of a Roman audience's experience of that space.

In a recently published work by Henri Lefebvre (2014) that prefigures *The Production of Space* (Lefebvre, 1991), the body, and in particular Lefebvre's body, is placed at the centre of the analysis of the new spaces of pleasure of the 1970s, such as Benidorm. What is revealed in this remarkable piece of analysis is how the subjective and the sensory were essential to Lefebvre's development of his writings on space, although the subjective was far from explicit in his later works. Indeed, the manuscript *Towards an Architecture of Pleasure* (the book's title) creates an intersection between intellectual thought on space and the sensory and/or sensual experience of the body. What Lefebvre saw, felt and heard in Benidorm informed his intellectual analysis, just as what we see, feel and hear affects our understanding of Rome. Physical distance is experienced by us today as we walk across the city of Rome (even within the confines of the ancient city space) and some interior spaces remain; so, methodologically, we can begin to access the residual haptic experiences of ancient Rome. This might be described as thinking through the body to create a better understanding of experiences of the past.

The Pantheon is probably one of, if not the, most famous pieces of Roman architecture that can still be experienced today. It is almost impossible to convey, with however many pictures, measurements, axiometric reconstructions and so on, what it is like to experience the building. In terms of visual perception there is the fact that the Pantheon, once inside, constitutes a volumetric space with the light from the oculus falling in a different manner according to the time of day (and time of year) at which a visit is made (Thomas, 2007, p. 68 interprets the interior space via a reading of Edmund Leach, 1983). The internal space is unlike, say, the Basilica Ulpia (today experienced via a visit to San Paolo fuori Le Mura, which was built on the same dimensions), that is a rectilinear space with a lower ceiling and an interior segmented by columns and vaults. In contrast, in the Pantheon the sense of the body in space is very different, and perhaps unique. Everyone can be seen, just as you would have been seen in the Curia (as rebuilt by Diocletian and visited by tourists today).

A key part of the haptic experience of the Pantheon is a particular soundscape that is moved into. This can be described as experienced on a busy Saturday evening (April 2014). The piazza outside the Pantheon is full of people; they are both seen and heard, even, to a certain extent, felt, as movement of the people is organised around seeing the Pantheon, meeting, chatting, passing through and so on. To step towards the Pantheon and to enter the porch amongst the granite columns is to enter another soundscape. For the most part, people do not stop here; they are moving across the space to enter or leave the rotunda of the building. It is quiet compared to the piazza, and there is also a perception of a change in either temperature or simple shelter from the movement of air around the piazza. Stepping into the interior of the rotunda, we enter a new space and another soundscape. It is far from quiet. People happily chat, take photos, tweet and text. No voice is distinctive; instead, there is a hum of voices. This is interrupted by the amplified message (in multiple languages) that the Pantheon is a place of religious worship and silence should be observed. The reaction is a drop in voices that then resurges to the previous pitch until once again the amplified announcement over the public address system is made. With a few hundred people inside, silence does not return; these people are too happy to be in this space and express joy. A couple embraces next to the sign advising silence. The experience of architecture in the Pantheon encapsulates Henri Lefebvre's articulation of an architecture of pleasure that depends on a consciousness of the body in space.

What is so interesting is that within the Pantheon silence cannot be maintained today. The building was said to have been used by the emperor Hadrian for public meetings to transact business, a function that continued through to the fourth century (Dio Cassius 69.7.1; *Theodosian Code* 14.3.10; Ziolkowski, 1999, p. 60). It is possible that the Pantheon was not a temple but an imperial *aula*, in which people could meet (Ziolkowski, 1999, p. 60; see also *Historia Augusta, Hadrian* 19.10; contrast Dio Cassius 53.27.2–3). It would seem that the Hadrianic Pantheon was primarily a building designed for dialogue between emperor and crowds within an interior space. The success of this space as a meeting place in which an emperor might be heard would require silence, but prior to that silence the Pantheon would have been filled with the noise of a crowd talking, a sound much like that heard today. The structure of communication in any public meeting would have required the crowd to become silent, something that did not always happen (Plutarch *Moralia* 207E).

The description above gives just one experience of the Pantheon. There are others that I know of, having visited the building in nearly every month of the year and at all hours of the day over the last twenty odd years. It has been a place of silence and contemplation with a sense of stillness not experienced in any other space in Rome. It has been a place of relief from the weather: cool in the heat of summer or shelter from Rome's torrential rain. Today, the separation of the Pantheon from the space of the piazza is foreshortened because the ground has risen, whereas in antiquity a flight of steps would need to be crossed prior to gaining access to the porch. There are other differences between ancient and modern experiences of this place of course. For example, on leaving the Pantheon in antiquity a view of the Mausoleum of Augustus would have been part of the realignment of the body to the exterior space of the Campus Martius. The intervisibility of monuments in the Campus Martius would have created a very different, and more interconnected, sense of urban space than is possible to attain in the modern city. This perceptual change should not be underplayed. In contrast, what is perceived inside the Pantheon is both the interior space and a sense of your own body existing within that space. This is not just a soundscape, but an architectural space in which sensory perception of the self–space interface is accentuated.

Silence in the city

The focus so far has been on noise, but there were also places in the city where there was no noise. Silence has a relationship to noise that has been described as 'the weird negative' of other spaces that make a noise, often associated with night, but also associated with particular places in the modern city (Bijsterveld, 2003; Tonkiss, 2003, p. 308). This conception that silence provides a contrast to noise is a means by which to begin to understand the value of silence in ancient Rome. Silence is merely relative to a range of noise found in other parts of the city and should not be taken literally as a complete absence of sound (Vincent, 2015b). Hence we should consider the urban soundscape as a textured acoustic space ranging from crowds and noise to isolation and silence.

Noise was certainly a key characteristic of the streets, and their traffic, that supplied the population of the metropolis with the stuff of urban living. In contrast, there were places of silence: the Fora were places without traffic and the Flavian Temple of Peace was associated with deep silence (*magno loci silentio*) in which to appreciate the works of art collected there for public display (Pliny *Natural History* 36.27; see Ramage, 1983, p. 89). There is an elite value in formal quiet that is set in contrast to the streets of the city (the best example of which is Seneca *Letters* 56). Other sources present night-time in the houses of the wealthy as a period of silence that might be disturbed by the sound of doors or windows being opened, or a person at the door (Ovid *Loves* 1.6; Plutarch *Caesar* 43.5; Plautus *Casina* 2.1, *Miles Gloriosus* 2.1, *Pseudolus* 1.1; Terence *Andria* 4.1, *Eunuchus* 5.7, *Phormio* 5.5).

Sounds in the night, just as noise in war, was to be feared and was associated with violence. Thus, the shift from silence to a sound signified the onset of violence and initiated a state of fear. A man killed in the night and found the next morning within earshot of others placed suspicion on those who had (purportedly) been asleep – because they should have been awoken by the noise of the attacker (Cicero *Pro S. Roscio* 64–65). Assaults on cities were to be begun at night, and only perceived by the noise associated with them (Livy 36.24). When the Gauls attempted a night assault it was the noise of them climbing the Capitol that disturbed the geese which woke Marcus Manlius. Interestingly, Livy notes that the dogs were not awoken on this occasion, even though, as he notes, dogs were clearly well adept at detecting intruders at night (Livy 5.47; or returning husbands in Horace *Satires* 1.2). A sudden noise could paralyse a sleeper with fear (Livy 7.36). On occasions the city could become a place of vigil followed by celebration filled with song, as in the case of Germanicus' illness and recovery. The sound of celebration woke the emperor Tiberius from his sleep (Suetonius *Gaius* 6), thus stimulating his sense of fear of Germanicus. Sounds at night turned situations of order into disorder and from sleep into fear.

Conclusion: The sounds of Roman culture

This chapter does not pretend to be an exhaustive account of Roman soundscapes, but instead opens up the possibilities of using literary descriptions of sound, sometimes alongside accounts of contemporary subjective experience, in order to gain a better understanding of places in the city of Rome. Sounds could represent both the order and disorder of the city, and could signify historic events as well as mundane activities. At times sound was to be confined, as in the examples of music and singing; at others it might be excluded to create the silence to contemplate art in the Temple of Peace. Scenes of war, whether

represented in literature or sculpture, would have been associated with a different set of imagined sounds which were not experienced in the city but were
fully represented in texts such as Livy. A conception of the noise of killing, of
flight and pursuit were written into the Roman sensory imagination (compare
Ihde, 2007, pp. 131–6). The meaning or significance of a sound depended, as it
does now, on the context of its position (Corbin, 1998, pp. 95–101). Rome had
a soundscape that included silence, sounds and noise that were spatially specific,
or even contained within space. We can visualise ancient Rome, but virtual
images need to incorporate the other physical senses; the difficulty is making
these culturally specific to the context of Rome. It would seem, even with this
volume, that we are still scratching at the surface of, rather than knowing, the
senses of the Roman empire. We are some way away from being able to advise
sound engineers of historical films such as *Gladiator* what was heard in ancient
Rome, but what these films and ancient texts share is that they both use sound
to draw out human emotion.[1] Any visualisation of antiquity, whether academic
or popular, needs to face up to the challenge of recreating the sounds of the city.

Note

1 http://web.archive.org/web/20010123034400/http://www.prostudio.com/studio-
  sound/july00/post_glad.html; http://web.archive.org/web/20050307174915/http://
  www.editorsguild.com/newsletter/mayjun01/sound_gladiat.html

2 The multivalency of sensory artefacts in the city of Rome

Eleanor Betts

Sensory archaeologies invite us to scrutinise what we take for granted by inviting us to focus in detail on the multisensory human body and the phenomenologies afforded by landscapes and material culture, to explore their interrelationships so that we might gain a more nuanced understanding of past societies (compare Rodaway, 1994, p. 6; Howes, 2006, p. 161; Skeates, 2010, pp. 2–3; Hamilakis, 2014, pp. 127–9). This chapter explores the extent to which phenomenology can be used to recover the sensory properties of Roman urban landscapes and material culture, and how these were experienced, with a focus on the embodied interrelationships of people, objects and places in ancient Rome. Sensory studies of Roman urban spaces and places give us a more complete understanding of lived experience, the social rhythms of the city and aspects of everyday life (compare Lefebvre, 2004, pp. 15–17, 2014, p. 10).

Blurring the boundaries

If we are to understand life in the Roman city from a fully sensory and embodied perspective, we must acknowledge some of the ways in which 'the senses blur the boundary between need and desire, biology and culture' (Stewart, 2005, p. 61), and the potential problems this creates when investigating the past. Stewart notes that '[w]e may apprehend the world by means of our senses, but the senses themselves are shaped and modified by experience and the body bears a somatic memory of its encounters with what is outside of it' (2005, p. 61). Both biological and cultural responses to sensory stimuli need to be taken into consideration if we are to use sensory archaeologies to better understand Roman urban life, and whilst both are difficult to recapture from such a temporal and cultural distance, this chapter demonstrates that it is possible to do so.

The problem of recording sensory experience and understanding its affectiveness[1] has been grappled with by philosophers including Husserl, Heidegger and Merleau-Ponty. Taking an essentialist standpoint for a moment, human physiology is broadly the same across the species and we therefore each have a clear point of reference through which to access past experience. The human body is a 'universal measurement' in the sense that we can expect each one to have a prescribed set of physical parts and systems, including a particular set of sensory apparatus (the sensorium). The criticisms most often levelled against archaeologists following this form of essentialism are, on the one hand, that it is broad brush and does not take into consideration the uniqueness of every human body, but on the other, that it is too subjective, based on the experiences recorded by an individual observer (Brück, 1998; Skeates, 2010, p. 2; Hamilakis, 2013, pp. 411–12). Nevertheless, more recent fieldwork has taken such differences into account and used them to form a more nuanced impression of life in past human societies (see, for example, Ingold, 2000; Hamilton and Whitehouse, 2006, forthcoming). We each have varying degrees of acuity when it comes to mobility, hearing, eyesight, sense of smell, palate and so on, and the quality of these can vary widely within the lifespan of an individual. These potential differences between bodies, accompanied by variations in sensitivity to sensations, must be explored when attempting to reconstruct Roman lived experience. As Lefebvre puts it, studying the rhythms of the human body is '[n]ot without risks: the leap from the particular to the general is not without the danger of errors, of illusions, in a word, of ideology' (2004, p. 15). In addition, there are numerous culturally specific differences to be taken into account, not least those relating to environment, social context and memory, all of which are significant factors in distancing us from understanding the ways in which individuals in ancient Roman cities perceived their sensory experiences (compare Knappett, 2004, pp. 45–6; Skeates, 2010, p. 3; Tilley, 2010, p. 474; Day, 2013b, p. 6). We must be careful not to make assumptions that our subjects of study reacted intellectually or emotionally in the same way that we do to sensory stimuli, so one caveat of sensory archaeologies must be that we acknowledge the limitations of reconstructing every aspect of past human experiences. One of the challenges of taking a sensory approach to the past is recognising the point at which experience diverges and, consequently, where the limits of our understanding lie. The starting point for sensory archaeologists is therefore to recognise that the past people we aim to understand are 'culturally constructed individuals whose personhoods differ while possessing a universal body' (Tilley, 2010, p. 487). From this starting point we can begin to consider the nuances of experience of everyday life according to the age, gender, status, sensory acuity, level of fitness, and so on, of both inhabitants of, and visitors to, the Roman city.

The senses, or sensations if we follow Lefebvre (2014, pp. 114–15), both shape the body and are shaped by it; part of this shaping is the relationship of the body's interactions with physical space and material artefacts (both animate and inanimate). Living is written into and onto the body as somatic memory, and includes a person's interactions with other people, their physical environment and the objects within it, influenced by the emotional impact of those interactions and of the different stages of the life course. As Lefebvre notes earlier in the same volume, '[m]ost people ignore their body and misunderstand it. . . . But the body is there: mine, yours, ours. A kind of pedagogy of the body, its rhythms, a kind of teaching, will fill the enormous gap' (2014, pp. 33–4). This chapter begins to explore how an understanding of the 'pedagogy of the body' can bridge the gap between modern and ancient Roman experience of the city, and the extent to which our subjective pedagogies influence our perception of the past. We must remain aware of the temporal nature of embodied experience, with respect to both linear and cyclical time, as it alters during daily, seasonal, annual and life cycles (see also Laurence, Veitch, Graham, this volume). If we approach sensory archaeologies of Roman culture from the perspective of the emitter of sensory stimuli, by establishing the sensory properties of specific objects, buildings and spaces ('sensory artefacts'), we can understand better how people would have interacted with their material world. This perspective overcomes the problem of the dislocation between Roman and modern perceptions, which is created by cultural specificity and the uniqueness of an individual's life experience, since the human perceiver is no longer the reference point. Instead, the body is the receiver of external, measurable sensory stimuli, some of which are controlled by human agency and the built environment, others of which have 'passive agency' (Stewart, 2005, p. 61), an ability to cause unintended, or unconscious, physical responses within the body. The approach taken in this chapter is to focus on the sensations effected by sensory stimuli rather than on human emotional and intellectual perceptions, with the overall aim of increasing our understanding of social interactions in ancient Rome. We may not be able to recapture the memory associations a particular smell had for an individual living in the city (contrast Morley, 2015, p. 119), nor make a definitive judgement about whether people were disturbed by the noise of the baths or activities in the street (Seneca *Letters* 56; see also Veitch, this volume), but constructing phenomenologies of sensations as they relate to the physical body, material culture and urban space makes it possible to characterise the interrelationships of people, structures and objects within specific locales and moving between places. This chapter presents a series of approaches through which sensory data can be extracted from our evidence, enabling us to recover sensory artefacts. These approaches, which focus on written evidence, material culture and architectural remains from ancient Rome, may then be used in combination to better understand aspects of everyday life in the city.

Reading against the grain: Text mining for sensory artefacts

As will be discussed below, sensory artefacts are best reconstructed from material culture, and sites such as Pompeii and Vindolanda (see Derrick, this volume) offer a wealth of artefacts for analysis. Material culture rarely survives to the extent that it is found at these two sites; therefore, sensory artefacts will often need to be resituated in Roman urban spaces via comparative approaches. One such approach is to text mine the sources for both direct and indirect sensory data (for a specific case study, see Vincent, this volume). Literary sources can aid interpretation, giving clues to the presence and uses of particular objects and areas in Rome's urban landscape. The sensory properties of the material referred to or described may be inferred, though there may be irretrievable nuances in the detail. For example, Martial invites Julius Cerealis to dine with him, listing several foods they will consume, all of which have sensory properties which may be broadly inferred (appearance, taste, smell, texture) because similar foodstuffs remain available today, but do we really know how olives from Picenum smelled, looked or tasted? (Martial *Epigrams* 11.52.11; see also Dalby, 2000, p. 253.) Martial is attempting to entice his guest, so we might infer that the foods he lists taste good; in other words, they are intended to create a positive gustatory experience. It is possible to extrapolate from this invitation to understand the intended sensory affectiveness of a good meal, which was to forge or cohere social relationships, in this case of two social equals.[2]

We must, of course, remain cautious when applying sensory details from the sources to particular objects and architecture, and avoid anachronism. Not only do we have the usual caveats of a limited number of authors, all coming from quite specific social groups, all male and all writing within their particular genre, we must also bear in mind the perceived hierarchy of the senses prevalent at the time (see Stewart, 2005, pp. 61–2 for a summary). Influenced by Aristotle (*De Anima* 2.6–12 (418a–424b)), sight and sound were considered to be the 'higher' senses, whilst smell, taste and touch tended to be associated with base needs and with lower social groups, often with the further connotation that they were 'unpleasant or dangerous' (Howes, 2006, pp. 164–5; compare Weddle, this volume).[3] It is arguably for this reason that objects and activities associated with taste, smell and touch are more prevalent in Roman comedy and satire than in epic poetry or historical narratives (compare Betts, 2011, pp. 130–1). An example of text mining for sensory artefacts is presented in the case study in the final section of this chapter. The next section considers the concept of sensory artefacts and the types of sensory data that can be obtained when text mining is combined with material culture.

Sensory artefacts as objects with agency

David Howes has highlighted the 'importance of attending to the multiple sensory dimensions of objects, architectures and landscapes' as being increasingly central to material culture theory (2006, p. 161; compare Hurcombe, 2007, p. 539). The sum of the physical properties of an object and its sensory affordances may be termed a 'sensory artefact' (on sensory affordances see Hunter-Crawley, 2013a, p. 162; Hamilakis, 2014, p. 14; compare Knappett, 2004, 2005). For example, a Roman oil lamp emits a particular smell of (perfumed) oil, fire and smoke; creates a flickering light in a room or on the street (Justinian *The Digest*, 50.16.245; see also Marshman, this volume); and has haptic properties such that it sits comfortably in the hand. It often includes some decoration, such as the figure of a Thracian gladiator (Staatliche Museen zu Berlin, inv. 31291), which may contribute to the tactile experience of holding and using the lamp but also act as a mnemonic for a favourite gladiator or visit to the amphitheatre, which may in turn create a talking point for the people using the lamp (compare Wallace-Hadrill, 2008, p. 389). Knappett notes that the affordances of material culture are not only directly perceived, but also indirectly perceived through a cultural lens (2004, pp. 45–6). Material, on all scales, embodies memory; it is 'linked to socially or culturally mediated remembrance and memory' (Holtorf and Williams, 2006, p. 235). The 'sociality of affordances' (Knappett, 2004, p. 47; see also Ingold, 2000, pp. 3–4) means that a sensory artefact could, and most likely would, have been perceived and understood in different ways by different people, and it is this aspect of sensory affectiveness which can lead us to use sensory archaeologies to tackle new and existing research questions about Roman society.

An individual's response to a sensory artefact will therefore be affected by several factors, including their cultural context and degree of sensory sensitivity (compare Hall, 1966, p. 2). Individuals have differing degrees of sensitivity to sensation and there are many variables within this, such as the acuity of particular senses, the effects of disability or ageing on that acuity, habituation to particular sensory stimuli and emotional responses triggered by the evocativeness of some stimuli and/or the association of a certain sensory property with a particular memory. Several of these variables have a temporal aspect, such as daily or seasonal changes enhancing or muting some odours (extreme heat and cold both produce quantifiable odour effects; see also Porteous, 2006, p. 99) or partial loss of vision and/or hearing as a person ages (Ihde, 2007, pp. 243–50).

These permutations remind us that artefacts, architecture and landscapes have both materiality and agency (whether active or passive), and that sensory properties are often intangible, in the literal sense that they cannot be physically grasped; instead, they have a type of illusory materiality particular to their role in the sensory or sensorial field, such as the vibration of sound waves or the chemical components of a perfume (for a definition of the sensory field see Lefebvre, 2014, pp. 114–15; for the sensorial field, see Hamilakis, 2014, p. 16, p. 112; on sound, see Veitch, this volume). The sensory artefact also influences, and is influenced by, the physical space which it inhabits and any person who interacts with it. A lit oil lamp in an empty room has measurable properties and is a sensory artefact in its own right without the need for a human perceiver to interact with it (though see Vincent, this volume, on Berkeley).

A sensory artefact often occupies a different space from the material artefact to which it pertains; this is especially true of odours and sounds, which do not respect architectural boundaries (Betts, 2011, p. 123; Veitch, Flohr, this volume). In contrast, sensory artefacts relating to touch (haptic or kinaesthetic experience) acquire materiality through the body's direct connection to physical surfaces, although those connections are not necessarily static. For example, the act of walking up the Via Biberatica in Rome involves movement, but the sensory artefact is the combination of the material of the basalt paving, the connection of feet and/or footwear with that surface, and the muscular sensation of climbing an incline (for further discussion of kinaesthesia see Slaney, this volume). Sensory artefacts also have a temporal aspect: a taste stays in the mouth after the material object has been consumed, or the bowl set down; smells and sounds will linger in particular places, or dissipate quickly, often depending on climatic conditions (see Veitch, Derrick, this volume). For example, the odour of dried blood would have been noticeable on the arena floor of the Colosseum for many weeks after Titus' inaugural games, perhaps up to fifty days (Weddle, 2013, p. 146; compare Koloski-Ostrow, 2015, pp. 104–5).[4] The smell of fish waste putrefying in the sun outside a stall on the Vicus Tuscus would be stronger during the summer months (Horace *Satires* 2.3.227). The cries of an ambulant sausage-seller seeking business around the baths would ring in the ears; then, as he came closer, the smell of sausages would filter through the air to the nose. The aroma, then the cries, would gradually fade away, whilst a customer would taste the sausage after the purveyor had left the area and the sounds of his shouts would remain audible even after he had passed out of sight (Seneca *Letters* 56.2). To extrapolate from Seneca's text in this way means empirically recording the distances travelled by a male voice shouting (67–118 m) and the smell of cooked sausages (less than 17 m), which can be done in a variety of temporal and climatic conditions (warm and dry July in these examples; Hamilton and Whitehouse, 2006, p. 176, p. 178). Each of these sensory artefacts occupies time and space, and together they overlap and intertwine to create a sensorial landscape in which people lived, through which they moved and which contributed to the construction and navigation of urban space (compare Tschumi, 1996, p. 39; Hamilakis, 2013, p. 409, 2014, p. 12, 'sensorial assemblage' pp. 127–9).

The aim of this approach, then, is to add sensation to traditional interpretative methods of material culture, enhanced by the sensory data extracted from textual sources. It is only by exploring each of these material and sensory properties and their potential affordances that we can fully appreciate the complexity of taking an embodied approach to 'experiential space' (Thomas, 1996, p. 86). The situation of sensory artefacts in space is the focus of the next two sections.

Mapping sensory space: Sense loci

Sensory artefacts fill space with sensory data, their dominant elements creating sense loci, many of which are temporally specific. Here I refer to Norwegian architect Norberg-Schulz's (1980) concept of 'genius loci', 'the spirit of a place', which refers to the numinous Roman (and pre-Roman) belief that the divine imbued a place with its properties. More recently Jim Drobnick has used the term 'pungent loci' to refer to the smell of a place, its olfactory 'spirit' or essence which helps define it as a discrete locale on the periphery of 'sensory awareness' or perception (2005, p. 275); in other words, sense loci consist of an object (or objects) and its (or their) sensory properties, bounded in space, but usually habituated so as not to dominate the consciousness of the perceiver. Urban spaces, whether streets and fora or the rooms inside domestic, commercial and public buildings, had discrete sensory signatures, but the panoply of sensory artefacts in each of these spaces at a given time often placed them on the periphery of perception. Anyone living in the city would have been accustomed to the smells, tastes, textures, sights and sounds of its fabric and daily rhythms but would also have noticed variations in the urban sensescape, whether consciously or subconsciously. The architectural fabric of the city played a large part in this, helping to shape haptic and kinaesthetic sensations, and being visually affective.

The sensory artefacts created by sounds, smells and taste were more fluid, moving between spaces and mingling with one another, blurring the boundaries between architecturally discrete locales.

The concept of pungent loci can therefore be extrapolated to include other proximate loci, places defined by subtle sensory cues (if we continue to follow Drobnick, 2005, p. 275). Each of these sense loci must be defined in a way specific to the characteristic sensory properties of its particular part of the sensory field, and this is why identifying the sensory artefacts of places and objects is relevant. Edward Hall's concept of proxemics, whilst not without its limitations, has some valency here: sense loci overlap one another, each bounded by the distances reached in intimate, personal, social and public space (1966, pp. 107–22; compare Betts, 2011, pp. 122–3). For example, sounds carry differently than odour in terms of both distance and permeation of other materials (for examples relating to sound, see Laurence and Veitch, this volume; for smell, see Derrick, this volume), but both have clear relationships to space and further-reaching spheres of influence than either taste or touch loci, both of which are defined by the intimate physical contact between the sensory emitter and the perceiver's body (via touch, kinaesthesia and interoception, with that contact being via the external or internal skin surfaces; these are largely ignored by Hall). For example, the Forum Holitorium would have been a highly textured, odiferous and potentially gustatory space, where fruit and vegetables could be smelled, handled and tasted (Varro *On the Latin Language* 5.146). Its pungent loci emerged from the contrasting odours of a variety of fresh fruit and vegetables combined with the more putrid odour of detritus from damp and rotting produce trampled underfoot during the course of the day's market, mixed with the odours of pack animals and their excreta (compare Koloski-Ostrow, 2015, pp. 103–4).

Pungent loci such as this, but also other sense loci, acted in a similar way to buildings and other architectural features on a visual map. They were a means by which to comprehend the form of the city and to make decisions about how to move through it, as well as where to stop (compare Lynch, 1960, pp. 66–72, pp. 78–84; Malmberg, 2009, p. 41). The distances offered by Hall in his study of proxemics give some indication of the reach of different sense loci, dependent on the strength of the sensory artefacts within a space, but also on the acuity of the perceiver (Table 2.1). Only by establishing the sensory

Table 2.1 Distances of proxemic perception

Informal distance classification	*Intimate*		*Personal*		*Social*		*Public*	
	Close phase	*Far phase*	*Close phase*	*Far phase*	*Close phase*	*Far phase*	*Close phase*	*Far phase*
Distance in metres	Touch-ing	0.15–0.45	0.5–0.75	0.75–1.2	1.2–2.13	2.13–3.66	3.66–7.62	More than 7.62

Source: based on Hall, 1966, pp. 107–22

artefacts of a particular place in a particular time can the use of that space be fully understood. Significant factors in our interpretation of the extent to which particular sensory artefacts constructed space and influenced people's behaviour in it include not only the range of each sensory artefact but also the extent to which they were striking or habituated. Taking further the example of the Forum Holitorium, its complex smellscape, along with elements in the built environment, characterised it as a space, but that smellscape is likely to have been habituated by the people regularly using the market. Being inured to the sounds, smells, textures and sights of daily life would not have stopped biological responses to those sensory artefacts, but instead demonstrates the adaptability of people to their environment, to the extent that they could choose to actively engage with sensory experience or exclude it from consciousness (compare Morley, 2015, pp. 118–19). In other words, sense loci did not have to be striking to be distinct spaces; the majority were likely unconscious elements, on the borders of human awareness, but were nonetheless intrinsic to mapping the city.

Everyday life in the heart of Rome: *Tusci turba impia vici*

The final section of this chapter presents a case study which demonstrates how the three concepts and approaches outlined above may be combined to enhance our understanding of everyday life in ancient Rome. The study begins to establish and explore some of the sensory artefacts associated with the heart of the city and to consider the extent to which they may have constructed sense loci. Its focus is on the sale of goods in and around the Vicus Tuscus, which ran northwards from the western end of the Circus Maximus, through the Forum Boarium and Velabrum, entering the Forum Romanum between the Temple of Castor and the Basilica Julia (Papi, 1999, pp. 196–7; Dalby, 2000, pp. 213–14). This route is known primarily from late Republican and Augustan authors, who tend to associate it with Rome's legendary past (for example, Varro *On the Latin Language* 5.46; Propertius 4.2; Servius *Commentary on the Aeneid* 5.560; Livy 27.37.15; Tacitus *Annals* 4.65). The aim of the study is to demonstrate that the analysis of sensory artefacts and sense loci enables us to understand better the ways that the city altered according to a variety of cyclical daily and seasonal rhythms, and how this multivalency affected the perception, definition and use of urban space in the first century CE. The particular items sold in the Vicus Tuscus varied according to their 'areas of trade' (Frayn, 1993, p. 77, figure 7), seasonal availability and the length of the Mediterranean sailing season, as well as the presence of an elite market in Rome (Arnaud, 2005, pp. 26–8; Holleran, 2012, pp. 35–6). These factors will constitute the particular focus of the case study, but other variables could form the basis of a sensory archaeology of this area; for example, considering how its sensory artefacts altered the interpretation and use of the space when it functioned as part of the triumphal route (Favro, 1994, 2014; Beard, 2007, pp. 102–5).

Street architecture

Archaeological evidence for the Vicus Tuscus is limited, but sufficient to indicate that, in addition to being a significant arterial route from the Forum Boarium (and therefore connected to the Tiber) to the Forum Romanum, its function was primarily commercial, certainly by the late first century BCE and probably much earlier. Several inscriptions refer to businesses in the area behind the Temple of Castor (*CIL* VI.9872: *sagario post aedem Castoris*; VI.30748, VI.10024 *post aedem Castoris*; also VI.9177, VI.9393) and a fragment of the Severan Marble Plan represents a short row of shops across the street behind the temple (*FUR* Stanford fragment 18a).[5] The Marble Plan also shows the section of the Vicus Tuscus between the Temple of Castor and the Basilica Julia, where it enters the Forum Romanum, but no shops or other distinguishing architectural features are represented here (*FUR* Stanford fragment 18bc).[6] A series of twenty-nine *tabernae* incorporated within the east, west and south sides of the podium of the Temple of Castor are of Augustan date, preceded by Republican equivalents, but those on the Vicus Tuscus side are poorly preserved (Nilson, Persson and Zahle, 2008, p. 53). Some of these *tabernae* may have been used as shops, others as offices, and with dimensions averaging 4.30 m depth by 2 m width their businesses may have spilled out into the street (Nilson et al., 2008, p. 21, pp. 53–8; Poulsen, 2008, p. 254). These recesses in the podium facilitated trade in a 6 m wide street space which was otherwise unsuited to permanent shops, given the architectural design of the Basilica Julia with steps leading down to the Vicus Tuscus.

   The commercial nature of the street is more firmly attested by the evidence of the Horrea Agrippiana, which occupied the area between the Vicus Tuscus and Clivus Victoriae below the Palatine (Astolfi, Guidobaldi and Pronti, 1978, pp. 31–106; Astolfi, 1996, p. 37; Papi, 1999, p. 196–7; *FUR* Stanford 5Abcd;[7] see also *FUR* Stanford 5Aa, 5Aab, 5Ae, 5Af). The Horrea Agrippiana owes its name and foundation to Marcus Agrippa (*CIL* VI.10026: *horreis Agrippia*; VI.9972; XIV.3958: *horreis Agrippianis*) but also had Domitianic, second- and third-century phases (Astolfi et al., 1978, pp. 31–106; Astolfi, 1996, pp. 37–8). The Marble Plan shows three adjoining internal courtyards, with a row of individual shops opening onto the Vicus Tuscus and Clivus Victoriae. (By the Severan period, there was also a row of shops on the opposite side of the street (*FUR* Stanford 5Abcd).) The northern and eastern sides of the building have been excavated extensively, revealing several architectural and decorative features, all of which have measurable sensory affordances. The northerly courtyard was paved with travertine (a mosaic floor was added in the third century CE) and supported by travertine columns on arcaded piers, above which was a vaulted ceiling. This courtyard was surrounded by rooms built of tufa blocks in *opus quadratum*, some of which had wooden mezzanines with *opus spicatum* floors, reached by two staircases (Astolfi, 1996, pp. 38; Holleran, 2012, p. 83; *FUR* Stanford 5Abcd). The entrance was towards the Vicus Tuscus, but is not shown on the Marble Plan (Astolfi, 1996, pp. 37–8). Nothing remains of the street façade, but it has been suggested that it may have been similar to the exterior of the Theatre of Marcellus, which also had travertine columns on arcaded piers (Astolfi, 1996, pp. 37–8, figure 27, p. 394; Favro, 1996, p. 315, note 48; Holleran, 2012, p. 83). The activities associated with the *horrea* included the manufacture and sale of clothing (*CIL* VI.9972, XIV.3958, Martial *Epigrams* 10.87.9–10 and possibly 11.27.11; Larsson Lovén, 2013, p. 116) and it is likely that some of the adjoining shops were also used for the sale of these items. These literary and epigraphic sources therefore enable us to begin to reconstruct part of the sensescape of this stretch of the *vicus* and to evaluate the extent to which its sense loci affected those working in the street, their customers and passers-by (both inhabitants and visitors to the city). The light, temperature and acoustics of the internal spaces of the *horrea* would have been different from those of the adjoining shops, and temporary stalls different again from these, creating discrete sense loci for distinct parts of the street (compare Veitch, this volume, for a methodology to measure acoustic properties of architectural spaces).

Piscator . . . pomarius, auceps, unguentarius . . .

Whilst the archaeology offers glimpses of the spatial structure, architecture and functions of the Vicus Tuscus, the literary and epigraphic references to occupations of people working in and around the street combine to categorise it further as a place of commerce and artisanship, each source generating imagined sensory artefacts which can be placed in physical space. Horace catalogues some of the businesses present in the area during the Augustan period: 'fishmonger, fruitseller, fowler, perfumer, the Tuscan Street's vile throng, cooks and parasites, the whole market and Velabrum' (*piscator . . . pomarius, auceps, unguentarius ac Tusci turba impia vici, cum scurris fartor, cum Velabro omne macellum; Satires* 2.3.227–30). In the first century CE at least, the Vicus Tuscus was characterised by some strongly affective sensory artefacts, amongst them the slippery feel and pungent smell of fish, the exotic and heady scent of perfumes, the loud calls and powerful odour of live poultry, the sweet smell of fruit and the luxurious texture of silk (Horace *Satires* 2.3.227–30; Martial *Epigrams* 11.27.11; see also Betts, 2011, pp. 129–30). The strong odours of the street created by fish, poultry and fruit would have been common in Rome's urban context, and likely to have been habituated by a broader cross-section of the populace than the sensory artefacts associated with imports such as silk and perfume (see below), but would nevertheless have contributed to the characterisation of the space, especially in the heat of summer, as would associated sounds, including shouts from the vendors (compare Seneca *Letters* 56.2). Retailers were more likely to become inured to the sensory artefacts with which they engaged frequently, whereas anyone moving through the street would apprehend sensory stimuli (especially visual, aural and odiferous) which were singular, repeated or constant, invasive or ambient, situated or directional, even if these were not always consciously perceived. For example, the strong odour of a fishmonger's wares would be situated and constant, sufficient that anyone passing by would be able to identify the approximate distance and direction of the source of the smell.

The availability of fresh produce would have varied throughout the year, resulting in a nuanced sensescape as the seasons changed. For example, the species of fish and shellfish on sale would have varied according to where they were sourced, with river, coastal and farmed fish more readily obtainable than species from the open sea, the availability of which was dependent on the sailing season (Frayn, 1993, pp. 65–9; Wallace-Hadrill, 2008, pp. 340–1, 2014, p. 76). The variety of fruit and vegetables altered seasonally, although fresh produce was supplemented by preserved fruits and nuts (Frayn, 1993, pp. 61–4; Dalby, 2000, p. 28, pp. 247–55). Poultry and eggs would have been a constant in the sensescape of the Vicus Tuscus, since they were obtainable year round and affordable to the non-elite (Martial *Epigrams* 11.52.11).

Recognising the seasonality of particular types of produce draws awareness to the extent to which taste sensations, with changing flavours and textures, varied during the year. Particular types of food were also a marker of status or means, if we can find a grain of truth in the satirical accounts of Petronius, Martial and Juvenal (see also Wallace-Hadrill, 2008, pp. 342–9). Another factor was the 'area of trade'. To ensure its freshness, perishable produce could not be transported far, so sites of production needed to be in close proximity to the point of sale. Frayn argues for a maximum distance of 5 km for soft fruit and vegetables, and 15 km for other types of fruit, vegetables, curd cheese, poultry, sucking pig and spring lamb, to which we may add fish from the Tiber (1993, pp. 75–7; see also Dalby, 2000, pp. 27–33 and Wallace-Hadrill, 2014, p. 77 for sources and discussion of produce local to Rome). Ownership of villa estates in Latium and Campania gave the elite a supply of fresh produce that was unattainable by the majority of Rome's population, and when they resided on those estates in September and October there would have been less demand in the city for expensive foodstuffs (Dalby, 2000, pp. 30–41; Holleran, 2012, pp. 35–6). Much of the produce for sale in the Vicus Tuscus, notably fruit, vegetables, river fish and poultry, would therefore have been obtained locally, but the particular items on sale would have varied according to supply and demand. Throughout the days on which these items were sold the strongest odours would have been those generated by live poultry and fish, both of which carry further than the smells of horticultural produce. The quality of soft fruit, leafy vegetables, eggs and fish would have deteriorated over the course of a hot day, wilting and generating debris, which would have combined with the other odours to alter the pungent loci as the day progressed. Other varieties of fruit and vegetables, especially those brought into the city on the *nundinae*, may have remained on sale over the course of a week, their smell and taste altering as they aged (Frayn, 1993, p. 77, figure 7, p. 161).

This discussion of foodstuffs available for purchase in the Vicus Tuscus has shown that if daily and weekly cycles, seasonality and proximity are taken into consideration we can find a kaleidoscope of nuance in the sensescape of the street. At the same time, the sense loci generated by the colours, textures and odours of these perishable goods, the surrounding physical urban fabric and the sounds of voices, animals and wheeled carts would have been familiar to anyone frequenting the street, the sensory artefacts mingling to generate a 'spirit' of the place which defined it as a discrete locale (Drobnick, 2005, p. 275; Newsome, 2011, p. 41). The foodstuffs sold from the shops and stalls in the Vicus Tuscus, and by ambulant vendors, contributed to the 'essence' of the place, creating a multisensory backdrop for the specific activities taking place in the street, such as Martial buying cheese from the Velabrum, then visiting different shops or stalls along the Vicus Tuscus to purchase eggs, tuna, lettuce, leeks, rue and olives (Martial *Epigrams* 11.52.5–11; Horace *Satires* 2.3.227–9); or Lucius Plutius Eros bringing purple-dyed fabric down the street to sell from the Horrea Agrippiana (*CIL* XIV.2433).

Prevalent in the written sources for the Vicus Tuscus and surrounding streets (such as the Vicus Unguentarius and Vicus Iugarius) are trades concerned with textiles, perfume and incense. These were exotic items from the East, often from places beyond the borders of the empire (Dalby, 2000, pp. 182–3; Young, 2001, pp. 18–23, pp. 90–100; Wallace-Hadrill, 2014, pp. 70–4). The annexation of Egypt by Augustus enabled (or catalysed) an increase in this trade, which may account for the building of the Horrea Agrippiana; whilst the Domitianic restoration of the building may be reflected in Martial's references to the sale of silk and cloaks dyed with Tyrian purple (*Epigrams* 11.27.11; 10.87.9–10). Processing of raw ingredients and manufacture of the end product often took place *en route* to Rome, notably in Alexandria (Young, 2001, p. 23, p. 51), although the epigraphy from the city suggests that those men and women working in the perfume and textile industries were not only salespeople, but also active in at least part of the manufacturing process. Several inscriptions from Rome mention freedmen and women involved in the textile industry in the Vicus Tuscus and surrounding area (*CIL* XIV.2433: *purpurario de vico Tusco . . . et veturiae*; compare *AE* 1923, 59: *purpur(arius) de vico Iugar(io)*, *CIL* VI.9848: *purpurari de vico*; VI.9872: *sagario post aedem Castoris*, VI.9976: *Vico Tusco vestiarius*, VI.9972, VI.33923: *vestiarius tenuiarius de vico Tusco*, VI.37826: *[vest]iariis tenuariss de vico Tusco,* XIV.3958: *vestiarius de horreis Agrippianis*). Without space for manufacturing or evidence for fulleries in this area of the city, it seems likely that the *purpurii* were selling (rather than making) purple products in the Vicus Tuscus, and those products may have extended beyond clothing to include the meat of the murex and paint pigment, all of which were luxury items (Hughes, 2007, pp. 87–90; Larsson Lovén, 2013, p. 115–16; compare Flohr, this volume). Martial's reference to the sale of Tyrian purple cloaks from the Horrea Agrippiana (*Epigrams* 10.87.9–10) indicates that textiles affordable to the elite were stored, and perhaps sold, away from the street in the enclosed and more private space of the *horrea*, access to which could have been controlled. This may have included not only purple-dyed clothing, but also silk (Martial *Epigrams* 11.27.11). Larsson Lovén (2013, p. 115) notes that all epigraphic references to silk have their provenance in Rome or its immediate vicinity (Gabii and Tivoli), which suggests that once it reached Italy the textile was sold exclusively in Rome. It would therefore have attracted attention as a luxury item exclusive to the city's elite market. Vision and touch would have been the predominant sensations involved in the manufacture, buying and selling of textiles, with the different types of clothing, from woollen caps to purple cloaks and silk dresses, each having particular haptic properties generated by the weight and texture of the fabric (compare Flohr, this volume). Buying textiles necessitated touch in order to establish quality and so drew customer and retailer into proximate haptic space, which had the secondary effect of causing them to speak in comparatively hushed voices, carrying no further than 5 m (Hamilton and Whitehouse, 2006, pp. 177–8). If we give credence to the hypothesis that the façade of the Horrea Agrippiana was highly decorated (Astolfi, 1996, figure 27, p. 394; Favro, 1996, p. 315, note 48), the visual effects of the elaborate architecture would have acted as a signifier for the high status textiles available inside.

The Vicus Tuscus (or Turarius) was also widely associated with the sale of perfumed oils, ointments and incense (Horace *Satires* 2.3.228; Pomponius Porphryio *Commentum in Horati Sermones* 2.3.228: *Tuscus dicitur vicus, qua iter ad Velabrum, ubi harum rerum (thus et odores) mercatores, id est unguentari consistunt*; Pomponius Porphryio *Commentum in Horati Epistualae* 1.20.1: *in vico Turario*; see also *CIL* VI.36819 on the relationship between incense and perfume sellers). It has also been associated with the Vicus Unguentarius, which may have been the street running parallel to the Vicus Tuscus behind the Basilica Julia (Rodríguez Almeida, 1985–6, pp. 111–17). Smell may have been the dominant sensation in these shops, but buying and selling perfume was also an intensely haptic experience. Perfumes and ointments were kept in closed containers out of direct sunlight until requested by a customer. They were tested by being 'put on the back of the hand, to avoid their being damaged by the warmth of the fleshy part' (Pliny *Natural History* 13.3), so were affective at intimate and personal distances. Once in use, scents such as perfumed hair oil or incense burning on an altar travelled further, reaching social and sometimes public distances (Pliny *Natural History* 13.4, 13.20; Martial *Epigrams* 5.64.3–4, 8.77.3–4; Dalby, 2000, pp. 246–7). Temperature changes would have caused daily variations in the intensity of the scents once they were released, but their range would have been limited to a few metres around the shops. The smell of smoke permeates further than perfumed oils, and even a small amount of burning incense can be smelled at a distance of 6 m on a cool day. Within the shop, individual scents may have been difficult to distinguish, not only due to the intermingling of several products, but also because the majority of perfumes were compounds (Pliny *Natural History* 13.1–2). A customer choosing perfume would begin to differentiate scents and the decision to purchase could be based on a range of factors including the intended use, expense, fashion, cultural acceptability, personal taste and memory associations. For example, Pliny notes the popularity of rose oils for the hair and body, myrrh was used at funerals and also to flavour wine, whilst frankincense found widespread use in religious rituals (Pliny *Natural History* 13.6; Young, 2001, pp. 15–17; Wallace-Hadrill, 2014, pp. 77–8; compare Hope, Weddle, this volume).

The epigraphic and literary sources, in combination with the material evidence for the Horrea Agrippiana, indicate that textiles, perfume and incense were sold in shops along the stretch of the Vicus Tuscus behind the Temple of Castor, and the dominant sensory artefacts (for those who had access to them) were therefore a striking combination of powerful scents (perfume, incense, dye), strong colours (Tyrian purple) and varied textures (wool, silk, oils, alabaster, glass phials). Foodstuffs being brought into Rome would find a market at the Forum Boarium and Velabrum end of the street, but could also have been sold from the part of the Vicus Tuscus closer to the Forum Romanum, especially if temporary stalls were set up next to the Temple of Castor. There would have been a synergy between each of these spaces and the people who made their living from them, such as the cheese merchant in the Velabrum, the perfumer who ran his business from a shop in the Vicus Tuscus or the clothier in the Horrea Agrippiana (Horace *Satires* 2.3.227–30; Martial *Epigrams* 3.55, 10.87.9–10, 11.8.9, 11.27.11, 11.52.10, 13.32, 14.110; *CIL* VI.9972, XIV.3958). Consequently, the particular sensory artefacts afforded by each business formed landmarks which together constructed and characterised this street as a discrete urban sensory space (compare Lynch, 1960, pp. 78–84; Malmberg, 2009, p. 41). The street would have been noisy with the hubbub of commercial activity and would also have had a distinctive smell resulting from the mingled odours of the various produce on offer. These, along with the street's visual architecture, the textures of the building and decorative materials used for the shops and *horrea*, and the kinaesthesia of people and animals moving along the street, all combined to create sense loci. Having established the 'essence' of the street, the case study concludes with an investigation into the impact of seasonal changes on the sensescape of the Vicus Tuscus.

Seasonality

The supply of imported goods was dependent on a sailing season which ran broadly from April to October, with some possibility of travel in March and November, extending into the winter for certain places such as Sicily (Dalby, 2000, p. 111; Arnaud, 2005, pp. 26–8; Adams, 2012, pp. 225–7). Whilst many imports such as preserved fruits, spices, silk and other fabrics, dyes, perfumes and *objets d'art* could be held in *horrea* in Rome and Ostia, and released for sale during the winter, seasonal patterns of production and supply would have altered the sensory texture of the city (Dioscorides 2.160; Martial *Epigrams* 9.59, 9.62, 10.80, 11.8, 11.27.11; Wallace-Hadrill, 2008, p. 332, 2014, pp. 88–9; Holleran, 2012, p. 57, pp. 64–87, pp. 249–52). Claire Holleran argues that the absence of the elite from the city of Rome in September and October would have reduced the market for luxury foodstuffs and other items, and for manufactured goods (2012, pp. 35–6), causing another seasonal alteration in the sensescape of the city. The reduction in shipping and absence of the elite market in specific months would also have meant that fewer porters and pack animals were transporting goods within the city, although this reduction was likely made up for by an increase in construction traffic (*Tabula Heracleensis* 2.56–67; Frontinus *Aqueducts of Rome* 23; Martial *Epigrams* 5.22.5–8; Favro, 2011, pp. 344–5; Holleran, 2012, pp. 36–7). Each of these factors altered the seasonal rhythms of everyday life in the city, presenting a varied tapestry of sensory artefacts which changed according to the time of day, month, climate, availability of certain products and the nature of human, animal, wheeled and river traffic (see also Laurence, 2015, pp. 182–3; Malmberg, 2015, pp. 190–2). The result was a multivalent sensescape in which smells, sounds, tastes, and the visual, kinaesthetic and haptic affordances of objects, spaces and people were in constant flux, causing the inhabitants of, and visitors to, Rome to interact with and interpret the city in seasonally variable ways.

If the elite were the primary customers of expensive textiles and perfumes, these businesses may have closed during September and October. Even if they remained open, the absence of the elite and, in particular, the reduction of political business in the Forum Romanum and Imperial Fora may have reduced the flow of people along the Vicus Tuscus during these two months. Consequently, the route between the Argiletum and Circus Maximus would have been less crowded and less noisy, affording the opportunity for most inhabitants of the city to move around more easily. This seasonal change would have altered the patterns and pace of movement within the city and consequently the experience and perceptions of the centre of Rome, in particular for the non-elite. We might ask whether other businesses filled the gaps and how this change of sensory artefacts would have altered the landscape. Seasonality of both products and potential customers therefore affected the interplay between sensory artefacts, which together combined to create sense loci that altered according to the season.

Conclusion

This chapter has put forward three approaches for sensory studies of the Roman city, focusing on literature and epigraphy as sources of sensory data and on objects as sensory artefacts, which, when combined with the architectural elements of urban space, enable us to identify sense loci in which some or all sensations had active agency (Lefebvre, 2014, pp. 113–15). The case study of the Vicus Tuscus has demonstrated some of the ways in which these approaches can be used to comprehend the daily and seasonal rhythms of life in the city and the variety of experience of urban life, focusing on the relationship between status and use of space. The mutability of sensory experience offers a wealth of opportunities to archaeologists and ancient historians who wish to include a multisensory approach.

Investigating Rome's sensory artefacts enriches our understanding of the character and use of the city's spaces, and the rhythms of Roman daily life. Whilst it remains impossible to recapture entirely an individual's specific relationships to the urban fabric and its rhythms, a multisensory approach furnishes us with the essential context with which to repopulate the city and appreciate some of the effects of sensory artefacts on human experience. We have at our disposal a wealth of evidence with which to examine the characteristics of particular sounds, smells, tastes, textures and sights in ancient Rome, and to relocate them in space. Multisensory approaches to ancient Rome will help build a map of the city as experienced by the elite, urban plebs, freedmen and women, children, foreigners and slaves. It will help us to understand better how specific buildings, streets and areas of Rome were related to one another and how they were used by the city's inhabitants. Only by acknowledging, investigating, recognising and using situated sensory artefacts can we begin to understand the actions (and perhaps some of the motivations) of the human perceiver of Roman urban space.

Notes

1　On the use of 'affectiveness' as a sensory term, see Hamilakis, 2014, p. 4; Lefebvre, 2014, p. 83.
2　This example is presented with the caveat that both characters are personae, and with an awareness of the satirical edge of the epigram.
3　Though contrast Pliny, who comments that '[a]mong the senses, that of touch in man ranks before all the other species, and taste next; but in the remaining senses he is surpassed by many other creatures' (*Natural History* 10.191).
4　Note, *contra* Koloski-Ostrow, that animal remains seem not to have been left in the confines of the amphitheatre (MacKinnon, 2006, pp. 18–20).
5　http://formaurbis.stanford.edu/fragments/color_raw_reduced/018a.jpg.
6　http://formaurbis.stanford.edu/fragments/color_mos_reduced/018bc_MOS.jpg.
7　http://formaurbis.stanford.edu/fragments/color_mos_reduced/005Abcd_MOS.jpg.

3 Beyond smell

The sensory landscape of the Roman *fullonica*

Miko Flohr

It has long been held that the world of the Roman *fullo* was first and foremost a rather smelly affair, and that the malodorous nature of their businesses meant that *fullones* faced serious challenges in negotiating their social position, or were even obliged to conduct their work in the periphery of the city so that they would not disturb civic live with the smell of rotten urine. In the 1930s Mima Maxey claimed that fulleries were a 'public nuisance to some extent' (1938, p. 37). More recently, in his provocative article on the cultural position of the Roman *fullonica*, Mark Bradley has argued that fulleries stank, and were 'proverbially unpleasant places to be around' (2002, p. 35). Similar ideas can be found in the work of Fridolf Kudlien, who refers to the '*gesellschaftliche Ambivalenz*' of fulling in his work on Lucius Patulcius, the fuller who became Proboulos in Magnesia on the Maeander (Kudlien, 2002, p. 58). Likewise, Andrew Wilson suggested that the fulleries at Timgad were concentrated in a remote corner of the city so that their smells would be blown away from the city centre walls by the prevailing winds (2000, p. 280). Nevertheless, while some of the chemicals used in the fulling process brought nasty smells with them, it is clear that this did not impede fulleries, and sometimes rather large ones, to be built in the middle of cities like Pompeii and Ostia. Their business did not impede *fullones* from developing clearly defined and public occupational statuses, nor did it prevent them from playing a central and visible role in many urban communities throughout the Roman world, as is attested by the many inscriptions left by their professional associations in the cities of, particularly, Roman Italy and Asia Minor (see Flohr, 2013a, pp. 322–46). Moreover, a great deal of the literary evidence supposedly associating *fullones* with bad smells, or a bad reputation, on closer inspection presents a much more nuanced picture than past scholars have tried to sketch (Flohr, 2013a, pp. 185–6). Indeed, if we want to analyse the cultural and social positions of fullers and their work in Roman urban communities, or rather the way in which these were shaped by the work they actually did, we cannot afford to stick to our noses: we need to bring in the other senses as well.

The present chapter aims to do precisely this: to evaluate the work done by fullers from a multisensory perspective, and to discuss how this impacted on the social and cultural roles of fullers in their urban communities. The following discussion starts from the idea that the sensory landscapes of workshops like *fullonicae* provided an infrastructure that played a vital role in the cultural perception of the production processes and shaped the stage on which craftsmen and workers negotiated their occupational and social identities. This stage, the workshop, may have appeared profoundly different according to particular circumstances, and to various groups of people. It was most familiar to those actually working there, and for regular visitors such as business contacts and customers; but less familiar to other people in the community who were not directly involved, and who may have had to base their knowledge and their perception on an occasional glimpse – an incidental visit, or an accidental look in from the street. This has a couple of implications that need to be highlighted here. In the first place, it is reasonable to assume that the Roman elite, and more in particular the authors of Latin literature, generally belonged to the second group. Some may have had reasonably good knowledge of workshops out of sheer interest, but others much less so. In both cases, they were outsiders to the world of the craftsmen and workers populating the shop floor of *fullonicae* and other workshops. It is essential to note that this has an impact on the way their references to fulling and fulling workshops can be used in a cultural analysis of fulling and its sensory impact: literary evidence must be used with great caution, because it may reflect prejudices and stereotypes rather than providing reliable indications of the cultural position of fullers and *fullonicae*. Whatever Roman authors say about the cultural position of fulling and its sensory impact needs to be weighed very carefully against the physical evidence for the stage on which fullers negotiated their occupational identity, the *fullonicae*. In other words, any cultural analysis of fulling needs to give pride of place to the archaeology (*contra* Olson, 2014).

Secondly, it becomes relevant to distinguish between direct and indirect sensory impact – the first being the impact that people perceived themselves, the second being the impact they may have imagined other people to perceive. The perspective of the workers as well as that of the outsiders with whom they had to deal on a regular basis are therefore equally important. The question, then, is very much whose senses we are actually talking about. Modern scholarship on Roman urbanism has sometimes tended to assume the perspective of the visitor, who walks through the Roman city like modern scholars walk through archaeological sites, discovering the realities of the city very much like we discover their remains. While this may be useful when describing the ancient environment, socio-spatial realities in antiquity were of course much more complex than that, especially when one is talking about workshops instead of monuments, and that complexity should be taken into account. The sensory landscapes of *fullonicae* can be approached from a variety of perspectives. As this chapter focuses on the way in which the sensory landscapes of *fullonicae* played a role in shaping the cultural position of fulling, there will be a certain emphasis on the extent to which these landscapes were open to outsiders.

In what follows, the sensory landscape of *fullonicae* will be analysed in three steps. The first section of this chapter will look into the fulling process and analyse the sensory impact of its key phases; subsequently, the focus will be on the *fullonicae* and how their spatial layout conditioned the way the urban community had an idea of what was going on in these workshops. The third step in the argument will put the *fullonica* into perspective by comparing it to a set of other workshops and their sensory impacts (for a related analysis see Veitch on sounds in Ostia, this volume).

First, however, it is necessary to briefly introduce fulling and its evidence. The evidence for fulling is quantitatively limited but qualitatively rich (Flohr, 2013a, pp. 12–34). The core is made up by the material remains of *fullonicae* from Pompeii and Ostia: while fulling workshops can be identified in a number of other places as well, the *fullonicae* of Pompeii and Ostia stand out both quantitatively and qualitatively.[1] For most purposes it makes sense to subdivide the identifiable *fullonicae* into three groups: small-scale workshops situated in *tabernae*, medium-sized workshops situated in *atrium* houses and large-scale *fullonicae* situated in purpose-built production halls (Flohr, 2013a, pp. 74–9). Election notices referring to *fullones* on the façades of three Pompeian *fullonicae* connect the material remains of fulling workshops to the textual record, which consists of a limited number of inscriptions and a relatively modest quantity of literary references. These come from a variety of genres, including legal textbooks, and most are very short but provide essential information on both the technical aspects of the Roman fulling process and the social and cultural contexts in which it took place, as will become clear in the next section.

Fullers generally seem to have worked with finished garments, not with raw cloth, as in the medieval period (Flohr, 2013a, pp. 57–64). Rather than cleaning, the aim of the fulling process was to curate the surface of the garment, and particularly the nap, which gave the clothes a smooth surface, made them warmer and gave them a shiny appearance. The fulling procedure consisted of three main phases (see also Flohr, 2013a, pp. 98–121). First, clothes were treated with detergents to dissolve fats and remove pollution. This was done in tubs, in a rather labour-intensive process which involved trampling the clothes, scrubbing them and wringing them out. This phase has left rather typical remains in the archaeological record in the form of fulling stalls (Figure 3.1). Once the chemicals had been worked in, they had to be rinsed out. To this end, most *fullonicae* had purpose-built complexes of rinsing basins (Figure 3.2), though some small workshops at Pompeii seem to have relied on public fountains. The phase requiring the most skills was the last phase, which involved the raising, trimming and polishing of the nap by means of brushes and shears. Additional treatments, such as chalking and sulphuring, could be performed as well, but these do not seem to have been part of the standard procedure (Flohr, 2013a, pp. 117–21).

Figure 3.1 Fulling stalls in *fullonica* (VII.2.41), Pompeii

Source: Photo: Miko Flohr

Figure 3.2 Rinsing complex in *fullonica* (I.6.7), Pompeii

Source: Photo: Miko Flohr

Fulling and the senses

Four of the five senses are relevant to understanding the multisensory realm of *fullonicae*; taste played no meaningful role. This section sketches the potential impact of fulling sense by sense, concentrating purely on the process and not its embedding in urban space.

Sound

A fulling workshop was not really a quiet place, even though the amount of literary references to the sounds caused by fullers at work is extremely limited. The first two phases of the production process can certainly be assumed to have produced sounds; the finishing procedure is likely to have been a relatively quiet affair except for the occasional sound of brushing and of scissors, and perhaps the sound of a cloth press being operated. As to the work in the tubs, one of the fragments of Titinius' *Fullones* alludes to the sound produced by the procedure: 'That is earth, not water, in which you usually slosh with your feet while you compact the clay, you, who wash clothes' (Titinius *Fullones*, fragment 10).[2]

The verb used by Titinius (*argutarier*) suggests trampling cloths with liquids and chemicals caused rather typical, sloshy sounds. This first phase of the process was rather labour-intensive so it is not hard to imagine that there were also sounds related to human physical effort, such as gasping from the exertion (with the caveat that all was dependent on an individual's level of physical fitness). The wringing out of garments is also likely to have generated some physical expression of noise.

The second phase, rinsing, of course included the sounds of clothes being dropped into and taken out of the water, but these may be marginal compared to the sounds of the actual activities taking place in rinsing basins, many of which seem to have had working benches which were perhaps used for brushing. The sound of workers navigating through the basins and working with the garments must have been a familiar sound in many fulling workshops. The water system of rinsing complexes generated noise as well: in all fulling workshops where the water provision system of the rinsing complex is preserved, the mouth lay above the highest possible water table, so that any filling or refilling of the complexes created the sound of water falling into water. As some complexes were designed to have a continuous flow of water, this sound may have been present throughout the working day.

Sight

The fulling process provided a variety of remarkable things to look at for outsiders, and echoes of that can be found in Latin literature. Seneca's detailed description of a *fullo* moisturising a garment stretched out on a brushing installation is exemplary in this respect:

> Watch a fuller, if you like, and you will see the same thing happen sometimes. When he fills his mouth with water and gently sprays it on clothes

spread out on stretchers it appears as though the various colours which usually shine in a rainbow are produced in that sprayed air.

(Seneca *Natural Questions* 1.3.2)[3]

The fuller fills his mouth with water, and sprinkles it towards the garment; as it goes through the air, the water gives off all kinds of colours, like a rainbow.

An aspect of fulling that certainly was seen as visually remarkable was the work in the tubs, and the trampling of clothes under the feet – the 'dancing fuller'. Roman comic drama occasionally refers to this activity, suggesting that it could be exploited on stage (Flohr, 2013a, pp. 326–7). Besides the fragment by Titinius quoted above, there is a fragment from Laberius' *Fullo* in which it seems as if a fuller is being compared to a Balearic crane, a bird spending his life with his long legs in shallow water: 'Do you think this is a Balearic crane or a man?' (Laberius *Fullo*, fragment 2).[4] Seneca, too, refers to a '*saltus fullonicus*', which he describes (*Letters* 2.15.4) as rather intensive, while assuming that his readers knew approximately what it looked like. The iconography of fulling, such as the paintings of the *fullones* from *fullonica* VI.8.20–21.2 (Colour Plate 1), or the frieze with the *amorini fulloni* from the House of the Vettii at Pompeii, also highlights the peculiar nature of the work in the fulling stalls.

On the paintings from the House of the Vettii, the depiction of the two cupids trampling cloth emphasises the intensity of the procedure (Colour Plate 2). It may be suggested that the relatively rich (and varied) iconographic record for fulling compared to most other crafts is at least partially due to the variety of visually remarkable procedures that could be seen in a *fullonica* by both those occupied in the workshop and by passers-by. These included not only the tub work, but also the brushing and the inspection of clothes, as is clear from both paintings from Pompeii, and from other iconographic representations of the fulling process, such as the reliefs from Sens and Forlimpopoli (Flohr, 2013a, pp. 31–5).

Touch

While the things someone could see and hear were roughly the same for workers and outsiders, this is not true for the things one could physically feel: fulling was a very physical process for the people involved in it, but obviously much less so for the visitors to their workshops. For customers, one may perhaps imagine that part of checking the quality of the work involved actually touching the garment and checking the smoothness of the nap, but that barely counts in such a kinaesthetic process.

The most physical part of the process was undoubtedly its first phase; rinsing and finishing were not so physically demanding, though some people involved in rinsing spent part of their time standing in 0.5–0.75 m deep (cold) water. Finishing involved careful inspection of the surface of a garment, using the fingers. During the first phase fullers were continuously in direct contact with the garment under treatment and the chemicals used as detergents, both with their feet and with their hands. In the case of used clothes, they were also potentially in direct contact with all kinds of dirt, as Bradley rightly emphasised (Bradley, 2002, pp. 29–30). Moreover, working in the narrow fulling stalls, which often were organised in sets of two or three (see Figure 3.1, above) or in rows, probably also meant that fullers touched each other quite a lot: neighbouring stalls generally shared the walls used as supports by fullers, so whenever they used these workers had to negotiate the position of their hands with those of their neighbours. The bodily involvement of fullers had its effects too. Pliny believed that fullers could not suffer from gout because they worked with urine (*Natural History* 28.66); the key ingredient here is ammonia. In reality, however, as Bradley noted (2002, p. 37), the effect of standing in detergents on a daily basis is most likely to have been rather disastrous for the feet of *fullones*.

For outsiders, the bodily involvement of fullers during the first phase of the process played a significant role in the picture they had of fulling and the people involved, especially in circumstances when they themselves might need to touch the hands or the body of someone who has just spent a couple of hours with his hands and feet in the dirt. In this respect it is relevant to point to the concept of 'dirty work', which has been used in the social sciences in reference to occupations that are physically, socially or morally tainted (Hughes, 1958, 1962; Goffmann, 1963). In other words, the things that you touch while making a living can lead to an occupational stigma. There is no evidence at all to support a claim that people known to spend their days in fulling stalls were to some extent 'untouchable', but the possibility that touching dirty material on a regular basis had an impact on one's occupational identity should not be *a priori* excluded.

Smell

Despite the bad name of fulling as a rather stinky affair, the actual references to the olfactory nuisance caused by fulling are few and fragmentary. The most explicit text associating *fullones* with bad smells is an epigram of Martial: 'Thais smells worse than the veteran crock of a stingy fuller, recently broken in the middle of the road' (*Epigrams* 6.93.1–2).[5] The text invokes a situation in which one of the over-used amphorae which contained liquid chemicals – probably aged urine – was accidentally broken, either knocked over in the street or during transport by the *fullo*; liberated from this container, the odour circulated freely through the air. Evocative as this text is, and while the association of fulling with smelly chemicals is unequivocal, it also seems that fullers had the means to *contain* these smells if they wished to – for example, by not using over-aged *amphorae*. The implicit suggestion is that 'good' *fullones* did not cause smells, while 'bad', avaricious fullers could.

Beyond the epigram by Martial there is only a preserved quip from Titinius to possibly link *fullers* to bad smells, 'a nasty smell attacks the nose' (Titinius *Fullones*, fragment 4),[6] but the exact link with the fulling process is unclear. Thus, the idea that fulleries stank is not really very deeply rooted in ancient literary evidence. This does not, of course, directly imply that fulling did not produce smells. A second caveat is that *fullones* had a variety of detergents at their disposal, which did not necessarily all have the same olfactory impact. The ammonia won from aged urine had a strong and irritating smell, of course, but the quantities in which this was used by fullers is unclear. As I have argued elsewhere, past scholars have tended to overestimate the role of urine in the fulling process (Flohr and Wilson, 2011, p. 150). The most important detergent seems to have been fuller's earth, the *creta* referred to by Titinius. Remains of fuller's earth have been found in certain quantities in *fullonicae* in Pompeii and Ostia (Robertson, 1986). Critically, fuller's earth not only has a much weaker smell than ammonia, it also has the property of neutralising the odours of decomposing urine – the reason behind its modern application in litter boxes for cats. This has rather dramatic implications for our ideas about the smells caused by fulling. Suppose fullers used aged urine and fuller's earth in combination, which may very well have been the case: *fullonicae* may not have been such smelly environments after all, unless, as in the situation described by Martial, something went wrong and the ammonia ended up in places where it should not be.

The sensory impact of the *fullonica*

Now that we have analysed the possible effects of the fulling process on the senses of both participants and passers-by, the next step is to discuss how this worked in practice: how did the sensory landscape of *fullonicae* appear to passers-by? Given the large differences between the identifiable *fullonicae*, the best way to do this is by discussing a set of representative examples of small, medium-sized and large *fullonicae* – two from Pompeii and two from Ostia. One important aspect that has not really been discussed to date is the light situation in these workshops. Light would have had a significant impact on the sensory landscape, both for workers and outsiders. A second key issue concerns the relationship between the workshop and public space – the street – as this defined the extent to which the sensory landscape of fulling workshops was easily perceptible by outsiders who did not need to be *in* the fullery (on the relationship of streets and shops in Ostia, compare Veitch, this volume). In this respect it is relevant to mention a regulation defined in the *Digests* (43.10.1.4) which explicitly (and by exception) allowed *fullones* to use the pavement in front of their shop (if they had one) for hanging out garments, as long as they did not impede traffic. The extent to which this was actually done is of course unknown, as the practice is archaeologically unidentifiable, but it suggests that fulling workshops could be visible from some distance because of clothes hanging out in front of them.

Pompeii, fullonica *(VII.2.41)*

This small *fullonica* (VII.2.41) was situated in a *taberna* along the busy Via degli Augustali right in the heart of Pompeii's city centre (see Figure 3.3). The working equipment was entirely concentrated in the main room, and thus well visible from the street (see also Flohr, 2013a, pp. 250–2). The wide opening meant that the room was reasonably well-lit during daylight hours and its location on the

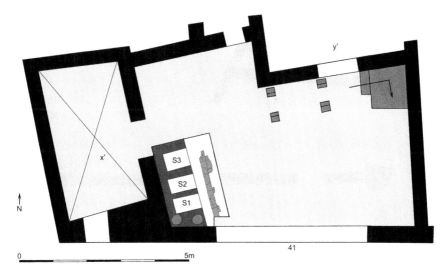

Figure 3.3 Plan of *fullonica* (VII.2.41), Pompeii
Source: Miko Flohr

north side of the Via degli Augustali meant that it received direct sunlight for large parts of the afternoon. The location of the fulling stalls (S1–S3) in the south-west corner of the shop meant that passers-by were almost in touching distance of the workers in the tubs. They could see the first phase in all its details and hear the sounds of the fullers working in the chemicals. Indeed, it is reasonable to assume that they could actually smell the substances with which the fullers worked. Remains of a finishing installation were situated along the north wall, and while the worker operating it stood with his back to the street, his work was plainly visible. In other words, the sensory landscape of this *fullonica* was a fairly public affair. It is relevant to note that it would have been possible to hide part of the process from the public by situating it in room 'x', west of the shop, but this option was not chosen. The layout of this *fullonica* is typical for the nine small fulling workshops of Pompeii, all of which have identifiable installations situated in the shop, even if other rooms were available. Whilst they were often situated in the interior, or back part, of the shop, the sound and sight of *argutarier pedibus* by *fullones* must have been familiar to Pompeians, and probably to the inhabitants of several other towns in Roman Italy.

Ostia, fullonica *(I.xiii.3)*

The *fullonica* in the *cardo* at Ostia (I.xiii.3) was slightly larger than the previous example from Pompeii (VII.2.41). It consisted of a shop and a back room in which the fulling installations were situated (Figure 3.4; Pietrogrande, 1976,

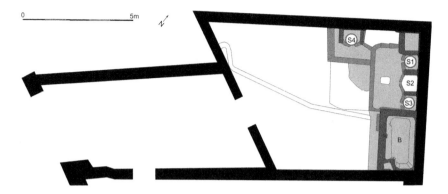

Figure 3.4 Plan of *fullonica* (I.xiii.3), Ostia
Source: Miko Flohr

pp. 9–13). This had implications for both the light situation in the workshop and for the perceptibility of the production process. As the back room was fully roofed, and there is no evidence for windows in the extant parts of the walls, the workshop is likely to have been a rather dark and confined place, its sensescape qualitatively different from the Pompeian example. There was a door between the shop and the workroom, but it must have been difficult to see whatever was happening in there, whilst sounds and odours would have been more concentrated and confined (see also Veitch, this volume, on acoustic architecture). This suggests that the sound, rather than the sight, of the tub workers dominated the space, together with the sound of the activities in and around the rinsing basin. It also suggests that the finishing part of the process, for which light was essential, was done in the shop, where there was much more light. Thus, in this workshop, the phases that were most culturally sensitive were invisible to outsiders and concentrated in a dark back room. The other small *fullonicae* at Ostia follow this model: that the portico belonging to the baths of Neptune consisted of only one room, but the fulling tubs were concentrated at the back of it, behind the rinsing basin (Flohr, 2013a, plan 5). In other words, the most characteristic phase of the fulling process was almost completely invisible at Ostia, which is a marked contrast with Pompeii.

Pompeii, fullonica *(I.6.7)*

The well-known *fullonica* of Stephanus (I.6.7) at Pompeii was situated in a house (Figure 3.5). There was a shop along the street (b) and a workroom (q) in the back part of the house, behind the peristyle and garden (p) but within the walls of the house (Flohr, 2011). The first two phases of the production process were carried out in the workroom, whereas the finishing procedure was done in the shop – as

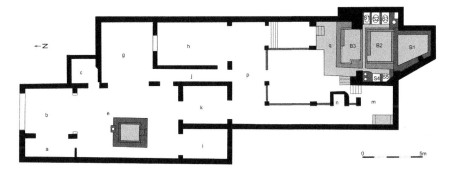

Figure 3.5 Plan of *fullonica* 'of Stephanus' (I.6.7), Pompeii
Source: Miko Flohr

is indicated by the objects found there, which included not only the remains of a cloth press but also several brushes and a set of shears (Della Corte, 1912, p. 246; Flohr, 2013a, pp. 162–3). The light in the two main work areas was profoundly different: the shop received daylight through its opening onto the street, whereas the workroom in the back part of the house was only indirectly lit through the garden. The workroom was a dark place and its limited size must also have made it rather noisy: the tub workers were placed directly around the small rinsing complex, which could have a continuous flow of water and had a spout between the first and the second basin (Flohr, 2013a, p. 141). This dark workroom is likely to have been dominated by the sounds of flowing water, of clothes being trampled in the tubs and of the voices of those present in this room. The shop, on the other hand, was not only much lighter, but also quieter. The distance between the shop and the workroom in the back part of the house meant that outsiders could not directly see or hear the back room activity, and it is reasonable to assume that it was visited only by a relatively limited number of people. This was also true for the work areas in the other two medium-sized *fullonicae* of Pompeii, which suggests that, to the outside public, the sensory awareness – and therefore the existence – of these larger workrooms was barely appreciated.

Ostia, fullonica (V.vii.3)

The three large *fullonicae* at Ostia, together with the *fullonica* at Casal Bertone in Rome and the workshop identified under the Piazza della Signoria in Florence, were situated in purpose-built construction halls. These were rather inaccessible environments: they did not have a shop and were therefore not generally visited by outsiders. Moreover, these fulling factories were generally invisible from the street. The best example is the *fullonica* of the Via degli Augustali in Ostia (Figure 3.6; Pietrogrande, 1976, pp. 55–89). This workshop was organised around

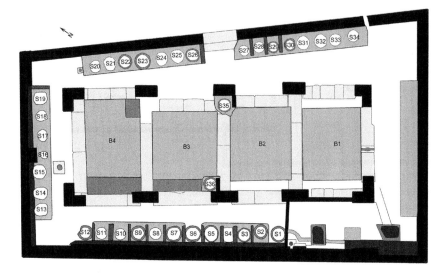

Figure 3.6 Plan of *fullonica* (V.vii.3), Ostia
Source: Miko Flohr

the four basins of its rinsing complex. While the details of its roof construction are not completely clear, the presence of large pillars on the borders of the rinsing basins suggests that the basins were either not roofed, or roofed in a different way from the surrounding space. Pietrogrande (1976, pp. 57–8), who excavated the place, argued that the main light source to the workroom was above the rinsing complex. This would mean that the visual focus of the complex was around its centre, while the sides, where the fulling tubs were concentrated, were slightly more marginal – though they were not necessarily very dark. The quantity of fulling tubs, and their layout in long rows along the walls of the hall, suggests the sounds related to the first phase of the process were a constant, dominant factor throughout the workshop, though it may be argued that the intensity of the noise also depended on the height of the ceiling, which is unknown. The only communication with the outside world was through the door on the Via degli Augustali; if this was opened, passers-by could perhaps hear what was happening inside, but they could see only a small section of the workshop, and mainly the rinsing complex. Of course it is not certain that the door was continuously opened, and it should be noted that the Via degli Augustali was not a main road with a lot of commercial activity around it; the number of passers-by was limited. The other two large *fullonicae* at Ostia did not even have direct access from the street, but were situated in the back part of a building, and only could be entered through these buildings. The *fullonica* at Florence was accessible from a dead-end road, while the workshop at Casal Bertone was situated outside the city, behind a necropolis. In other words, the existence of these large fulling workshops, and their sensory landscapes, may have been completely unknown by many people (Flohr, 2013a, p. 241).

These four case studies reveal that the sensory landscapes of *fullonicae* differed with the size and the layout of the workshops. Yet it should be pointed out that there is one general trend: the larger the workshop, the less visible it was to the outside public. The largest number of fulling tubs visible from the street in either Pompeii or Ostia was three; rinsing was rarely visible, and only in small workshops. The implication is that any cultural perception of the sensory landscape of the *fullonica* was based on the small-scale *fullonicae* situated in *tabernae*, and not on those larger workshops which, in theory, may have been much noisier (and perhaps smellier) than the smaller workshops. The general public had only very limited knowledge of this large-scale fulling.

Fulling and other urban crafts

Besides the intrinsic sensory artefacts of fulling (such as the smell of urine and fuller's earth, or the kinaesthetic movement of the fuller at work), and the way they worked out in urban space (such as the visibility of small workshops and the invisibility of larger ones), there is a third key factor to consider. In order to understand the ways in which the smells, sounds and sights of fulling shaped the cultural position of the trade, they must be compared to those of other crafts. Contrary to expectation, fulling does not really seem to stand out very negatively; for the most part it was neither particularly noisy nor smelly. The *fullonica* had a rather specific sensory landscape, but it was neither more nor less intrusive than those of other crafts. With this premise in mind, it is relevant to briefly highlight three aspects in which the *fullonica* was environmentally friendly compared to other workshops.

In the first place, it is essential to note that fulling, like all crafts involving textiles, was a relatively quiet process: it contributed to the soundscape of ancient cities only to a very limited extent. Indeed, the sounds coming from a fulling workshop could easily be drowned out by a cart or a horse passing by. It is unlikely that a fulling workshop could be heard from a great distance unless its workers were singing or talking very loudly. This is of course a rather big difference from, for example, workshops devoted to iron-working, or to the working of bone or wood, which produced sounds of hammering and sawing that could be heard at a considerable distance from the workshop (for further discussion of sounds on the streets of Ostia, see Veitch, this volume).

Secondly, it is relevant to observe that fulling, unlike many other manufacturing processes, did not use heat. This meant two things. In the first place, it meant that the temperature in *fullonicae* was not higher than it was in their immediate surroundings. In other words, while people passing a smithy or a bakery would sometimes feel the presence of a workshop from the heat of the furnaces or ovens, this was not the case when they walked past a *fullonica*. At the same time, the absence of heating installations meant that fulleries did not produce smoke or any other smells associated with burning fuel. This should not be underestimated: the two dyeing workshops in *tabernae* V.1.4 and V.1.5 at Pompeii had dyeing cauldrons standing on their thresholds. During working hours, considerable quantities of smoke and smells must have been coming out of these workshops, so they could probably have been seen and smelled from a considerable distance away.

Finally, as far as smells are concerned, other processes may have produced much stronger odours than fulling did. This is particularly true for the many outlets that sold warm food along the streets of Pompeii, and probably many other towns in Roman Italy (Ellis, 2004; Monteix, 2010, pp. 89–132). Bakeries, too, are likely to have produced odours that could be smelled in their urban environment. Their omnipresence throughout Pompeii suggests that the smell of fresh bread was a prominent part of the urban landscape. These smells are, of course, 'good' smells, in the sense that the smell of freshly prepared food tends to attract people rather than to offend them, but their role in the sensory landscape of the city must not be underestimated. These food smells may actually have been *stronger* than the smell coming from *fullonicae*, especially if ammonia and fuller's earth were used in combination. Moreover, even if *fullonicae* produced 'bad smells', these would not have been exclusive to the *fullo*. For instance, tanneries are also known to have produced strong and nasty odours, as in all probability did the shops commonly and incorrectly known as *lanifricariae*: while the nature of these workshops is disputed, the way they were embedded in the urban environment suggests their production process smelled extremely badly (Monteix, 2013; Flohr, 2013b, pp. 57–60).

Final discussion

Fulling was a visually remarkable process that produced rather typical sounds and needed chemicals that in theory could cause olfactory nuisance. Yet, in practice, things do not seem to have been so bad, and there were manufacturing activities with a much stronger impact on the urban sensory landscape. Most importantly, fulleries did *not* stink and *cannot* be seen as 'proverbially unpleasant places to be around' (*contra* Bradley, 2002, p. 35; Koloski-Ostrow, 2015, pp. 101–3; Bradley, 2015b, pp. 140–1). There was no cultural stigma attached to fulling because of its olfactory impact; past scholars have been unduly pessimistic in this respect. Indeed, in the cultural perception of fulling the technical peculiarities of the production process tend to receive most attention, both in the literary sources and in the iconography (see, for example, Colour Plates 1 and 2). In all probability the cultural image of fulling was not defined by how *fullonicae* smelled but by the sights and sounds they offered, and, perhaps, by the bodily involvement of the workers trampling clothes in the tubs. In other words, it is not just 'not enough' to stick to our noses when making sense of fulling, it is also wrong: to understand fulling and its cultural image in the Roman world, eyes and ears are more important than noses.

This also has implications for our view on the cultural history of fulling in the Roman world: if the idea that fulling stank is wrong, the idea that fulling was spatially or socially controversial also crumbles. True, fullers could be made fun of because of the odd nature of their everyday work, and there were certain aspects of their business – particularly the fact that they worked with other people's valuable property – that made their work socially sensitive, as is expressed by the many legal texts describing the legal responsibility of fullers in case something went wrong with the clothes that had been trusted to them (see Flohr, 2013a, p. 275). It is also true that some elite authors appear to show little respect for fullers; though they do not show much respect for other craftsmen either. At the same time, the tombs of some large elite households in Rome include epitaphs of people proudly commemorated for the fulling they did for the household (Flohr, 2013a, p. 71). In Pompeii, *fullones* could use their occupational status to recommend candidates in the local elections (*CIL* IV.7164), and did so more than any other occupational group. As the statue from the building of Eumachia in the same city shows, a group of *fullones* could pay and erect a honorific statue in a prestigious and probably highly frequented location in the heart of the city. At Ephesos, a successful athlete could be commemorated with reference to his nickname 'the fuller' (I.Eph. 1084). There is no evidence that all this was in spite of a cultural stigma. A well-functioning master *fullo* could simply use his occupational identity as an asset in social interactions within the community.

Paradoxically, this means that there may, after all, be no need for a 'cultural history' of fulling (see Olson, 2014, p. 598); at least no more than there is need for cultural histories of Roman baking, dyeing, smithing or woodworking. Fulling was a craft like most other crafts: it could work to your benefit if you were good at it, but if you were bad at it, it did not help your social status. There were some risks attached to it, and some tensions, but no more than there were to other crafts. Just as the sensory landscape of *fullonicae* was not significantly more or less culturally loaded than that of other workshops, so was the craft itself culturally more-or-less 'neutral'. In other words, looking for the cultural sensitivities related to fulling may, in the end, be simply looking in the wrong direction.

Notes

1 Twelve *fullonicae* have been excavated at Pompeii; five can be identified at Ostia. Also important are the (unpublished) *fullonicae* excavated in Casal Bertone and Florence. Two more workshops have been partially excavated in Rome. Small fulleries have been excavated at Herculaneum and Fréjus (see also Flohr, 2013a, pp. 20–30; for Fréjus see Rivet, Brentchaloff, Roucole and Saulnier, 2000, p. 259).
2 *Terra istaec est, non aqua, ubi tu solitus argutarier / Pedibus, cretam dum compescis, vestimenta qui laves.*
3 *. . . si quando observare volueris fullonem: cum os aqua implevit et vestimenta tendiculis diducta leviter adspergit, adparet varios edi colores in illo aëre adsperso quales fulgere in arcu nolent . . .*
4 *utrum tu hunc gruem Balearicum an hominem putas esse.*
5 *Tam male Thais olet, quam non fullonis avari / testa vetus, media sed modo fracta via . . .*
6 *. . . interea foetida anima nasum oppugnat . . .*

4 Soundscape of the street
Architectural acoustics in Ostia

Jeffrey Veitch[1]

Since the 1970s, the measurement of noise and its influence on everyday life has brought the field of aural architecture out of sound studios and into the commercial and residential buildings that line our streets. Alongside this, historical soundscapes and reconstructions of ancient sites have been produced for sixteenth-century England (Smith, 1999) and for the Hal Saflieni Hypogeum (Eniex, 2014). The aim of this chapter is not simply to reproduce a historic soundscape, nor to reconstruct historic noises (compare Laurence, Vincent, this volume), but to use archaeology to set the framework for discussions of sound in the Roman city. Sounds happen at specific times and in specific places, and the physical structures of these times and places impact on the sounds. Large spaces are perceived by long *reverberation times*,[2] while small spaces have sharp *frequency responses* (Blesser and Salter, 2007, p. 21), demonstrating that acoustics provides the information required to perceive spatial volume. In hearing, volume and area remain primary, while physical boundaries are secondary to the experience of the space (Blesser and Salter, 2007, p. 21; Betts, 2011, p. 121). This contrasts with the essentially visual concept that physical boundaries demarcate space. Whilst the standing remains of Ostia no longer echo with ancient sounds, their acoustic characteristics can be interpreted through analysis of the size, shape and material structure of the buildings. In this chapter, my knowledge of aural architecture is applied to the historical site of Ostia to develop methods for understanding the relationship between physical buildings and sound. The intention is to present some practical methodological premises for the interpretation of aural architecture, sounds shaped by and produced in the built environment. In many ways, sounds are the easiest sense data to recover, although, as will be shown, this is not as straightforward as is often thought.

The first sections of this chapter lay the foundations for reconstructing the acoustics of built structures, taking as an example the common one-room shops lining the northern section of the *cardo maximus* in Ostia. The acoustic properties are drawn from traditional archaeological analysis and site publications, with the important proviso that the measurements are used in quite different ways from those associated with archaeological reports and publications. A room's measurements, construction and decoration provide the basic features from which its architectural acoustics can be analysed, but to understand the influence of architecture on the soundscape (the combination of sounds particular to a given area) one must also take note of the characteristics of sound itself (Schafer, 1977). Most significantly, the ability of sounds to transfer through materials acoustically links visually distinct spaces. The production and perception of sound are just as important as the architectural space in which sounds were heard, and the physical properties of space can only be related to social interactions through the mapping of sounds and acoustic properties. Therefore, the physics of sound is emphasised in this methodology to recover the experience of architectural acoustics.

Sounds are ephemeral and momentary in nature, changing as the circumstances around them alter. The final section of the chapter considers the potential sounds and their temporal setting on the street, in order to better understand the social systems that structured everyday life in the ancient city. Time and setting are important features of sounds; they aid in navigation and produce forms of knowledge about urban areas (Betts, 2011, pp. 122–3). Thus, a better understanding of the urban soundscape of Ostia reflects the everyday rhythms of the city.

Setting the scene: *Portico di Pio IX* and *cardo maximus*

The shops along the *cardo maximus*, north of the Capitolium, form the main buildings along the street leading from the Forum to the Tiber (Figure 4.1). Construction of the *Portico di Pio IX* is remarkably uniform, with very similar building techniques and materials used throughout. The bricks were supplied from the *figlinae Caepionianae* (*dominus* C. Curiatius Cosanus) and the *figlinae Brutianae* (*dominus* Rutilius Lupus), with two-thirds of the brickstamps dated to 114–116 CE (DeLaine, 2002, p. 96). This building project was the likely occasion for the realignment of the north *cardo*, as the earlier first-century BCE Forum temple respects the earlier *cardo* location leading to the gate in the *castrum* (Calza, Becatti and Bloch, 1953, p. 104, pp. 130–2).

The change also resulted in a considerable rise in ground level, from 1.40 m to around 2.40 m above sea level, which corresponds to a section of road under the east portico flanking the Capitolium (DeLaine, 2002, pp. 96–7). The raised ground level suggests that the *cardo* and the inner pomerial road, located under the Capitolium portico, originally intersected under the later Capitolium (DeLaine, 2002, p. 97). The Capitolium is not centred with the realigned *cardo*, suggesting that it was a later building than the *Portico di Pio IX* (DeLaine, 2002, p. 99). Thus, the realignment of the north *cardo* linking the Tiber and Forum, and the building of the *Portico di Pio IX*, began a process of reorganisation that ended with the later Capitolium and extended Forum porticoes (see Lavan, 2012). The overall dating points to the *Portico di Pio IX* being completed not later than 116 CE, with the other structures completed in 117–118 CE (*Piccolo Mercato* (1.8.1), *Caseggiato dei Misuratori di Grano* (1.7), *Caseggiato del Balcone e Mensole* (1.6.2) and the *horrea* at 1.8.2; Figure 4.1). The Capitolium and flanking porticoes have a later date, possibly in the 120s CE (DeLaine, 2002, p. 64).

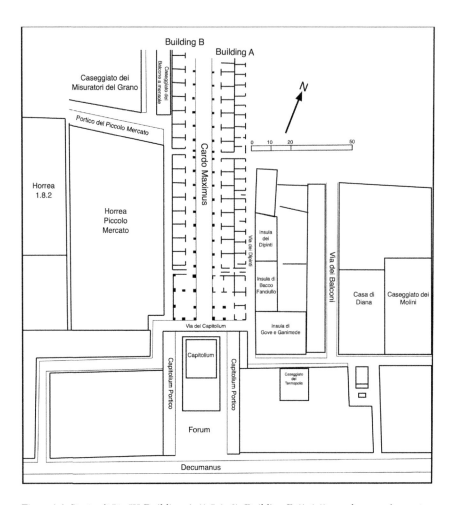

Figure 4.1 Portico di Pio IX, Building A (1.5.1–2), Building B (1.6.1), northern *cardo maximus*
and the surrounding area

Source: Jeffrey Veitch

The *Portico di Pio IX* buildings (Building A, 1.5.1–2; Building B, 1.6.1; Figure 4.1) are composed of eight shop blocks with stairways to upper levels, passages through to the other side and a continuous portico lining both sides of the street (Figure 4.1). At the southern end of the street were two *loggia*, open spaces with four brick piers supporting the ceiling. There is some indication that the *loggia* had basalt paving and could have been for the stabling of animals (Calza et al., 1953). The *loggia* fronted directly onto the street, while the rows of shops to the north had porticoes marking the transition from the street to the shop front. Doorways at the end of the porticoes led into the shops and *loggia*. Although the street has not been excavated in its entirety, it may be assumed that the same arrangement continued along its length, and that the porticoes and shops would have lined the street to the Tiber, with the structures covering an area of nearly 4,700 m² (DeLaine, 2002, p. 67).

The shops are very similar to one another in construction, size and decoration, and these architectural parallels make them acoustically the same. Each of the shops along the northern *cardo maximus* has six surfaces, all of which reflect sound energy to create a complex *sound field*. The internal dimensions of the shops are roughly 5.5 m by 6 m. A wide doorway, on average 3 m, was set at the front and the thresholds indicate the use of wooden shutters to close off the space. A 'night door', or hinged plank, was set on the right-hand side so that with the shutters in place access was still available to the inhabitants (Packer, 1971, p. 21; Ellis, 2011, pp. 164–5). The lintels for the front doorways are set at a height of 3.5 m, the average in Ostia (Meiggs, 1973, p. 240). The groove widths average just under 0.04 m, which means that the wooden planks were of similar width (measurements by Paula Lock). This gave the front doorway a wooden area of 10.5 m², standard for shops in Ostia.

The walls were made of brick-faced concrete and *opus reticulatum*, with an *opus caementicium* core (Figure 4.2). This concrete core was made of slaked lime, sand or pozzolana (volcanic ash) and aggregate pieces. The standard sizes of Roman bricks meant that walls also tended to be of standard widths. In the case of the *Portico*, the average width of the walls is 0.60 m (measurements by Colin Runeckles), just above Ostia's site average of 0.56 m (Storey, 2003, p. 16). The measurements recorded in these studies make it possible to establish the acoustic properties of these architectural spaces, as will be illustrated below.

In terms of vertical space, there are remains of stepped platforms and mezzanine structures in several shops (Figure 4.2). These spaces were reached by ladders, placed on low platforms a step or two off the ground, and were supported by cornices made of projecting *bipedales*, approximately 3.40 m above the floor (DeLaine, 2002, p. 67; Figure 4.2). The mezzanine floors consisted of a wooden base overlaid with a layer of mortar around 0.15 m thick (Ulrich, 2007, pp. 112–13; Figure 4.2). Above the mezzanines, the roofs were barrel vaulted, which is evident from the remaining roof sections visible in several shops (Figure 4.2). The vaults were set at a height of approximately 7 m above the floor, leaving around 3.6 m of space above the cornices (Packer, 1971, p. 146). Above the doorway, a small window measuring 1 m by 0.60–0.80 m lighted the mezzanine space.

The evidence for the flooring in the shops of the *Portico di Pio IX* is limited, but there are indications of *opus spicatum* flooring (herringbone-shaped tiling set in mortar) along the portico and passages between the buildings. The *loggia* on the west side (1.6.1) has the remains of *selce* blocks, which were also used for paving the carriageway of the street. Travertine thresholds remain between several of the piers of the portico, indicating that sections of the portico could be closed off.

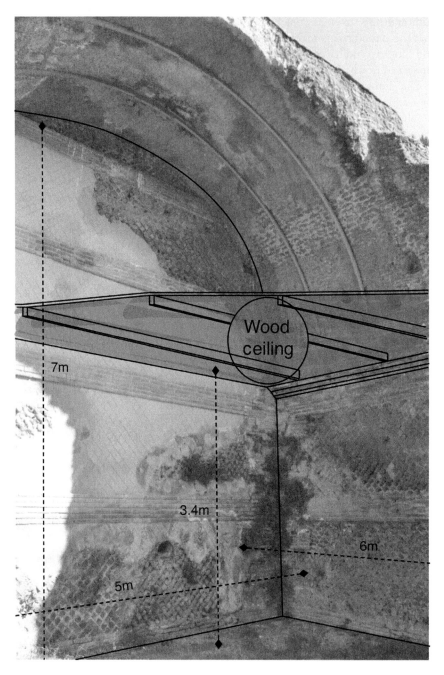

Figure 4.2 Portico di Pio IX shop. Internal dimensions and acoustic properties

Source: Jeffrey Veitch

Architectural acoustics

The acoustic properties of a given architectural space are based on the physical structures (such as those described above) and the way sound reacts to those structures. Sound functions as a wave and can pass through solids, liquids and gases, including materials like cement, glass or wood; in short, all the materials used in Roman construction (Everest and Pohlmann, 2009, p. 3). These basic physical properties of sound waves mean: (1) all materials in the ancient world can be acoustically measured; (2) acoustic hierarchies, based on acoustic measurements, have different correlations than visual hierarchies; and (3) acoustic boundaries are always relative to the sound levels in the area. These foundational properties of sound enable acoustics to offer insight into the social utility of space.

We can often 'see' physical structures with our ears (Blesser and Salter, 2007, p. 2), a phenomenon described as *echolocation*. A brief example will help to further clarify the aural qualities of architecture. Clap loudly in a room and you will hear the sound of the clap, as well as the reflection of the sound off the surfaces of the room as an echo. The distance from the wall determines the delay of the echo (in cathedrals the delay can be noticeable), the area of the wall determines the intensity of the reflected sound, and the material of the wall determines the *frequencies* perceived in the echo (Blesser and Salter, 2007, p. 2). The physical facts about the wall (distance, area and material) are interpreted through hearing sounds within the space.

The difference in materials in the *Portico di Pio IX* buildings – brick-faced concrete, *opus reticulatum*, wood and tiling – alters the acoustic properties of the space, as does opening or closing the shutters. The acoustic properties of a space transmit a variety of information about the space through the physics of sound. Again, clap loudly in the room where you are (if you are able). Depending on the size of the room the reflection of sound off the various surfaces will produce different effects (clapping in a cupboard will be perceived differently from clapping in a cathedral). When sound strikes a surface some of the energy is transmitted or absorbed by the surface and some is reflected. Dense or heavy materials tend to reflect more energy than lighter materials and the reflected energy is always less than the energy striking the surface. As the sound bounces around a room, energy is absorbed when it strikes a surface. In the case of the Ostian shops, the brick-faced and *opus reticulatum* walls would absorb minimal amounts of sound and reflect the majority, whereas the wood would absorb more sound, allowing it to pass into the neighbouring spaces. Thus, by measuring the reverberation of different sounds in the architectural spaces of the shops we can begin to build up models of their possible soundscapes.

The measurement of the absorption or reflection of a material can be quantified as the *absorption coefficient* (designated $\propto$). The absorption coefficient varies based on the frequency of the sound and is usually given at six standard frequencies (125, 250, 500, 1,000, 2,000 and 4,000 Hz; Everest and Pohlmann, 2009, p. 181). Absorption coefficients range between 1.0, indicating perfect

Table 4.1 Absorption coefficients for modern building materials and other materials that correspond with ancient materials

Material	125 Hz	250 Hz	500 Hz	1k Hz	2k Hz	4k Hz
Brick (natural)	0.03	0.03	0.03	0.04	0.05	0.07
Brick (painted)	0.01	0.01	0.02	0.02	0.02	0.03
Plaster (gypsum or lime, on masonry)	0.02	0.02	0.03	0.04	0.05	0.05
Concrete block (coarse)	0.36	0.44	0.31	0.29	0.39	0.25
Wood flooring	0.15	0.1	0.1	0.06	0.04	0.04
Doors (solid wood panels)	0.28	0.22	0.17	0.09	0.1	0.11
Marble or glazed tile	0.01	0.01	0.01	0.01	0.02	0.02
Glass (small pane 3 mm)	0.08	0.04	0.03	0.03	0.02	0.02
Benches – wooden (empty)	0.1	0.09	0.08	0.08	0.08	0.08
People – adults	0.25	0.35	0.42	0.46	0.5	0.5
Water or ice surface	0.008	0.008	0.013	0.015	0.02	0.025

Source: Everest and Pohlmann, 2009, Appendix; SAE Institute, 2014, http://www.sae.edu/reference_material/pages/Coefficient%20Chart.htm

absorption, and 0, complete reflection (Table 4.1). An open window serves as a perfect absorber as no sound returns into the room, giving it an absorption coefficient of 1.0. Although counterintuitive, defining absorption as the lack of reflection of sound back into the room is helpful in gauging the potential sound filtered into neighbouring spaces. Perfect absorption, therefore, does not automatically indicate complete diffusion of sound, or that the sound is no longer heard elsewhere. If the wide doorways were completely open in the shops, the sound from inside the shop would reflect off five surfaces and would emanate from the open front unimpeded.

The absorption coefficient for an entire room can be calculated based on the materials, area and known absorption coefficients. The sound absorption (A) provided by a given area of the material is calculated by multiplying the material's absorption coefficient ($\propto$) by the surface area (S, in m^2) of the material exposed to the sound, or $A = S\propto$. Therefore, the entire absorption coefficient for the room is the sum of all materials multiplied by the materials' absorption coefficients. There are a variety of measured absorption coefficients for common modern building materials and many of these can serve as estimates for the coefficients of ancient materials (Table 4.1). Since absorption coefficients vary based on frequency, the *noise reduction coefficient* (NRC), a single-number rating based on the average of the mid-range frequencies that pertain to speech, is often used for individual materials.

The NRC rating for modern wood flooring (similar to wooden planks used on the shutters) is 0.162 (Table 4.2). This gives the closed wooden shutters an absorption unit of 0.169, although when open the space would completely

Table 4.2 Basic acoustic elements in shops, plus absorption coefficients and reverberation time calculations

Surface	Area (m²)	Noise reduction coefficient (NRC)	Absorption units (sabins)³
Brick-faced concrete[4] (E–W walls)	20.4	0.042	0.86
Brick-faced concrete (back wall)	18.7	0.042	0.79
Wooden shutters (doorway)	10.5	0.162	0.169
Wooden planks w/mortar (ceiling)	33	0.082	2.71
Opus signinum (floor)	33	0	0
		Total absorption	6.05 sabins
		Reverberation time	2.38 secs

absorb the sound. The absorption units can be calculated for the other surfaces of the shops: the three walls have surface areas of 20.4 m² (east and west) and 18.7 m² (back), whilst the NRC for brick is 0.042, giving the walls absorption units of 0.86 and 0.79 respectively (Table 4.2). But what is the practical application of this? Once we know the absorption coefficients for each of the six sides in the space (four walls, ceiling and floor), we can calculate the time it takes for a sound to dissipate, the reverberation time. Take for example someone shouting in one of the shops. A loud shout of 80 dB will drop to 20 dB (effectively inaudible) in 2.38 seconds as the floor, walls and ceiling absorb the sound reverberating in the shop.

As mentioned above, the opening or closing of the doorway will change the acoustic character of the space. The reverberation time of 2.38 seconds is measured with the wooden shutters closed. If the shutters were open the reverberation time would drop to 1.11 seconds as the noise would not reflect off the wood but would dissipate through the opening. This is a relatively short reverberation time, similar to that of the mezzanine space, which has a reverberation time of 1.29 seconds. The reverberation time would be further reduced if the shop space were full of goods, especially textiles, furniture or other absorbent materials.

A comparative study was made of the eleven shops within the hemicycle of the Markets of Trajan in Rome. These shops are slightly smaller in size than those of the *Portico di Pio IX*, averaging 3.6 m deep and 5.5 m wide. They lack mezzanine levels and have open barrel vaulted ceilings. These differences in dimensions and internal arrangement account for the variation in reverberation times measured at the two sites: 1.07 seconds in the Markets of Trajan compared with 1.11 seconds in the *Portico di Pio IX*, although a difference of 0.04 seconds between the two is hardly noticeable. The calculated measurements for the Markets of Trajan were slightly lower, at 0.98 seconds, indicating the minimal change due to atmospheric pressure. The difference of 0.09 seconds between calculated and physically measured reverberation times also confirms the accuracy of the acoustic model and the relevance of contemporary measures for calculating measures of ancient materials.

Another measure allows for the quantification of sound energy that passes through the walls of the shop into neighbouring spaces. *Transmission loss* is the technical measure of the amount of sound energy that passes through a material, and the calculation of the transmission loss is based on the mass of the material; greater mass corresponds with higher transmission loss. Wood has a lower transmission loss rating (between 17–34 dB) across the same frequencies as the absorption coefficients. In comparison, the concrete walls have a transmission loss rating of 45–71 dB. Sounds produced in the shops would, therefore, if loud enough, pass through the concrete walls and be audible in the neighbouring shop; for example, ten or more people (80+ dB), hammering, mill grinding or other production noises, or brass instruments. The frequency response indicates that lower frequency noises, such as those associated with production, would be louder than higher frequency noises.

The acoustic properties of the shops are only one side of the discussion of sounds. The other side is to focus on the listener's experience, exploring how the physical spaces in which sounds happen influence the perception of those spaces, as well as the ways in which humans perceive sound, both of which characterise the soundscape (see Laurence, this volume). Thus, we turn from the description of the acoustics of the shops to the sounds produced along the street and explore how the nature of sounds can offer insight into the daily rhythms along Ostia's north *cardo*. The aim is to explore how the acoustics of the shops may have affected the perception of the street and characterised this area of the city.

Before this can be done, it is necessary to explain some of the basic qualities of the physics of sound and human perception of sounds. An understanding of these acoustic principles is essential to my methodology and its application to ancient Roman contexts. The issues raised in this chapter are dependent on the interaction of sounds with structures (such as buildings or rooms) and movable objects (for example furniture, carts or people). The methods are not aimed at recreating all the sounds in a given context (compare Betts, this volume); instead, they indicate potential ways by which to gain a better understanding of the everyday rhythms of ancient sites through the archaeological remains.

Some physics of sound and hearing

Taking away the physical encumbrances of buildings, people and materials, one is left with a *free field*, a theoretical space where sound travels unimpeded and free of any physical influences (Everest and Pohlmann, 2009, p. 33). In a free field sound travels out from a particular source, referred to as a *point-source*, spherically, and the sound is of uniform intensity in all directions. As the sound travels outward in all directions at the same sound power level, the sound is spread over an increasingly greater area as the radius increases, resulting in a decrease in the sound energy (Everest and Pohlmann, 2009, p. 34). Simply put, the sound energy decreases the further away it travels. Thus, as one doubles the distance from the sound point-source, the *sound pressure level* (SPL) is reduced by a factor of four, or decreases by 6 *decibels* (dB), but it must be remembered that we are dealing with a free field, a theoretical space, and not physical space (Everest and Pohlmann, 2009, p. 36). The inverse-square law will not provide the actual SPL of sounds in the shops, only a theoretical estimation of the level from a certain point-source at a given distance, like a shout from one end of the street.

Not all sounds emanate from a single source or point-source. Ancient examples of multi-source sounds include processions, the triumph being the largest and possibly loudest (Favro, 1994; Beard, 2007). In this case, the sound functions as a *line-source*, or many point-sources acting in line. Sound spreads from the line cylindrically, resulting in a reduction by a half, or 3 dB, when the distance is doubled (Everest and Pohlmann, 2009, p. 36). With a line-source the sounds and movement work together and the acoustic quality of the action changes; but the way a person interprets the action also varies. Other factors affecting the utility of the inverse-square law are the reflection of the earth's surface outdoors. In this case, the reflection from the earth's surface will make the SPL somewhat less than that indicated by the 6 dB free field approximation. In outdoor situations, the 6 dB approximation is usually closer to a decrease by 4 or 5 dB with the doubling of distance (Everest and Pohlmann, 2009, p. 38). Thus, quantifying distances with measured sound pressure levels offers only half the auditory picture.

Since sound functions as a wave, its basic measurements are related to the waveform. The number of cycles per second is referred to as the *frequency*, f, and is measured in *hertz* (Hz). Frequency is related to *pitch*, the perceived tone, but not in a linear fashion. Pitch is a subjective unit, whereas frequency is a physical unit. This means that a soft 1,000 Hz signal will remain 1,000 Hz even if you increase its SPL. The pitch of a sound, however, will often depend on its SPL. The *intensity* of sound, calculated as the sound power per unit of area in dB, is not the same as the *loudness* of a sound (Everest and Pohlmann, 2009, p. 1). Loudness is another subjective term that is used to describe the perceived magnitude of the sound. In the audible range, a sound is not noticeably affected by its intensity or frequency, nor by changes in atmospheric pressure, meaning that ancient sounds functioned in the same manner as modern sounds and that calculated measures remain constant.

Sound interpretation is also the perception of noise by people, or the sensation of hearing, which involves psychoacoustics and subjective judgements of taste. The process of understanding the sounds of the ancient word therefore consists of analysing both the physical acoustics of spaces such as Ostia's shops and the way these acoustics shape what people perceive. The ear and brain together take the combined sound waves and separate out certain sounds, such as specific instruments in a symphony orchestra or a particular conversation in a crowded room, referred to as the 'cocktail party' effect (Everest and Pohlmann, 2009, p. 63). We often unconsciously turn towards the direction of a sound. Because the ears are located on the side of the head, slight changes in hearing time enable the brain to triangulate the source of the sound. In this process, directional data is transmitted with the sound signal and interpreted by the brain.

The SPL of sounds when picked up by the ear also transmits information about the distance of the sound. Sound, as wave motion, has a relative speed of 1,235 km/hr. This is dramatically slower than the speed of light and it takes sound about 3 seconds to travel a kilometre. Again, the relative speed of sound means that humans perceive the distance over which sound travels, unlike our perception of light. This feature of sound says much about the way it interacts with the visual world and the implicit information sounds carry with them. These processes are fundamental to human interpretation of place and navigation.

The specific structure of the human ear shapes the way humans hear and perceive sounds; and the audible spectrum of frequencies for humans is between 20 Hz and 20,000 Hz (Everest and Pohlmann, 2009, p. 14). The human ear can detect about 280 discernible steps in intensity and some 1,400 discernible steps in pitch (Everest and Pohlmann, 2009, p. 54). The perception of sounds by the human ear is not based on arithmetic differences between frequencies but on frequency ratios, perceived logarithmically. This means that the interval between 100 Hz and 200 Hz is perceived as being larger than the interval from 200 Hz to 300 Hz. In terms of sound pressure levels, the minimum change in level the human ear can detect in the important mid-frequency range, the speech range, is 2 dB (Everest and Pohlmann, 2009, p. 54). Short sound pulses are perceived differently. A short sound, 3 milliseconds, must have an SPL 15 dB higher than a 0.5 second sound to be perceived at the same loudness (Everest and Pohlmann, 2009, p. 53). Random noises and tones function in a similar manner, in terms of perceived loudness. The nature of the human ear and the process of hearing are tailored to the frequencies of speech and attune humans to easily hear and interpret these mid-range frequencies.

The combination of physical characteristics of the human body and the physics of sound are important in developing particular methods for analysing the soundscape of ancient sites. In summary, the physics of sound, as they pertain to architecture, can be stated:

- All six surfaces in a room influence the acoustic character of the space.
- Sound can travel through air, water and gas, as well as physical materials like concrete, wood and glass.
- A point-source, like a single person, will function differently to a line-source, a procession of people.
- In outside spaces, as the distance doubles from a point-source the SPL decreases by 6 dB, or by 3 dB in the case of a line-source.
- Humans perceive sound logarithmically, so different frequencies are perceived at different levels of loudness despite having the same intensity (SPL). Certain frequencies will be perceived as louder than others, whether they actually are or not.

Street sounds

A wealth of studies since the 1990s has provided a more complete understanding of what happened along Roman streets and the social behaviours that influenced interactions therein (most recently, Laurence and Newsome, 2011), but the roles of sounds, either their production or their effect, have been only briefly discussed (Betts, 2011, pp. 126–9).

The north section of Ostia's *cardo maximus* was exceptional in certain respects: at roughly 130 m in length it was the only street with porticoes fronting it on both sides for the majority of its length, and at 8.11 m it was the widest street in the city apart from the *decumanus*. Connecting the Forum and the Tiber, with the possibility to stable animals in the *loggia*, the street was used by residents and visitors alike (DeLaine, 2005, p. 33). The sounds and levels of noise along the *cardo* can further quantify the social importance of the street.

The rhythms of everyday life, and the associated rhythms of sound in the city, were a key element in the production of urban knowledge (Lefebvre, 2004). Sounds are mediated by time and the temporal rhythms of activity are reflected in the rhythms of sounds. Daily rhythms influenced the Roman soundscape (as they do the modern), as people got ready for work, opened shops, went to the Forum, baths or back to their houses for dinners. As Martial complains, schoolmasters are heard in the morning and bakers make noise at night, whilst during the day moneychangers, metalworkers, religious groups, beggars and pedlars make a racket (12.57.4–14). Some of these sounds can be located in specific places, such as the *Caseggiato del Termopolio* (1.2.5) and the Forum, or the noise of bakers working in the *Caseggiato dei Molini* (1.3.1), three streets over from the *cardo*.

Sounds reflected the events of the day, evident in Martial's complaints about Rome, and also helped people to locate where in the city those events took place (Betts, 2011, pp. 122–4, pp. 129–31). The majority of events recorded in Roman daily life relate to elite duties structured by clock-time; spatially, they often ranged across the city (Laurence, 2007, pp. 161–2; Riggsby, 2003, p. 185). For members of the non-elite, such as the inhabitants of the shops of Ostia's *cardo*, daily tasks were more limited both temporally and spatially (Laurence, 2007, p. 166). Work and home were located in the same space, requiring minimal movement, although the associated sounds would be different. The peaks in noise would relate to peaks in activity along the street during the day and into the night, whilst the types of sounds related to the tasks and duties being performed.

At dawn the shops would open; the wooden shutters would be taken down and merchandise arranged outside, possibly spilling onto the street (Papinian *Digest* 43.10.1.3–5; Martial *Epigrams* 7.61). The noise of opening wooden shutters and moving various goods would have dominated the street. Beginning in the early morning, porters (*saccari*) loaded and unloaded ships moving between the Tiber and warehouses in the area. Unloading of ships would indicate noise at the north end of the street along the Tiber while the movement would bring noise down the street to the warehouses to the west of the *cardo* (Figure 4.1). The warehouses would have been active with the sound of workers piling and storing goods. It is likely that day labourers would have loitered around the street looking for work, filling the portico and street side with conversation (Matthew

20:1–16; Holleran, 2011, p. 253). By the second hour, the shops would have been open; games started around this time and the law courts were in session from the third hour (Suetonius *Claudius* 34.2; Martial *Epigrams* 4.8; Laurence, 2007, pp. 159–60). From the second to sixth hours the Forum to the south of the *cardo* would have been busy and noisy (Cicero *For Archias* 6; Horace *Odes* 3.29.12, *Epistles* 2.2.79–80; Pliny the Younger *Letters* 1.9.7; for discussion of *strepitus* see Laurence, this volume). The *Portico of Pio IX* would, therefore, have been relatively active in the morning, especially with the movement of goods from the ships on the Tiber to the warehouses in the area and to the south in connection with the Forum.

Activity in the shops and stalls would have created a highly textured, noisy soundscape throughout the day, both within the premises and along the street. The more transient cries of hawkers and street traders selling goods acquired from the docks or warehouses in the vicinity would have filled the street and porticoes (Holleran, 2011, p. 255). Seneca famously complains of the food vendors hawking in the bathhouse below his apartment (*Letters* 56.2). The competition for attention (something Seneca points out) motivated sellers to cry out so that they might stop passers-by. Haggling and bartering were commonly used in settling the prices for goods, and these interactions of buying also produced sounds (Seneca *On Benefits* 6.17.1, *Letters* 42.8; see also Betts, this volume).

The architectural acoustics of the *Portico di Pio IX* enable some of these actions and sonic events to be reconstructed. Whilst we may not be able to replicate these sounds perfectly, they can be approximated and their impact on the aural architecture of the shops modelled using the acoustic properties outlined earlier. Normal conversation falls in the range of 55–66 dB, whilst shouting tends to be between 72–80 dB, sometimes higher (Olsen, 1998). The sound distribution of a conversation in the middle of the street (65 dB) would decrease to 40–45 dB between 58.5 m to 71.5 m along its length; at thresholds of 44.5 m and 84.5 m it would be 35–40 dB, and at 97.5 m and 32.5 m the SPL would be between 30–35 dB. The shops within the 58.5–71.5 m range, with the shutters closed, would reduce the SPL to 6–28 dB, while the furthest shops would reduce the SPL to 0–13 dB. In the portico itself, there is a minimal reverberation time (between 0.6–0.7 seconds). The frequency response indicates that low and mid-range frequencies would resonate the most within the portico space.

There is a noticeable shift in the frequency range for loud and shouted speech, especially for men (Hamilton and Whitehouse, 2006, p. 176). This means that at louder conversation levels sound energy is produced at high frequencies. The frequencies do not reach the levels at which absorption increases, as the highest energy is in the range of 1,250–1,600 Hz, meaning that although higher in perceived pitch, the shouts are not absorbed in higher levels by the buildings along the street. A shout at 80 dB at one end of the street would be reduced to 38 dB at the other end, simply based on the distance travelled and air impedance; the higher frequency of the shout would mean that the sound would be more intelligible to listeners at the opposite end. The frequency response in the portico, however, would absorb more of the frequencies at either end of the spectrum, reducing the intelligibility of the sounds heard outside the portico. Adding more shouts to the mix will not double the SPL, as sound functions logarithmically. Two people shouting, both at 75 dB will, therefore, increase the SPL by 3 dB; doubling the number of shouts will increase the SPL another 3 dB, totalling 81 dB. The potential number of people can be used to predict relative sound levels on the street.

The soundscape of the street would alter in the evening as members of the elite went to their houses for dinner and those of the non-elites went to the baths or bars. The sounds relating to these activities would migrate to elite houses and apartments, such as those in the *Insula dei Dipinti* (1.4) and the upper stories of the *Portico di Pio IX*. Just around the corner from the *cardo* was the *Caseggiato del Termopolio* (1.2.5), a large food vendor taking up three shops on the ground floor. Late in the day, the bar would be busy serving food to those in the area to the east. Thus, the soundscape of the *cardo* was nuanced, varying according to the time of day (and its relative climatic changes) and the activities taking place in the wider neighbourhood.

The rhythms of sounds that structured the street activity were also dependent on the number of people on the street. James Packer studied the majority of ground floor accommodation in Ostia and calculated the population by totalling the number of bedrooms (*cubicula*) in multi-room apartments, also giving each shop four inhabitants (1967, pp. 85–6). While Packer's total population count seems unreasonably low, based as it was on the standing remains identified at the time, he did estimate the population totals for each individual building. Packer notes that the buildings flanking the north *cardo* were densely populated, having some of the highest population totals of any buildings in the city (1967, p. 87). Using Packer's building totals, the noise in the building can be assessed in terms of the number of people. Packer suggests Building A (1.5.1–2) of the *Portico di Pio IX* was four stories, with twenty-nine ground floor units, eighteen on the first floor and twenty units on the second and third floors (1971, p. 80). This gives the building eighty-seven total units and a population of 348. Building B (1.6.1) had fifteen units on the ground floor, seven on the first, and nine on the second and third, making a total of forty and a population of 160 (1971, p. 80).

The 'crowd' noise of Ostia's total population can be predicted in an outdoor setting (Table 4.3; Hayne, Taylor, Rumble and Mee, 2011, p. 2). Several different variables influence crowd noise, such as the size of the group, direction of the sounds and the ages and genders of the individuals, so several predicative equations have been formulated to account for these different characteristics (Hayne et al., 2011, p. 2). The predicative crowd noises are divided into two components: 'babble' produced by groups of people interacting with one another, and 'transient' noises like laughing, shouting or cheering, which cause peaks in sound levels (Table 4.3). When measuring crowd noise over a long period of time, the babble component of people interacting with one another in various groups would produce a quasi-steady noise level, while the transient noises range from one second, for example a shout, to several minutes, in the case of cheering. In terms of the total population, the quasi-steady noise level

Table 4.3 Predicative crowd noise for the *Portico di Pio IX* buildings

Equation	Total population (dB(A))	Building A (348 people) (dB(A))	Building B (160 people) (dB(A))
Max (Transient)	110.58	83.54	83.2
01 (Transient)	106.58	79.54	79.2
10 ('Babble')	107.58	69.54	69.2
EQ ('Babble')	104.58	66.54	66.2

Source: based on population numbers in Packer, 1971

is in the range of 104–107 dB, a loud noise level. The peaks could potentially hit 110 dB, which is comparable to noise levels at modern sporting events and rock shows. If the crowd noise predictive measurements for Buildings A and B in the *cardo* (Table 4.3) are compared, we see that the relative noise levels are lower than the total population predictions but still in the top 24% for average predictive measures in buildings (41 out of 171 units). The acoustics of the shops would filter out some of this 'crowd' noise, evident in the transmission loss analyses.

By calculating the sound *decay rate*, based on the reverberation time, the influence of the buildings on noise levels can be seen. With a reverberation time of 2.38 seconds, with the shutters closed, the sound decay rate is 25.21 dB/s (decibels per second). This means that if the crowd noise were to stop abruptly it would decrease by 25.21 dB per second in the shops. With the shutters open, the decay rate increases to 54.05 dB/s, meaning that the sound would decay at a higher rate. This suggests that the relative noise of the north *cardo* when full of people going about their business would reach noticeably high levels, but the buildings could dampen various levels of sound by closure of the shutters. The sound distribution in the street also indicates that sounds at the level of the crowd prediction would remain at levels of 65–70 dB at the opposite end; if the noise were produced in the centre of the street, it would be around 70 dB at either end. This noise could leak into neighbouring streets but sustained interaction (at the point-source or in the proximate locale) would be necessary if they were to remain perceptible in the neighbouring areas. Thus, it was noise generated by the regularity of street activity that signalled the social importance of the *cardo* and its central location within the soundscape of the city.

Conclusion

The aim of this analysis of the *Portico di Pio IX* has been to show the potential for sensory studies of Ostia, and other Roman urban contexts, by paying attention to aspects of the acoustics and soundscape of a particular neighbourhood. The buildings of the *Portico di Pio IX* reshaped the northern *cardo maximus*, reorienting the street and directing people to the Forum or the Tiber. Along with the reorientation of movement, the new buildings shaped the soundscape of the street in the second century CE. The acoustic property of the street, spilling out so as to be heard in the surrounding areas, is indicative of its importance in the social and economic spheres of the town. The inhabitants had the ability to produce high levels of ambient noise, which would undoubtedly have been punctuated by momentary and sporadic louder noises. These ambient noise levels are at odds with the relative quietness of the site today. This is not to say that Ostia had the levels of traffic and background noise of contemporary cities, only that at certain times of high activity the level of ambient noise could reach peak levels which could act as a landmark, orientating a person within the multisensory cityscape. In the terms of navigation, the street noise would offer an immediate means of placing oneself in urban space as the noise increased or decreased with distance from the neighbourhood. The ability to direct one's movement based on hearing is key to navigating unknown cities, as well as cities with limited signage or visibility (Betts, 2011, p. 123). The ambient noise along the *Portico di Pio IX* would have served to direct people to the Forum and the centre of the city.

Replicating this study in other locales in Ostia can give us a knowledge of the town's soundscapes that is necessary if we are to better understand the nuances of Roman urban life. These might be further studies of the sounds of daily life on the city's streets (see also Flohr, this volume) or studies of special occasions, such as events in the theatre, a passing procession or festivals (see Bruun, 2009, 2015). The particular sounds of such events would likely advertise their presence, drawing people to their source, but this hypothesis can only be tested by taking into account the aural architecture of the affected locales. As further studies of the soundscapes, both literary and archaeological, are undertaken, the everyday life of ancient cities and the sounds that shaped them will enable ancient historians and archaeologists to understand better the complex relationship between buildings and social interactions. In the case study presented here, sounds emanating from the everyday rhythms of the city highlight Ostia's important connections with both the river Tiber and Rome, connections that helped characterise each of these places.

Acoustic glossary

Absorption coefficient: The fraction of sound energy that is absorbed by any surface. It has a theoretical value between 0 and 1 and varies with the frequency and angle at which the sound hits the surface.

Decay rate: A measure of the decay of acoustic signals, expressed as a slope in decibels per second.

Decibel (dB): A unit measure of the intensity of a sound, based on a comparison with a logarithmic reference scale. The decibel is one-tenth of a bel, although the bel is rarely used as a unit any more.

Echolocation: The ability to discern objects in space through the echoes reflected by the object. Both animals and humans, especially the blind, are able to navigate by producing sounds and perceiving the audible changes in echoes.

Free field: A theoretical space in which sound emanates spherically in all directions at uniform intensity without any interference.

Frequency: The measure of the alterations of a periodic signal, expressed in hertz (Hz). Frequency response: The changes in amplitude or sensitivity of a circuit or device with frequency.

Hertz (Hz): Unit of frequency; the same as cycles per second.

Intensity: Acoustic intensity is the average rate of sound energy transmitted through a unit area normal to the direction of sound transmission.

Line-source: A series of point-sources acting in line. Sound emanates cylindrically from a line-source and decreases by 3 dB with a doubling of distance.

Loudness: A subjective term for the sensation of magnitude of sound.

Noise reduction coefficient (NRC): A single-value rating for the absorption coefficient of a particular material based on the average of the absorption in the frequencies 250 Hz, 500 Hz, 1,000 Hz and 2,000 Hz.

Pitch: A subjective term for the perceived frequency of a tone.

Point-source: A single sound producer in a fixed location. Sound emanates spherically, in all directions, and decreases by 6 dB as the distance doubles (inverse-square law).

Reverberation time (RT60): The time it takes for the sound pressure level to decrease by 60 dB from its original intensity in an enclosed space. Calculated from the surface area and absorption of the room. The RT is directly proportional to the volume of the room and inversely proportional to the room's effective surface area.

Sabin: Unit of measure for the absorption of sound. One metre square of open window has the absorption of one metric sabin.

Sound field: Area in which a sound can be heard.

Sound pressure level (SPL): Sound pressure expressed in decibels, dB, above the standard sound pressure.

Transmission loss (TL): Decrease in sound intensity (in dB) as it passes through a material or space.

Notes

1 Thanks to Eleanor Betts, whose conference Senses of Empire inspired much of my work on acoustics, and Ray Laurence. Both read early drafts of the chapter and have continually offered helpful comments, criticisms and insights. Any remaining faults are my own.

2 *Italicised* words are explained in the Acoustic Glossary at the end of this chapter. Based on Everest and Pohlmann, 2009, pp. 483–94.

3 The calculated absorption unit is measured in *sabins*, which do not directly correspond to decibel measures.

4 Absorption coefficient for brick-faced concrete and *opus reticulatum* are the same.

5 Sensory archaeologies

A Vindolanda smellscape

Thomas J. Derrick[1]

Studies of urban smellscapes are often based on detailed contemporary reports and social studies and, crucially, are informed by geographical theory (see, for example, Classen, Howes and Synnott, 1994; Cockayne, 2007; Reinarz, 2014), but reconstructing the smellscapes of archaeological sites for which we cannot conduct these types of survey presents challenges. Recent publications have drawn attention to ancient smellscapes, and highlight the challenges of understanding how these may have been perceived in the past (Henshaw, 2014; Koloski-Ostrow, 2015; Morley, 2015). Henshaw writes that 'cities in the past were highly odoriferous sites fuelled by gatherings of large numbers of people in concentrated areas and supported by a cycle of food and goods supply, waste production and removal. . . . [C]ities can be identified by their very nature as having always been sites of olfactory conflict, where negatively perceived odours combined with those that were more culturally acceptable' (2014, p. 11), a description which generalises but encapsulates the smellscape of past urban spaces. This chapter explores the case study of the Roman fort and *vicus* at Vindolanda in order to demonstrate that it is possible to better understand the way in which individuals experienced the smellscape afforded by this Roman fort. This study will demonstrate that a sensory approach can further nuance our understanding of life at Roman military sites in the northern frontier region. This sort of study is possible at any archaeological site where a sufficient amount is known (or hypothesised) about the use of space via the site's material culture (as demonstrated by other chapters in this volume).

The reason for choosing Vindolanda as a case study is that the site's (third-century CE) ground plan is well known. Additionally, the nature of recent archaeological work at the site, in both the fort and the *vicus*, coupled with favourable taphonomic conditions, has contributed to a good understanding of the use of space at the site. Although this study limits itself to one fort, it is hoped that many of the issues and potential conclusions raised within it have wider implications and applications.

Olfaction as a potential archaeological heuristic tool

Porteous (1990) describes the interaction between space and olfaction as an 'olfactory geography' with distinct and discontinuous smell 'events'. A smellscape is therefore a space structured and described through reference to the relationship, or multitude of relationships, between the perceiver and the odours in a given space (Porteous, 1990). Visual landscapes and, to a lesser extent, soundscapes, happen at a distance from the individual, but smellscapes can be conceived of as occurring in closer proximity to the perceiver (Rodaway, 1994, pp. 63–5). The smellscape is conceptualised, and only understood, internally. The methodologies discussed by Porteous and Rodaway are specifically designed to suit case studies in their fields, and the same is true of Henshaw (2014). The fragmentary and culturally distinct nature of archaeological and ancient literary evidence does not permit such detailed approaches as theirs. This chapter nevertheless offers a preliminary engagement with the 'olfactory geography' of Vindolanda, with the aim of illustrating a new way of engaging with the archaeological record of the site in order that we might consider, if not better understand, the 'sense of place' felt at this Roman military site (and perhaps others).

Reconstructing how people in an ancient society will have perceived something is inherently problematic. How one senses and evaluates the world around them is essentially culturally constituted (Day, 2013b, p. 6; Morley, 2015, p. 113; Bradley, 2015a, p. 3) and, given the plurality of possibilities even within distinct existing communities, it might seem impossible to begin to attempt to approach questions of perception in the diverse Roman military community. This pessimism is unwarranted and enquiries into ancient sensorial experience need not be dismissed outright. With the combined tools of a shared biological reality and the Roman material and literary records, we have a reasonable foundation for future enquiry (Betts, 2011, p. 122).

A visitor to a Roman fort in the Hadrian's Wall area is often greeted by a more or less exposed ground plan and, occasionally, accompanying partial reconstructions. At Vindolanda the visual power of the partially reconstructed rampart and timber fort wall, constructed with the help of local school children, is testament to the stark contrast of what is missing. The post-excavation consolidation work at these sites has to make the site safe to visitors, preserve other non-parietal features and minimise upkeep costs. This work is, of course, essential to make sites a viable heritage concern, but it can limit our imagined sensory perception of the archaeological site (Foster, 2013, pp. 371–89). Particularly adept curators can in some cases make up for this by commissioning and displaying visual reconstructions, structural mock-ups or replica items of material culture at the site or in an accompanying museum. Professional reenactors are occasionally involved in specific events at many sites, but these are usually sporadic for reasons of practicality. Vindolanda's own Chesterholm Museum is an example of a well-planned educational experience where concessions have been made for increased sensory perception, such as the recreation of typical *vicus* scenes in the museum gardens. Chesterholm Museum is close to the site itself, but in many cases the distance between archaeological site, museum collection and interpretative material creates a real sensory and cognitive disconnect. At many sites there is no museum or interpretative material available (as at nearby Carrawburgh); at others the collection is presented in an antiquarian or simple fashion (such as Chesters).

The latter situation is a perfect contrast to the current display at Vindolanda; if multisensory experiences at archaeological sites are ultimately desirable, then we still have a long way to go.

Field archaeology deals with material in a largely visual and haptic way. We draw, photograph and describe what we are able to identify visually, and sometimes note additional physical traits, such as the weight or texture of the remains and artefacts we survey (compare Day, this volume; also Day, 2013b, p. 21). Field archaeology is, on the whole, olfactorily sterile; not because an excavation has no smellscape, but because that is the smellscape of the present not of the past. A tenet of field archaeology is to recover and record material data from the past, and the olfactory data from the past is just not there in a direct form. Consequently, the fact that every ancient site would have been filled with olfactory stimuli is often marginalised in studies of everyday life in antiquity, whether by omission or an assumptive estimation of the audience's capacity for imaginative reconstruction.

Olfaction often loses out in historical discourse, in most cases, to vision (Reinarz, 2014, pp. 209–18). Sigmund Freud certainly considered the sense of smell to be largely vestigial, and pinpointed its importance to a less developed time where the selection of food and pheromonal pursuit of a mate was much more important to human survival (1990, pp. 99–100; Gilbert, 2008, pp. 58–60). Vision is intrinsically linked with literature, architecture, art, love and physical attraction, and other romanticised aspects of human culture, whereas olfaction is linked with the selection of food, luxurious excess and excreta (Henshaw, 2014, p. 10). Hierarchical groupings of the senses (largely based on Aristotle) were traditionally rooted in colonial discourse in the eighteenth and nineteenth centuries, and later in racial discourse in the first half of the twentieth century (Day, 2013b, p. 4; Reinarz, 2014, pp. 85–112).

Our sense of smell is fundamental to our understanding of place, and positive or negative olfactory reception can alter our attitude towards, or use of, space. Many modern urban landscapes are increasingly sterile, in olfactory terms (Reinarz, 2014, pp. 209–18; compare Morley, 2015, pp. 111–12, who warns against over-emphasising the alien nature of past smellscapes). The Roman towns and cities of Britain, even the large ones, would have had a stronger smellscape than the towns and cities of the present day (following Henshaw, 2014, p. 11). The location of industrial processes such as smelting, textile and leatherwork within or close to these settlements, coupled with a less sophisticated approach to the disposal of waste and pollutants, made for a diverse smellscape in the Romano-British town; one that was, perhaps, distinct from the smellscapes of the countryside or of towns in other parts of the Roman empire (compare Koloski-Ostrow, 2015; Morley, 2015 on Rome).

Roman military scholarship

James (2002) has demonstrated that Roman military scholarship traditionally did not engage with archaeological theory. It was slow to adopt and adapt approaches applied in other areas of classical (and other) scholarship. Roman military studies have traditionally favoured structural processes such as troop movement, equipment, offices, laws, garrison sizes and economic frameworks. More recently, work has begun to focus on the lives of the military community, seeing its members as humans rather than quasi-monastic automata (James, 2002, pp. 7–9). Work on the artefact records from forts has fundamentally changed the way we view these sites. We now possess a greater understanding of the population and nature of life in Roman forts, the demographics indicating variety in sex, age, ethnicity and status (Allison, 2013). Some of this pioneering work has been undertaken at Vindolanda itself. Carol van Driel-Murray's work on the leather from the site has shed important light on the presence of women and children at Roman forts (van Driel Murray, 1993, 2001); and the doctoral work of Andrew Birley has proven, through artefact analysis, the presence of these groups within the walls of the fort, a situation previously thought improbable (Birley, 2010, pp. 193–5). We are therefore beginning to understand much more about the make-up and behaviours of military communities, and a logical extension of this for the discipline would be to consider them from an experiential perspective; this study focuses on the spaces which they inhabited and utilised.

Recording and evaluating the Vindolandan smellscape

'Smellwalking' is a technique, described by Henshaw (2014, pp. 42–56), whereby at various times of day the modern urban landscape is experienced from a phenomenological standpoint by various members of the study team, and smells and their strengths are recorded. In simple terms the reception of scent can only be subjective as the chemical receptors in the olfactory system compare the compounds to previously experienced odours (Gilbert, 2008, p. 25). Furthermore, the biological, cultural and individual differences in people increase the potential variation in recorded olfactory sensation (Day, 2013b, p. 6). Machines that measure smells in terms of compound concentration in given volumes of air can suggest a certain amount, but the human olfactory system is still required if we wish to discuss lived experience (Digiscents: Marks, 2002, pp. 113–14). It is not just the reception of odour that is variable, however; the smellscape of a given environment is massively variable dependent on atmospheric conditions and the activities undertaken in particular spaces. Smellscapes are not static and consequently they are not something that one individual can measure entirely, even in a modern environment (Henshaw, 2014, pp. 42–56). Archaeological smell maps can therefore only be an interpretation, the data for which is based on the inferred odours of particular activities (where those activities are evidenced by material culture).

How, then, can we consider and potentially evaluate an archaeological smellscape? We can consider the activities that may have occurred in given spaces, based on archaeological indicators about the use of the space and the given atmospheric conditions at the site. Taking what is known archaeologically about the given environments of the fort and its *vicus* smellscape, we can overlay smell data, either by recreating or imagining the potential smells which may have characterised the site. This allows the construction of an archaeological smell map (or olfactory geography). An urban environment is made up of smell environments of differing scale. Enclosed spaces, to which only certain sections of the populace had access, or wished to access, whether a barrack room, small *vicus* house, workshop or commander's house, would have become distinct smell environments; for the purpose of this chapter, these buildings will be referred to as micro-environments. Conversely, there were environments to which larger groups of people had access; these characteristically open or communal spaces had smell environments which were necessarily collaborative, although often not through choice. These macro-environments, such as the inter-vallum space, the roads and the workshop areas, were sites of interaction characterised by the various processes which occurred in these different areas of the site.

In order to assess the olfactory geography of Vindolanda it is important to consider the ways in which we might characterise the individual smell emitters at the different parts of the site. Technological and scientific advances and cultural change have altered the way in which we typically characterise certain olfactory stimuli. For example, recent debates about pollution, and in particular carbon emissions, have recontextualised the way in which smoke is viewed. In the same way, medical advances in toxicology have led to legislative restrictions on tobacco smoking and a widespread alteration of public opinion about the smell of cigarette smoke. Something similar can be said about the smell of refuse and excrement and modern understandings of pathogens. That is not to say that the ancients did not understand that these 'miasmas' were unhealthy, only that they did not understand the mechanisms through which they did harm (Scobie, 1986; Scheidel, 2003; Morley, 2005; Henshaw, 2014, pp. 11–12). Whilst it is difficult for us to assess how certain smells would have been received, we can suggest what sort of odours may have been created (Morley, 2015, p. 113).

Experimental archaeology may have a lot to tell us about the experiential impact of ancient technology and social practice, but its results are often recorded in terms that follow schema of techniques and processes rather than the sensory perception of these activities. One could of course attempt to recreate some of the smells that may have occurred on site, but any recording or interpretation of them will inevitably be subjective since we can never step away from our own contextualisation. As with the other sensory methodologies which are being established for use in the field, such as smellwalking, a large team of active perceivers would help even out bias. Another option would be to consult a large number of experimental archaeologists. Some of the main groups of smells which are likely to have been present at the fort are: refuse (of all sorts), human and animal excreta and body odour, leather, rust, food preparation, tanning and fulling odours, smoke (from workshops and the bathhouse) and probably, given the Northumbrian climate and the furnishings at these sites, damp.

Traces in the archaeological record enable us to reconstruct the various processes that would have produced olfactory stimuli at the site. A discussion of the sorts of odours that likely characterised the fort and the sorts of possible reactions to them, positive or negative, follows. The savoury odour of cooking food, especially the type of food that the particular group has chosen to prepare, is likely to have been viewed positively although, as with all odours, there is the possibility of associated memories, positive or negative, evoked by smells (Crowder and Schab, 1995; Marks, 2002, pp. 14–15). The odour of refuse and excrement (which were deposited together in fort ditches) is understandably disliked across cultures. Smoke from the burning of solid fuels, made acrid due to their inherent toxic compounds, was likely avoided where possible. The burning of perfumed oils, incense and plant material, such as local heather, would have altered the olfactory nature of the spaces in which they were used. They could also ward against insects or be used in religious rituals. Oil- and fat-based lamps were, of course, lit at some parts of the site. Each of these types of burning usually happened in enclosed spaces and were undertaken in order to influence the micro-environment around the individual, whether in an olfactory sense or in a practical sense which has an olfactory corollary, such as the level of lighting or discouraging insects.

The site of Vindolanda can therefore be broken into micro and macro smell environments. Both were influenced by the military community as a whole but the micro-environments were controlled by the specific members of the community who commonly used their enclosed spaces. Colour Plate 3 illustrates the sorts of micro- and macro-environments that existed at Vindolanda, and the relationship of odours to them. This is an impressionistic map of the olfactory geography of the fort; it does not map exactly the strength and reach of each smell – this requires further experimentation in the field. Consequently, the shapes superimposed on the map represent the zone in which stimuli are produced and not the extent of their impact, which was likely not limited to the coloured areas.

Case study: Third-century CE Vindolanda

Vindolanda offers an array of evidence for anyone who aims to explore, and potentially reconstruct, lived experience at Roman military sites. This study focuses on Vindolanda's third-century CE fort. This period of the site's occupation has the most exposed and archaeologically explored ground plan of any of the fort's construction and habitation phases. Similarly, the most detailed analysis of the material culture from Vindolanda focuses on the third and fourth centuries (Birley, 2010). Combining these architectural and artefactual data offers an excellent opportunity for sensory studies. The information the site can provide is specific to its context as part of the Stanegate frontier system in northern Britain, but it is hoped that the interpretation made here of a snapshot of Vindolanda's history will have wider implications for our consideration of ancient smellscapes.

Smoke and the wind

Roman fort design was rather formulaic, at least in terms of the way in which the site was laid out. The *vicus* was a rather more free-form affair, with greater potential for building and activity differentiation. The fort at Vindolanda was likely situated where it was because of local resources. Its industrial processes were located close to the site, in the *vicus*, although there is a possibility that additional industrial processes occurred outside this zone. This proximity was probably for the practical reasons of supervision, logistics and protection.

The topography of the site means that a prevailing south-westerly wind whips across Vindolanda much of the time. In the third century some allowances were made for this wind direction. The activities of the site that produced the most acrid smoke, such as the workshops (1a, 1b) and the main bathhouse (10), are in alignment with the prevailing wind (Colour Plate 3).[2] The same can be said of the furnace for the governor's residence (12), which is located in its north-east corner, the direction from which the smoke escapes away from the site. The locations of the workshops and the bathhouse in the *vicus* seem to respect, and therefore avoid, the central buildings of the fort: the granary, *principia* and *praetorium* (west to east). With this prevailing wind smoke would not have flowed over the southern cavalry barracks; this choice of site may have been due to the higher status of cavalry over the infantry in the northern barracks, or a simple coincidence. The tavern is located close to the workshops and would have been in a rather smoky and dingy part of the extramural settlement. The *vicus* buildings to the south of the road, and thus away from the path of most of the smoke, are larger and have courtyards. These buildings appear to have been occupied by the more literate occupants of the fort, people of higher status perhaps, as evidenced by the distribution of styli (pens) compared to other areas of the *vicus* and the fort (Birley, 2010, pp. 210–12). The alignment of these buildings within the *vicus* appears to have been a conscious decision, likely made by those who typically inhabited the spaces that avoided the worst of the smoke in the third century CE. Their aim appears to have been to avoid polluting the dwelling spaces of the fort's commander, the cavalry and the more salubrious parts of the *vicus*.

Influencing external parties

Vindolanda did not simply sit in the landscape only influencing its own inhabitants and quietly supplying nearby military installations and its own soldiers. In an area of Britain which had not seen urbanism prior to the arrival of the Romans, a site as large as Vindolanda would have been quite the visual spectacle from afar. It would also have had a smellscape which bore resemblance to, but also contrasted with, those of the existing settlements. This would have been particularly noticeable to visitors to the fort, or at least to those visiting for the first time. Many individual smell events at Vindolanda would have been the same or broadly similar to those encountered by indigenous communities: for example, the burning of local woods and plants, coal, metalworking, brewing, leatherworking and tanning, fulling, the preparation of food (although differences in diet are likely), animal and human faeces, butchery remains, refuse, human habitation, haymaking, the collecting and storing of plant materials, mould, mud and stagnant water. The concentration of these competing odours, due to the scale of the fort and *vicus*, would have made the Vindolandan smellscape striking within the context of the local landscape. Unfamiliar odours would have increased the distinctiveness of the site's smellscape, with use of foodstuffs such as olive oil, wine and cattle contributing to this (amphorae: Bidwell, 1985, p. 182; cattle compared to sheep and goat: Bennett, 2014). Roman corporeal behaviours were very different to those of indigenous communities: the residual smells of the bathhouse, and the use of perfumes and incense for either personal or religious use, must also have factored into the mixture of odours at the site.

The topography of the southern Northumbrian landscape is such that particularly pungent odours can be smelled from great distances. In 2001, with the outbreak of the foot-and-mouth crisis in the United Kingdom, the scent of destroyed animals travelled several miles in this terrain (Birley and Blake, pers. comm.). This was reportedly an acrid odour which, owing to the thankful infrequency of these events of livestock destruction, was quite unlike anything smelled before. This might be how we can conceptualise the Vindolandan smellscape in terms of its external influence. Although the smell produced in the crisis was obviously different to any ancient one, it is likely that the smell of large-scale burning of fuel was markedly different than any previously experienced by indigenous communities. This would have been especially true in the final quarter of the first century CE, when the fort was established, but also throughout the site's life. The lack of archaeological indicators of the native landscape in the frontier region make it hard to know much more than this, along with not knowing the exact work schedules and the amount of processing which happened at Vindolanda (even though the facilities are substantial and the indicators of industrial activity frequent).

It is also important to note that the smoke of industry from the site would have drifted along the Stanegate on the northern side of the fort, the most prestigious of its entrances. We might imagine military officials being impressed by this display of industry as they came to inspect the site. The same can be said of those approaching through the *vicus*, who would have had to walk along the west gate approach to the fort, which seems likely to have been an area which trapped commercial odours. The way that the space is structured at the site seems to force anyone who comes to it from the outside to engage directly in sensing an element of the site's smellscape; whilst those inside may have been fully habituated to that same smellscape.

Macro smell environments

The industrial areas (1)

Industrial activity has been identified in two main areas, both in the *vicus*. The first is a row of buildings immediately facing the western fort rampart, excavated from 1970–76 and identified by the common presence of crucibles, industrial waste, evidence for burning, fire resistant stone floors and fixtures (Birley, 1977, pp. 16–25) (Colour Plate 3, 1a). The second grouping is in the south-western corner of the *vicus*, uncovered in two phases of excavation, in 2003–4 and 2007–12 (Birley and Blake, 2005; Blake, 2014) (Colour Plate 3, 1b).[3] The 2003–4 excavations uncovered three or four workshops with similar archaeological indicators to those uncovered in the north-western rampart facing row (1a). Two workshops, one with an apsidal feature, were discovered to the south-east of these (Birley and Blake, 2005, pp. 1–38). In the western industrial area the evidence for residential living is unsurprisingly sparse, although further excavation in this region, particularly in the area to the east of the 2003–4 group (north of the 2007–12 group) may provide more information. The results of a geophysical survey seem to confirm this relative sparsity in comparison with the eastern *vicus* (Blake, 2014, pp. 21–4). Heavy industry is traditionally considered to have been located in liminal areas, but the north-western workshop group seems to disprove this somewhat, as it is situated well within the *vicus*, in close proximity to the fort. These open-fronted masonry workshops face onto a rampart covered with a stone wall, and were therefore a reasonably low fire risk. The main considerations involved in the situating of the north-western industrial area were probably linked to safety, but the topography of the site and its atmospheric conditions (notably the wind direction) would have caused smoky by-products created at the site to be taken away to the north-east. Testimonies of industrial processes and their surrounding commercial and logistical activities are recorded in several of the Vindolanda tablets (Bowman, 1994, pp. 37–8). The tablets make it clear that Vindolanda was an important industrial centre in its early phase (to which the tablets refer), as well as in the archaeologically better known third century. But why was this the case?

Strategically speaking Vindolanda is perfectly situated for industrial activity. The east–west line of the Stanegate constituted a form of frontier system prior to the construction of Hadrian's Wall, and was first and foremost a way of controlling crucial communication and logistics in the region (Bowman, 1994, pp. 14–16; Birley, 2010, pp. 60–1). Contact between the Stanegate forts and towns was common and the correspondence between them was, and continues to be, revealed by the tablets (Bowman, 1994, pp. 14–26). Vindolanda was also surrounded by sources of fuel and other natural resources which were required for the functioning of the fort itself but also for the military community in the region. Lead, silver, iron and high quality low-sulphur coal were all mined in the vicinity of the fort and the wider region (Birley, 2010, pp. 60–1). In addition, heather and moss, likely collected from nearby hillsides, was burned along with softwood charcoal processed at the fort or nearby (Birley, 2010, pp. 60–1). Charcoal degrades if it is transported over a long distance, so a ready supply of this was likely crucial for the fort's industrial output (Sim and Ridge, 2002, p. 17). Low-sulphur coal and charcoal are particularly suited to different applications: charcoal for smelting, coal for forging (Sim and Ridge, 2002, p. 57).

The west gate approach (2)

The flagged road that approaches and enters the west gate of the fort is flanked on either side by *vicus* buildings, which were likely two stories high. This part of the third-century *vicus* is the best known due to the excavation history of the site to date (Blake, 2014, pp. 13–18). The archaeological evidence suggests that these buildings were hubs of commercial activity and constituted a row of shops. This row included a probable butcher's shop and a tavern, which have been inferred due to the nature of the spaces and the fixtures within them, and it is almost certain that the other buildings fulfilled less archaeologically visible trade purposes (Birley, 2010, pp. 97–9). The granary just inside the west gate was also clearly a hub of commercial activity, and it seems as though it and the *vicus* shops formed a sort of 'commercial zone' at the site; the commercial importance of the granary, based on the coin evidence, seems to increase in the fourth century (Birley, 2013, pp. 44–5). Some of the shops are likely to have sold food, either prepared or otherwise, and other goods required by the soldiers, citizens of the *vicus* and visitors. This area was a rich multisensory space and we might see scaled down parallels in recent rich descriptions of similar environments in imperial Rome (Koloski-Ostrow, 2015; Morley, 2015; Bradley, 2015b). The sounds, sights and smells associated with wheeled and pedestrian traffic would have been frequent. The noise of the industrial workshops facing the northern half of the western rampart, coupled with the general sounds of life in the fort, would have made it loud. The overall impression would have been one of activity and, therefore, prosperity. The smellscape of this area would have been diverse and variable, depending on the activities being undertaken at a given time and the climatic conditions. The height of the *vicus* buildings and the direction of the prevailing wind would have resulted in the area being a bottleneck for multifarious aural and olfactory stimuli.

The fort ditches (3)

The third-century ditches at Vindolanda do not drain away from the site. The accumulation of various sorts of effluvia and refuse in them would therefore have had to be emptied periodically to stop the ditches overflowing. This periodical disturbance must have produced a rather strong odour, and those working in the *vicus* immediately to the west side of the fort, and south of the road, would have been subject to it; whilst those inside the fort were somewhat better protected by the fort wall. The latrines within the rampart wall would also have contributed to this aspect of the smellscape, generating a pungent odour in their immediate vicinity. Further evidence suggests that the south-west ditch of the fort was prone to flooding, and the flow of effluvia from north to south can be illustrated by the three corresponding joining pieces of so-called 'gladiator glass' found in the ditch at various points of the southwards flow (Birley, 2010, pp. 119–22).

The cavalry barracks (4)

Vindolanda's cavalry barracks are not as well known as its infantry barracks, which are themselves not wholly excavated. To state the obvious, the main difference between them is the smell of a large powerful animal, its food and its excreta. A cavalryman and his groom were likely inured to these smells and provided that the stabling was relatively well kept there are no grounds to assume that this would have been particularly offensive to the nose. In fact, it can be posited that the smellscape of this area, a combination of equine scent and fodder combined with the usual scents of human occupation, may have afforded this area a certain status within the fort due to the association of horses with power and military prestige.

The barrack environment (5)

The external environment of the barracks would likely have had a smellscape similar to many of the groupings of *vicus* houses, or like any densely populated residential area in Roman Britain at the time. Primarily, this would have been a concentration of the odours of people and their excreta, of cooking, of mud and disturbed earth, and of refuse. We know from the archaeological record that these spaces were populated by men, women and children. The walls of the fort were seemingly not a barrier; their permeability is evidenced by finds of military equipment in *vicus* houses, as well as shoes and jewellery belonging to women and children in the barracks and their environs (Birley, 2010, pp. 106–12).

The inter-vallum path (6)

Their height and proximity to one another created an enclosed space and an isolated smell environment in the inter-vallum area between the rampart wall and perpendicular barrack buildings (Birley and Blake, 2007, pp. 35–40). A large amount of jewellery (attributable to both women and men) was found in and around this area, perhaps because it was a well-used social space where inhabitants of all ages and genders could interact and fraternise. It may have been that the jewellery was lost during the preparation of bread and other foods for cooking in the rampart ovens, or that minor metal repairs were undertaken here (Birley and Blake, 2007, p. 39). The high wall and the narrowness of the passage meant that, even in the north-western corner of the fort, this space avoided the worst of the odours emitting from the workshops (1a), as the smells of industry would have been carried overhead.

This space would have been characterised primarily by the smells of baking and other cooking, the latrines (a further area for social interaction), oven rakings and their smoke and, in the north-western corner, the smells emitted from the temple of Jupiter Dolichenus (Colour Plate 3, 11a; Birley and Birley, 2012, pp. 231–58). These were clearly dynamic spaces which were frequently used by the diverse military community, including women and children. There is also an element of exclusivity inherent in the use of the inter-vallum path, as with all locations within the ramparts, as access was likely controlled by sentries.

The principia (7)

The large open court of the *principia* was a space where all the soldiers at the garrison could muster, and that environment would have emphasised communality and a sense of common duty. When used, the space would have been olfactorily characterised by the smell of the men. The fort's strong room, situated in the centre of the rear of the *principia,* housed the regimental coin and displayed the all-important standards. Regimental standards had a quasi-religious status within the Roman army and they were cared for in many of the same ways that effigies of deities were (Marcu, 2007, pp. 75–105; Birley, 2010, pp. 30–1). The anointing and perfuming of Roman standards is attested in literature and it is not hard to imagine incense being burnt around them (Marcu, 2007, pp. 75–105), although both perfume and incense are difficult to detect archaeologically at Vindolanda. The sense of communality fostered by the space would have been bolstered by the olfactory and visual awe inspired by the golden standards: they could be glimpsed at the rear of the *principia*, their perfume emanating from them across the room. Sadly, not much is known of this structure's material culture as few records have survived its 1930s excavation (Birley, 2010, pp. 210–11).

Micro smell environments

The smellscape of an enclosed space is constructed by the community of individuals who use the space and the activities they undertake there. If you were to recall the distinctive smells of your friends' houses when you were a child in contrast to your home smellscape (to which you were habituated), you will probably have been able to point out consistent and jarring differences in your sensory reception of their homes. The housekeeping routines of a given family, coupled with the food cooked there and the activities undertaken in the house create an individualised smellscape, which is habitually perpetuated. We can never recapture these historical smellscapes, but if we consider the different micro smell environments at Vindolanda we can begin to consider the way in which social interactions could be structured within them and the site more generally.

The barrack room (8)

If we take the barrack *contubernia* as an example we might expect certain commonalities of smell. Many individuals are thought to have slept in these tiny rooms, which very often had minimal ventilation, so the collective smells of human habitation would have been a dominant odour. The reed matting which often covered the floor was only periodically replaced and would have held damp odours as a consequence of the cold and damp climate of the region (Birley, 2009, pp. 78, 93–5; Birley, 2010, p. 122). It is entirely possible that some, if not all, members of a *contubernium* had little regard for the smell of their environment, but the evidence for the presence of sweet-smelling herbs and prepared perfumes in and around barrack rooms would indicate that some did; and that they took measures to alter their micro smell environment. The Vindolanda site archive clearly records several unguentaria from multiple phases and locations at the site.

The potential strength of the *contubernium* smellscape may be corroborated by a particularly gruesome discovery under the floors of one of Vindolanda's *contubernia*. A shallow grave under the flagstones of one barrack room contained the remains of a pre-pubescent girl of North-African extraction (Wilson, 2011). This highly illegal act of burial was apparently not discovered at the time, despite the odour of decomposition, which suggests that this unexpected odour was sufficiently masked by the familiar smellscape of the barrack room and did not rouse suspicion.

The vicus house (9)

The internal workings of the typical *vicus* house or apartment may have been fairly similar in nature to the barrack rooms, resulting in a similar smellscape; but a more detailed comparison of these two micro-environments warrants further study. The *vicus* dwellings are likely to have been inhabited by a wide range of people: active soldiers and their dependants, retired soldiers and their dependants, traders and those involved in the supply chain, and perhaps individuals with no military background who chose to live in these communities.

Inside the bathhouse (10)

The sensory nature of the Roman bathhouse has been well explored, and does not need too much embellishment here (Yegül, 2010, pp. 6–9). What is important to point out, however, is the contrast between what would have been considered the norm in Roman-period Britain. Most studies concerned with the sensory impact of baths consider them in an urban context, usually with reference to Italy. Furthermore, Koloski-Ostrow has recently emphasised that the rather idealised and sanitised picture we have of the baths should be replaced by one more often punctuated with grime and filth (2015, pp. 104–5). Although Vindolanda should not be described as non-urban, it is certainly not Rome or Pompeii. Roman bath design created internal architectural spaces in which atmospheric conditions were carefully controlled and the main sensory impact of the baths was, of course, related to the impact of heat and cold, wet and dry. In addition, the baths were a place where social differentiation could have been expressed through the use of scented oils and unguents, and this seems to have been the case at Vindolanda.

The temples (11)

The south-western workshops operated in a liminal space and shared the fringes of the *vicus* with buildings which have been identified as temples (11b, 11c). This is a common situation in Roman Britain and it was somewhat of a surprise when the temple of Jupiter Dolichenus was excavated in the north-western corner of the third century CE fort (11a) (Birley and Birley, 2012, pp. 231–58). The *cella* of the temple may have provided an escape from the smellscape of the fort at large. When in use for a sacrifice or festival, the micro-environment of this temple would have had a distinctive smellscape which included the scents of sacrifice and offering, such as incense, burning and animals (compare Weddle, 2013, especially pp. 155–6).

The praetorium (12)

The Vindolanda tablets refer to the second-century CE *praetorium* (governor's house), mentioning slaves and a varied list of household items, including food-stuffs and items of personal care. A diverse array of foods were prepared and consumed here, including garlic, anise, pork skin, spices (*condimenta*), fish sauce, oil and wine, olives, caraway and thyme (Bowman, 1994, pp. 64–6). This clearly Mediterranean diet was supplemented with locally brewed beer which, given the number of references to it in the tablets, was clearly held in high regard. All this suggests that there was a degree of luxury in the living conditions within the *praetorium*, certainly when compared to a barrack room, centurion's quarters or *vicus* house (Bowman, 1994, pp. 60–72). These differences would have mani-fested themselves in the micro smell environments of each of these buildings.

The *praetorium* had many facets that would have made its smellscape a micro-cosm of the fort: for example, the building had its own kitchens, baths, latrines and stables. Smells that were usually present in communal environments were made personal and controlled by the governor and his household. To be invited into the *praetorium* and experience its sensescape was surely a mark of status or privilege (Birley, Blake and Birley, 1998). We know, for example, that the pro-vincial governor and other commanding officers were frequent guests in the *praetorium* of Flavius Cerialis (Birley, 2009, pp. 65–70).

Conclusion

Although pragmatism and an adherence to a general spatial and structural order-ing of things at military sites are arguably the main attitudes that informed the way in which the site of Vindolanda was used, this preliminary study of the fort's third-century CE smellscape suggests that certain concessions were made in terms of spatial planning to account for the olfactory geography of the site. The clearest of these is the tendency to route smoke away from the central admin-istration buildings, the larger southern *vicus* buildings and, perhaps, the cavalry barracks. In other words, the higher status individuals who inhabited those areas wished to avoid being subjected to the effects of smoke.

We can also begin to see how the individuals who inhabited the fort and *vicus* may have experienced the parts of the site that they used (both their macro- and micro-environments). The individual micro-environments were places where a small or closed community using that space for a given period of time had agency over their immediate surroundings. This could be expressed in different ways, depending on the socio-economic status of the individual or group and their role within the constraints of the military framework (higher status indi-viduals had greater opportunity to affect their sensescape).

This study is just the beginning and its aim has been to highlight avenues for further research into the Vindolanda smellscape. The detailed ground plan and wealth of material recovered from the site make it a rich data source for sensory fieldwork, with the overall objective of learning more about the living condi-tions of the population of the fort and *vicus*. In addition, a detailed study of the references to olfactory stimuli in the Vindolanda tablets could be used to inform and nuance what this chapter has shown is possible to deduce from the architec-tural and artefactual remains. Whichever methods we use, further investigation of the olfactory geography of Vindolanda and other sites will enable us to bet-ter understand their smellscapes and the impact these had on their populations. This chapter has, I hope, illustrated the potential of Vindolanda as a case study for multisensory research.

Notes

1 Unreserved thanks are owed to Andrew Birley for his enthusiasm for this research and hospitality on site, and also his valuable feedback on a draft of this chapter. Thanks are also due to Anna Walas for her esteemed and detailed explanation of Roman fort dynamics, and to Harold Johnson for his help with specific details of Vindolanda's topography and excavation history (further information about his 3D reconstructions of this and other sites is available at twitter.com/stori3d_past). All shortcomings are my own.
2 Numbers refer to locales and buildings illustrated in Colour Plate 3.
3 Excavation is ongoing in this area of the western vicus, the map polygons, however, are based on more recent topographical plans. This area is awaiting full publication.

6   A sense of grief

The role of the senses in the performance of Roman mourning

Valerie M. Hope[1]

> In the beginning of the summer Agricola suffered a domestic blow: he lost the son born a year before. He took the loss neither with bravado, like most strong men, nor yet with the lamentations and mournings of a woman. Among other things, he turned for comfort to the war.
>
> (Tacitus *Agricola* 29.1)[2]

Tacitus constructs his much-loved father-in-law as the perfect mourner. Agricola neither suppresses his grief nor augments it, though he distracts himself with state business; war against the Britons is one remedy for grief. Tacitus' identification of extremes in how grief could be expressed (the stoical self-controlled male versus the wailing female) reflects the challenges of understanding Roman mourning. It was an emotive subject, one that could create polarised opinions and judgements which were often underpinned by stereotypes. What was acceptable and expected in bereavement was largely dictated by social status and gender. This stereotyping is also suggestive of the tension, and even uncomfortable relationship, between grief and mourning. It may be possible to provide definitions that separate grief and mourning: grief as the emotional, uncontrolled and primarily private reaction to loss, and mourning as the public expression, or processes and actions that accommodate loss; but in many cultures and periods the two overlap and collide somewhat haphazardly.[3] Tacitus suggests this in his characterisation of Agricola: his loss is like a wound (*vulnere*) that needs to be both shown and concealed. His genuine grief must be publically acknowledged, but his mourning must not reveal too little or too much grief; the emotional dimension to mourning is problematised. Getting mourning right was a cultural and social challenge in the Roman world. Grieving was perceived as natural or human (Seneca *Letters* 99.16, *Marcia* 7.1), but grief was not just private. The expected rituals placed the bereaved in public and, like it or not, they had to act as public mourners for whom there was a ready audience waiting to evaluate, and even judge, their performance. Funerary rituals marked the mourners as temporarily different and the appropriate enactment of grief was expected before their reintegration back into society (for the staging of grief in funerary ritual see Richlin, 2001; Prescendi, 2008).

Funerary rituals could involve numerous people, all of whom had specific roles, and demanded set actions accompanied by expectations of how the people involved should behave. It is these expected roles, rather than the emotional responses to bereavement, that are explored here. In particular, this chapter investigates the embodied aspects that affected, controlled and manipulated both the senses of the mourners and those who came into contact with them. The state of mourning involved sensory cues, both for the bereaved and the non-bereaved, which signalled mourning as an altered state: put simply, mourners looked, sounded and smelled different. This chapter considers the range and nature of those cues, and how they may have shaped people's perceptions of their own bereavement and the bereavements of others.

Recent work has sought to recreate some of the sensory aspects of the Roman funeral, in particular seeking to reconstruct the spatial context and progression of the funerary cortège, including imagining some of the sights, sounds and smells experienced by the participants (Favro and Johanson, 2010; Johanson, 2011; Potter, 2014, pp. 36–44). These approaches remain largely grounded in elite Roman funerals and have also noted the role of the senses in reinforcing, or renegotiating, the social hierarchy within such elite rituals (Potter, 2014, p. 43). Here the focus is placed not just on the funerals of the well-to-do, but on a broader range of peoples and contexts, in order to investigate how the senses were used to shape and define the mourning experience for different participants.

Evidence

At the outset the nature of the evidence needs to be addressed. We have few written literary accounts or descriptions of Roman funerals and wider funerary and mourning rituals. What we do have is often coloured by specific agendas and is almost exclusively the product of the wealthy male elite. The evidence ranges across a wide time span and varied genres. To build up a picture of events we can be forced to combine, for example, Polybius' account of an elite funeral in the city of Rome held in the mid Republic (6.53–4) with Lucian's satirical Greek treatise on mourning written in the second century CE (*On Funerals (On Mourning)*). Therefore, recreating Roman funerary ritual often produces a composite account that lacks any real geographic and chronological specificity. These shortcomings can become more pronounced when focusing on mourning, since mourning could be viewed as inherently female, and a sign of moral failings (see below). Many accounts of mourning behaviour are about mythological figures (for example, the mourning characters in Seneca's *Trojan Women*), are philosophical critiques (such as Plutarch's *Consolation to His Wife*, written at the death of their daughter), or are satirical works (for example, Lucian's treatise on mourning or Petronius' Widow of Ephesus: *Satyricon* 111–12). Thus, understanding what real mourners did and how they behaved is difficult to recreate. Mourners could, for example, be described as carrying out acts of self-harm (cheek scratching, breast bruising or hair tearing), and such gestures were common literary mourning motifs, but we can be less certain as to by whom, or to what extent, these acts were actually performed. In addition, when evaluating the role of the senses, sight often takes priority within literary sources (Hamilakis, 2011, p. 210). Ancient society was an oral and aural one, and the other senses of touch, smell and taste, though far from ignored, were often less well explored (Betts, 2011, pp. 118–19; Toner, 2014b, p. 3).

Complementing the literary sources are a number of sculpted reliefs which depict funerary and mourning scenes. The best known are the so-called Amiternum relief and the Haterii relief (Figures 6.1 and 6.2). The Amiternum relief (probably later first century BCE in date) shows a funeral procession, with a bier carried by eight pall-bearers; musicians lead the procession, accompanied by nine mourners, some of whom raise their arms (see Bodel, 1999, pp. 264–65; Hughes, 2005; Hope, 2007, p. 100; Potter, 2014, p. 39). The relief from the tomb of the Haterii (late first century CE) shows a woman laid out at home, with a musician present and mourners beating their breasts; incense burners and garlands also fill the space (Bodel, 1999, pp. 267–8; Leach, 2006; Hope, 2007, p. 98). In addition to these reliefs are a number of decorated sarcophagi that show mourners gathered around the deathbed, and also mythological scenes depicting mourners attending corpses (for examples see Zanker and Ewald, 2012, pp. 57–70). It needs to be emphasised that the Amiternum and Haterii reliefs are highly unusual in their level of detail, and thus it is unclear how representative these images are. These images also place limits on recreating sensory experience, prioritising the visual; although depictions of food, flowers, musical instruments and gestures evoke movement, sound, taste and smell.

Scholars have reconstructed aspects of Roman funerals, remaining sensitive to changes across time and social status, and are cautious about what can be securely established (for example Toynbee, 1971, pp. 43–64; Bodel, 1999; Hope, 2009, pp. 65–96). This chapter follows that tradition, identifying traits and making assertions about mourners whilst remaining mindful that accessing all peoples, places and times across the Roman era, and the full range of mourning experiences, is not possible.

Figure 6.1 Funerary relief from Amiternum showing a funeral procession

Source: Drawing by Jerneja Wilmott; copyright Maureen Carroll

Figure 6.2 Relief from the tomb of the Haterii (Rome)
Source: Drawing by Jerneja Wilmott; copyright Maureen Carroll

Mourning bodies and spaces

Roman mourners were not just found at funerals. The funeral was one element, but not the first or final aspect of the mourning process. The acknowledgement of a death meant that the family became a *familia funesta*, obliged to undertake the disposal of the body and also prohibited from usual activities (Servius 6.8, 11.2; Cicero *On the Laws* 2.22.55; Livy 2.47.10). What this meant in practical terms is difficult to establish. It can be assumed that members of the bereaved household faced restricted movements and social interactions and were precluded from sacred, public and economic activities until the time of the funeral, and possibly longer (Šterbenc Erker, 2011, p. 41). This was due, at least in part, to a sense of spiritual pollution (somewhat ill-defined) brought by death (Lindsay, 2000; Lennon, 2013, pp. 136–66). The degree to which pollution and restricted movement actively affected all members of the household is, however, uncertain; the extent of pollution (and also mourning) may also have been dictated by who had died. The death of a small child, for example, could cause minimal disruption to the family, whereas that of the *paterfamilias* would be a major disruption. If the family chose to display the body there would have been several days between the death and the funeral, and this time was not marked by inactivity or complete isolation. The funeral needed to be arranged, others informed of the death, undertakers hired and visitors greeted.

How quickly the bereaved transitioned into their role, or at least took on the guise of a mourner, is unclear. A household in mourning was supposed to be recognised as such. A cypress or pine branch was placed outside the house (Pliny *Natural History* 16.18. 40; 16.60.140), and inside there would have been clear visual and audible cues to identify the mourners. The bereaved were supposed to don dark clothing; some may have had clothing already of the requisite colour (due to previous bereavements), but others may have needed to purchase or acquire the cloth. A cheaper and more rapid solution was to dirty existing clothing or to dye it (for mourning dress see Olson, 2007). The mourners might also cultivate an unkempt appearance by not washing and leaving hair uncombed; women might also let their hair down and men not shave. In addition, faces, arms and chests might be deliberately bruised and scratched, hair and clothes torn and tugged at (for the appearance of mourners see, for example, Lucian *On Funerals (On Mourning)* 12; Petronius *Satyricon* 111; Richlin, 2001). Aspects of such a dishevelled appearance could be adapted rapidly (the loosening of hair, for example) or achieved by the application of dirt and ashes, but the overall impact, especially of aspects such as bruises and facial hair, may have been a cumulative one; as time passed the alterations to the mourner's appearance became increasingly pronounced.

The way the mourners carried themselves, their actions and gestures, also announced their state. Mourners could raise their arms (in supplication of the heavens) or use their hands to beat their cheeks, chests and arms, pull at or tear hair and clothing, or use fingernails to scratch exposed skin. Mourners could also fall to the ground, roll on the floor and bang their heads (for gestures see, for example, Petronius *Satyricon* 111; Apuleius *Metamorphoses* 8.7–8; Lucian *On Funerals (On Mourning)* 12; Corbeill, 2004, pp. 67–106; Figures 6.1 and 6.2). Self-inflicted physical pain was an enactment of emotional pain. How often, or precisely when, these gestures were enacted or deemed appropriate is unclear; such actions could be characterised as extreme, unnecessary and false by elite, male authors. The gestures could be seen as being triggered by the initial shock at a death. For example, at the passing of Priscilla her husband cried wildly, drew a sword and threatened to harm himself (Statius *Silvae* 5.1.198–200). Other authors suggest that such actions were performed only when there was an audience; for example, Seneca notes that people cry louder, hurt themselves and fall to the floor when others are in the room (Seneca *Letters* 99.16). Dramatic gestures might also be demanded of certain mourners; Lucan paints a picture of a mother instructing female slaves to beat their breasts at the death of her son (Lucan *Pharsalia* 2.24).

A household in mourning was also expected to be noisy. The range of sounds was diverse, from incoherent sobs, shouts, groans and wails, to speeches and sung laments accompanied by musical instruments (Lucian *On Funerals (On Mourning)* 12–13; and for instruments see Figures 6.1 and 6.2). The noise level ranged from muted sighs and moans to loud horn blasts. Again, some of these sounds were easily created by the bereaved, but others were orchestrated and demanded the summoning of trained musicians and those versed in lament (Varro *On the Latin Language* 7.70). The soundscape would have reflected different stages of the mourning: shouts and groans accompanied the announcement of a death, more formal musical laments were sung around the laid out body and during the funeral, and the *nenia* (a soothing lament thought to encourage the dead to leave this world) was sung at the graveside (Dutsch, 2008). It is also worth noting that just as the noise levels varied, there may also have been periods of silence, and periods when the majority of the mourners were expected to be quiet. Lucan notes the stunned silence that could follow the moment of death (*Pharsalia* 2.22), and for laments to be heard, if not interrupted, some of the mourners needed to reduce their noise and listen.

The corpse, mourners and house may also have had distinctive odours. Those in mourning may not have visited the public baths or used perfume, the corpse may also have had a changing and deteriorating smell, especially if left on display for several days. Bad odours could be viewed as polluting, even dangerous (Toner, 2014b, p. 3 and p. 19), and the use of perfumes on or near the corpse, and the burning of incense were expected (Pliny *Natural History* 12.41.83; Statius *Silvae* 2.6.84–93; the Haterii relief, Figure 6.2). This scenting of the house involved the purchase and consumption of the requisite goods. On the one hand the mourners' neglect of personal hygiene may have rendered them increasingly malodorous; on the other, their clothing and hair may have been suffused with the sweet smell of incense.

The sensory transformation of both mourners and house was a process, not instantaneous. Within the house certain areas were probably affected by death and mourning more than others. If the death had occurred at home the room in which the corpse had breathed its last would have been an initial focus for activity and change, marked by the actions and sounds of the new mourners. In houses of the more affluent the body was then moved to the atrium for a period of display. The atrium had to be prepared, a space allocated and a suitable couch or bed (presuming that of the deceased was not used) obtained and positioned. It is possible that expensive materials would have been used to cover the couch and draped in other areas of the atrium; candles, garlands and incense burners would also have been positioned (see, for example, Figure 6.2), as well as seating for those attending the corpse. The atrium would have been filled with the sights, sounds, smells and gestures of both death and bereavement; it was a space temporarily altered by the presence of the corpse and the mourners who attended it; for the inhabitants of a house the familiar space of the atrium was made alien.[4] The presence of the corpse and mourners, and the physical changes to the bodies of both, created a mourning environment. To enter this space was a marked experience that heightened the senses.

The mourning environment was not a confined or entirely separate space, however. People were mobile and would have carried their mourning with them. We cannot assume that in the immediate aftermath of the death all the household would have been equally restricted in their movements; people would have entered and left the building, and this mobility was probably influenced by the nature of their relationship with the dead person. Pliny the Younger noted that he was kept indoors by the loss of his wife, but still wrote to a friend inviting her to visit him to discuss a legal matter (*Letters* 9.13.4); two days later (probably post the *cena novendialis*) Pliny seems to have been back in circulation and able to attend the senate (*Letters* 9.13.6).

Following the display of the body mourning was taken from the house onto the streets through the funeral procession (*pompa*), which moved the body to the cemetery (in some cases via the forum). Mourners were part of this procession and the cortège was marked by clear sensory cues that announced its presence to a wider populace. The procession was highly visible and audible; the gestures, appearance and sounds of the mourners continued as before, but were now mobile and presented to a wider audience (Figure 6.1).[5] Elite funeral processions could mimic aspects of triumphal processions, with the *imagines* (masks) recalling the family pedigree, and placards, *fasces* and military standards indicating a career's high points (Bodel, 1999, p. 261). Such processions were designed to stimulate the senses, to entertain and inform the viewer. The onward movement of the cortège was punctuated by moments of stationary display. If a eulogy was given in the forum the mourners would have stopped their dramatic gestures, shouts and laments and gathered around the speaker; attention shifted from the cortège to the orator and any familial masks displayed on the rostra (Polybius 6.53–4). Nevertheless, eulogies could be interrupted by the shouts and cries of the listeners, and these could be deliberately incited by the words of the speech (see, for example, Appian *Civil Wars* 2.141). The participation and performance of the mourners did not stop but could be adjusted to fit the context. Both the streets and forum temporarily became mourning environments, and must have been spaces which were regularly affected by such events.[6]

The end point for the cortège was the cemetery, where the body would be buried or cremated, and the remains marked. The necropolis was a space defined but not confined by death and mourning. Burial areas were beyond city walls, but rarely carefully planned and laid out. Tombs could jostle for road frontage and thereby access to the eyes of the living. The cortège would have crowded around the pyre or grave associated with the family tomb, or the new burial space obtained following the death. The mourners may have continued with the same sounds and actions but were confronted with some additional sensory experiences, such as the smoke of the pyre, the blood of sacrificial animals and the smell of burning flesh (compare Williams, 2004; also Weddle, 2013). Post funeral the tomb or cemetery, unlike the atrium, the streets or the forum, remained a mourning environment. It was the focus for return visits by mourners on anniversaries and set festivals for the dead (Graham, 2005; Hope, 2009, pp. 99–102). It provided a setting for the continuing relationship between the living and the dead, and aspects of its sensory environment must have reinforced the mourner's identity. The incense, flowers and foodstuffs associated with commemorative rituals, and in the case of inhumation tombs, the smell of decay, marked the tomb and cemetery as specific spaces, linked but separated from the everyday (Avery, 2013). A visit to the cemetery had the power to evoke and even return the individual temporarily to their former state of mourning.

Post funeral, the mourners would have returned to the house, which had been swept out (Festus 3L), an act of ritual purification which may have been coupled with tidying the atrium and the removal of the mourning accoutrements. The mourners also underwent purification by fire and water.[7] The corpse was no longer in residence, but the mourners' changed appearances and actions may have continued, even if paid undertakers, musicians and lament singers were no longer present. Nine days after the death a feast and further purification rituals were held (*cena novendialis*). For some, and probably primarily men, this may have marked the end of the formal mourning period. This was the time to put aside dark clothing, to shave, wash properly and resume public life (for example Cicero *Against Vatinius* 13.31), and thus re-establish the expected sensory order. However, this setting aside of mourning was not formally prescribed and men, at least, could opt to mourn for less or more time. There were famed examples of men who curtailed their mourning because they gave priority to state demands and responsibilities (see below). Those who prolonged their mourning risked criticism, such as the emperor Gaius who, in mourning his sister, repeatedly trimmed his beard but then allowed it to grow again (Seneca *Polybius* 17.5). If a man expressed his mourning dramatically, or for too long, he risked being called womanish or, with a negative play on the sense of touch, soft (*molliter*, Seneca *Letters* 99.1).[8]

There were certain rules which stated how long mourning for children, parents and husbands should be (Plutarch *Numa* 12; Paulus *Opinions* 1.21.2–5). Such rules seem to have been primarily aimed at women, especially ensuring the paternity of any child born soon after widowhood commenced. Seneca implies that whereas tradition dictated that women could mourn for a year, no restrictions were placed on men since it was best not to mourn at all (Seneca *Letters* 63.13) and the *Digest* notes that husbands were not obliged to mourn for their wives (*Digest* (Paulus) 3.2.9). Paulus suggests that those (women) who broke the restrictions could be placed in disgrace, but we cannot be certain how this was policed or if anyone was ever so punished. In this context, what did mourning for up to a year really mean? Paulus notes that mourners should avoid dinner parties, jewellery, adornments, and purple and white clothing. Women could continue to indicate their bereaved state through their physical appearance and restricted activities. Dramatic gestures, wailing and the like were supposed to lessen with time, but continuing to wear dark clothing marked the female, especially the widow, as still being in a state of social transition; for women certain sensory cues for mourning continued. This is one of the areas where grief and mourning could separate. Grieving could persist (or indeed come to an end), but the outward symbols of mourning, including sensory cues, were supposed to conform to certain time-defined expectations. Further, women were expected to continue mourning the longest, and primarily for their male relatives, while women may not have been mourned for at all.[9]

Mourning had a temporary impact on certain environments and locations, and a transformative, cumulative effect on mourners' bodies, which were used as canvases for the exterior expression and enactment of expected grief through mourning dress, gestures, sounds and smells. There was also a certain fluidity in the parameters and definition of mourning bodies and spaces; there were clear sensory cues, but the extent to which these were adopted and for how long differed according to the identity of the mourner.

The centrality of the corpse

The focus in this chapter is upon mourners, but we cannot overlook that a major player in funeral ritual was the corpse. Emma-Jayne Graham has explored the idea of the materiality of the Roman corpse and its potential agency (2011a). On the one hand the corpse was inanimate and readily manipulated in the hands of the living; on the other, it had the power to affect strongly the senses of the living. The corpse had an appearance, odour and touch that marked it as different from a living body, something which was experienced by those preparing, washing, dressing and moving it. Even those at further remove could see, and perhaps smell, this sense of difference. Up to and including the funeral the corpse took centre stage, both affecting and defining the mourners. It was a relationship (or former and now altered relationship) that made someone a mourner and dictated their level of contact with the corpse. To be in the presence of the corpse, to share space with it, was the expected duty of a mourner and provided a heightened sensory experience.

A corpse is notable for the absence of its senses (for characterisation of this in Latin literature see Walter, 2013). It is silent and static, it cannot hear, speak, move, taste, smell or touch. In the Roman world this sensory absence was readily acknowledged by the living survivors who did things to and for the corpse, such as washing, dressing, perfuming, positioning and carrying it. In tending the corpse the bereaved did for the body what it could no longer do for itself. Simultaneously, there was almost a denial of the absence of the senses. Corpses were touched and kissed, spoken to and offered flowers, perfumes and food. In many respects these actions emphasised the betwixt and between state of the corpse; that it both was and was not the person who had died (Synnott, 1993; Nilsson-Stutz, 2003, p. 58). These actions appealed to the vestiges of the corpses' senses, even though no response was expected, and the hope or belief that the person or soul, if not the corpse, might be entering an afterlife that allowed some sort of continuing existence. The possibility of sensory continuity of the soul, however, could be readily challenged: 'But apart from the body there can never be either eyes or nose or hand by itself for the spirit, nor tongue apart from the body, nor ears; therefore spirits by themselves cannot either have sensation or exist' (Lucretius 3.31–3).

A series of oppositions existed between the corpse and the mourners (Ochs, 1993, p. 48). The mourners were in a liminal state, with responsibility for the removal of the polluting corpse from the world of the living. For mourners, usual expectations were reversed and sensory experiences turned on their head (Hope, 2009, p. 122). So the corpse was tidy and clean, the mourners were dishevelled and dirty; the corpse wore pale clothing, the mourners dark; the corpse was silent, the mourners were noisy; the corpse was motionless, the mourners could move often and rapidly (raising arms, beating bodies, falling to the ground); the corpse touched nothing (although it may have had things brought into contact with it), the mourners touched multiple surfaces (the corpse, their hair, faces, bodies); the corpse experienced no physical pain, the mourners might cause themselves physical pain; the corpse was perfumed, the mourners were unwashed; the corpse could be offered food and drink, the mourners may not have eaten.[10] In some respects the mourners were marked as more polluted, more abhorrent, than the dead and soon to be rotting body.

Elite family mourners

The mourning about which we know the most is generally that of the elite, although it is often coloured and defined by expectations of, and to some extent prejudices against, the behaviour of other social groups. This was epitomised by philosophical ideals that dismissed mourning as unsuited to elite men, and as a characteristic of foreigners, women and the ill-educated (Seneca *Marcia* 7.3; Plutarch *Moralia: Consolatio ad Apollonium* 22). There were popular anecdotes of famous men who were admired for putting duty before emotion and who, when struck by grief, carried on with their public duties. For example, Lucius Bibulus, consul in 51–50 BCE, lost two sons but resumed his official duties the day after he heard of their deaths (Seneca *Marcia* 13.2; compare Valerius Maximus 5.10.2). The point of these anecdotes is not that such men were callous or unfeeling, but that showy, dramatic or prolonged mourning, a mere performance, could be incompatible with male identity; as Martial put it, he who grieves properly grieves alone (*Epigrams* 1.33).

On a practical level the elite male may have been more readily removed from the sensory extremes of death and bereavement. Direct contact with the corpse may have been minimalised. The washing, dressing, perfuming and general arrangement of the corpse was the responsibility of others.[11] Indeed, the sense of spiritual pollution attached to the corpse may have made it unsuitable for male heads of households to touch the dead any more than necessary. A death in the family was particularly problematic for men with a public religious role. For example, in 82 BCE, when the dictator Sulla was presiding at the festival of Hercules, he was unable to visit his dying wife and was forced to divorce her and have her removed from his house (Plutarch *Sulla* 35). This is not to underplay the role of men in funerary ritual. Images depict men as well as women sitting with corpses and performing mourning gestures (Figure 6.2). Lucian's treatise on mourning also focuses on the father's response as much as that of the women of the household (*On Funerals (On Mourning)* 13–15). There were also specific roles attached to the closest male relatives of the deceased. They might be expected to carry the bier. Valerius Maximus records, for example, that Quintus Metellus Macedonicus (consul in 143 BCE) was carried through the city on the shoulders of his sons and sons-in-law (7.1). Any eulogy, whether delivered in the forum or at the grave, was also made by a close male relative (Polybius 6.53). An elite funeral was about public display. It could be a 'civic event' (Bodel, 1999, p. 261) where the male relatives of the deceased needed to be seen to be putting on the event properly and fulfilling their expected public roles as lead mourners. The direct handling of the corpse might be limited, but unless bound by religious office men could look at and touch the corpse, and must have been readily affected by the corpse's altering state.

In terms of the elite male's own body, modifications may have been relatively slight. An educated man should not wail, fall to the ground, tear his hair or injure his body; but nor should he be devoid of grief (Tacitus *Agricola* 29.1). Donning dark clothing, being unshaven and shedding a few controlled tears was acceptable. Judging the correct amount of emotion, the appropriate display of grief, must have been difficult. Pliny the Younger, for example, admires and accommodates the grief of his close friends (*Letters* 5.16, 8.5), but dismisses that of his enemy Regulus as excessive and false (*Letters* 4.2, 4.7).

Mourning was often characterised as feminine (Cicero *Letters to Friends* 9.20.3; Seneca *Marcia* 2.3.4; Plutarch *Moralia: Consolatio ad Uxor* 4), and traditionally it was the women of the household who would give the dying a final kiss, close the eyes of the corpse, call out the name of the dead person and then wash, dress and perfume the body (Hope, 2009, pp. 125–6). Women had more direct contact with the corpse initially, and the amount of time they subsequently spent in its presence may have been greater than men; sitting with it, crying, wailing, moaning and singing, as well as performing dramatic gestures, including self-harm. These sounds and gestures could continue during the procession and at the pyre, although silence and control may have been expected for the male performance of the eulogy. Women may also have been expected to stay by the pyre, and collect the remains (Suetonius *Augustus* 100, *Tiberius* 1.3.5–8). Unlike men, women could be expected to retain the outward symbols of mourning, especially dark dress, for longer (see above). The parallels between women's roles in birth and death have recently been highlighted (Corbeill, 2004, pp. 67–106; Dutsch, 2008; Hope, 2010). Women performed important functions in overseeing and guiding entrances and exits into society. In many respects women were both elevated and demeaned by their associations with death and mourning. They were performing an important task, symbolising both familial and state loss, but the dirty and polluting tasks associated with death were assigned to them. The fact that female mourning was controlled and time limited, and excessive displays were in theory prohibited (Cicero *On the Laws* 2.22.59), suggests that the importance, power and even dangerous nature of female mourning was acknowledged (for discussion see Richlin, 2001; Corbeill, 2004, pp. 67–106; Mustakallio, 2005; Hope, 2009, pp. 125–6).

We need to be aware, however, of changes across time. Bodel has suggested that funerary ritual may have become more oriented on family, private and internal display following the change from Republic to Empire. Under the emperors the funeral procession lost some of its potency and relevance for the elite, and the main venues for the performance of mourning may have shifted from the streets and forum (the funeral procession) to the home (display of the corpse) and cemetery (disposal and commemoration) (Bodel, 1999). The championing of these more private aspects of the ritual, and the importance of family, may have caused some softening of the philosophical ideals for male elite mourning, as the poetry of Statius explores (Markus, 2004, p. 126; Gibson, 2006; Hope, 2011a, pp. 111–15). It may have become more acceptable for men to acknowledge, if not enact, their grief in public (the paradigms of extreme male control date mainly to the Republic). Bodel has also argued that there was an increase in use of hired help by those who could afford it, especially from the late Republic onwards (Bodel, 2004). Individuals other than the female members of the household could be hired to wash and prepare the body, to lament over it and act out the expected mourning gestures. The more dramatic and noisy performance of mourning may have become increasingly inappropriate for elite women. The marked sensory impact of handling the corpse and using their own bodies as a physical representation of familial grief may have been curtailed, although women may have retained the authority in delegating these tasks to others (Šterbenc Erker, 2011, p. 48). Thus, there may have been some convergence of gendered mourning expectations, and we are left to wonder whether the performance of mourning in an elite household was really that dramatically different for men and women. The basis of traditional roles (and their gender distinctions) may have continued, but as mourners men and women did similar things in similar environments, donning dark clothing and facing the challenge of figuring out how much emotion was really appropriate for their mourning display. We can be fairly sure that elite men and women experienced others performing their grief for them, and were exposed to the sensory aspects, especially the sights and sounds, of that performance. Elite mourners were thus both participants and spectators in the expected mourning rituals.

Non-elite family mourners

Unable to afford help (or as much help), those who were less well off may have performed more of the traditional and expected roles themselves. Washing and dressing the corpse, and lamenting over it, may have led to more direct contact with the dead body. As such these mourners may have been more readily exposed to and affected by the corpse and changes in its appearance, smell and touch. Display of the body (prior to disposal) may have been shorter due to lack of appropriate space and the cost of disguising decay. The perfumes and incense, sound of musical instruments and extended lament singing may have been less, or different from, those used by the wealthy, resulting in a different sensory experience; whilst the dramatic gestures and sounds of mourning cost nothing and may have been readily performed by the family, especially its female members. There may have been informal support networks within communities, which shared the burden of mourning; people skilled in laying out a corpse and experienced in composing and leading lament, who did not charge for these services but used reciprocal arrangements. Regulations for *collegia* indicate that members could be paid to attend funerals (*CIL* XIV.2112), suggesting some structuring of support networks.

For the less well off it may also have been the case that sensory deprivation and experiences, and the contrasts with normative sensory experience, were felt less acutely in the face of bereavement. A woman of low status, for example, may in mourning have been much as she was in normal life – dirty, dishevelled, in dark clothing and very much responsible for the bodies of others. Indeed it can be suggested that in particular the adoption of dark clothing by wealthy mourners deliberately evoked poverty (Richlin, 2001, pp. 241–2). This is not to claim that the poor did not mourn for their dead, but their daily sensory experiences may have meant that the expected mourning environment was less of a sensory shock.

Non-familial mourners

Amongst those attending the funeral, and possibly visiting the corpse while it was displayed, were more distant relatives, friends and members of the wider community. The people in this wider mourning group were distanced from the corpse because they did not touch, handle or carry it, and were thus less affected by its materiality. They were probably physically further away than the family and/or hired mourners who surrounded the corpse. The bodies of these mourners were probably less adapted to the mourning state. Dark clothing may have been donned, some tears shed, and these mourners may have joined in laments or expected responses to eulogies, but they were less likely to indulge in mourning gestures. Their actions were also confined to the funeral and any pre-funeral visit to the corpse. These mourners could exit the mourning environment and were not defined by it. Nonetheless this wider mourning group was affected by both the presence of the corpse and the other mourners. In some ways it was this wider group who were the target audience for the mourning performed by or provided by the family; it was they who saw and judged whether the family had publically discharged their duty to the dead person in an appropriate manner. They experienced the mourning of others, and were affected (to the point of participation) by the sights and sounds.

Hired mourners

Those who had the most contact with the corpse and displayed the loudest and most dramatic reactions may have been those most immune to the impact of both the corpse and grief. The undertaker's retinue could include people to wash, prepare and perfume the corpse, musicians, lament singers and female mourners. These were slaves who were supplied by the undertaker to handle the corpse and perform those tasks which could be deemed dirty, polluted or demeaning, and these specialists were regarded as polluted by death and the profit they made (Bodel, 2000, 2004; Lennon, 2013, pp. 147–53). The increasing use, from the late Republic, of such help in mourning tasks further underlined the low status associations that were attached to the performance of mourning.

The full impact of the sensory experience of these hired mourners is difficult to gauge. For them exposure to a corpse was a daily occurrence and the sights, sounds and smells of mourning were their normative experience and sensory environment. For such people their own body presentation, in terms of dress, appearance, gestures and sounds, was that of a mourner. They were actors of mourning; they could turn the tears, shouts and laments on and off. In some respects they defined and could never fully be separated from the mourning environment. But in terms of an individual death they, more than any other mourner (rich, poor, familial or more distant), could enter and exit the mourning environment with relative sensory ease.

Mourning was work for hired mourners and presumably their senses were habituated and hardened to the sights, sounds and smells of mourning. Yet they were amidst people (the family of the deceased) for whom bereavement was not the normative state. They may have moved among and mixed with the bereaved, showing them what to do and vocalise, encouraging them to give vent to their emotions. Simultaneously, the presence of hired mourners may have meant that some of the genuinely grief stricken (men in particular) were removed from some of the sensory extremes; they became spectators as their own grief was enacted or represented in front of them. Horace suggested that hired mourners put on more of a show than those grieving in their hearts (Horace *The Art of Poetry* 431). We should not assume, however, that all aspects of the performance were false and somehow distanced from the corpse. Emma-Jayne Graham has argued that sensory-driven memories could have shaped an individual's encounters with death and mourning (2011a, p. 30; compare also Graham, this volume). Previous experiences of loss, grief and ritual affected how one reacted and behaved; those hired may have been reliving, remembering and re-enacting their own losses, and their own mourning, but were also confirming their identity as funerary workers (Graham, 2011a, p. 33).

Extended household as mourners

The extent of the slave *familia* varied depending on the wealth and status of the owner, and this may have dictated the degree to which slaves and ex-slaves grieved for, and were then expected to mourn for, their owner or ex-owner. In some households slaves may have been used to perform funerary functions such as the washing and preparation of the corpse. Female slaves may have been expected to follow the lead of the mistress of the house or hired mourners and lament singers in giving physical and audible expression to the family's grief (Lucan *Pharsalia* 2.24).

The freeing of slaves in a will was a known strategy for swelling the number of mourners attending a funeral, and it was expected that such ex-slaves would show their gratitude by publically displaying their respects to the dead, and possibly their sorrow (for example, Petronius *Satyricon* 42). Legislation attempted to limit the number of slaves that could be freed via the will (Carroll, 2011). Bequests in wills could also be dependent on the recipient attending a funeral (for example *Digest* 32.10; 35.1.9). Thus, slaves were expected to be part of the mourning performance and the nature of such performances helped confirm social positions; it is likely that a freed slave would be expected to perform more exaggerated mourning at the funeral of his patron than a patron would have performed at the funeral of his freed slave (Šterbenc Erker, 2011, p. 57).

Bystanders

Horace observed that a funeral done in style was something that a community enjoyed, appreciated and commented upon (Horace *Satires* 2.5 105–6). Funerals would have been a frequent and familiar street occurrence, and those going about their daily business, who did not know the deceased or follow the bier, were anyway exposed to its sights, sounds and smells. These spectators could be drawn into the event, evaluating the deceased and the family, but they might also empathise with the bereaved. Mourning was a performance with a deliberate emotional element. Polybius noted that at the funerals of distinguished men, the population of the city had their sympathies engaged, 'the loss seems to be not confined to the mourners, but a public one affecting the whole people' (Polybius 6.53.4). More modest funerals also played with the emotions of those present, and the spectators were reminded of their own losses and mourning experiences. Juvenal noted that passing cortèges, especially those of the young, could draw natural tears from all that saw them (Juvenal *Satires* 15.138–40; see also Seneca *On Anger* 2.2).

Conclusion

Roman mourning created a unique sensory environment in which mourners took their bereavement with them: they were mobile and communicated their state to others via a number of embodied experiences. At the same time, certain contexts and physical environments were associated with death and mourning: the deathbed or room where the death occurred, the atrium of the house where the corpse might be displayed, the streets of the town through which the funeral procession passed, and the cemetery. These spaces could be filled with the sights, sounds, smells and gestures of death and bereavement. The presence of both the corpse and the mourners, and physical changes to their bodies, characterised these spaces. To enter one of these environments was to challenge the senses; to move from one sense world and enter another.

Anyone paying their respects to a corpse, attending a funeral or seeing a funeral procession pass by on the street engaged in a multisensory experience. A funeral procession was probably heard, and possibly smelled, long before it was seen. There was also a unique sensory interplay between the bodies (dead and alive; bereaved and non-bereaved) of those involved. The corpse affected those who came into contact with it. In response, the mourners adapted their own bodies, often presenting them in opposition to the corpse to symbolise suffering, grief and pollution. These body modifications of the mourners in turn affected the bodies and senses of fellow mourners and the wider populace. By being loud, dirty, dishevelled, smelly and dramatic, mourners presented an inversion of the everyday norms of the respectable. Sensory cues announced the altered state of the mourners, alerting others to death pollution but also allowing them to spectate, empathise with and participate in the display of grief. Mourners were integral to creating the sensory dimension of Roman funeral ritual. The mourners manipulated their own senses in their performance of mourning, and in the process manipulated the senses of others.

Mourning was a multisensory experience, and mourners of all different types (men, women, hired, bystanders and so forth) were united by sharing aspects of this experience. Even those on the sidelines, those present only from duty or stopped by a passing procession, could be drawn into the event. The specific details of how a given individual should mourn was, nonetheless, dictated by societal expectations. Mourning could be codified and dictated by who you were in terms of age, status, relationship to the deceased and gender. Not everyone chose, or was allowed, to mourn in the same way. There was a hierarchy of mourning which affected how mourning was experienced, and thus what an individual saw, heard, said, touched, smelled and did; and the extent to which he or she interacted with the corpse and the other mourners. There was also a scale of permissible expressiveness: at one extreme were elite males who might shed a single tear; at the other were low status women who could exhibit a range of frenzied behaviour. These extremes were often stereotyped and exaggerated, and formed part of moral dialogues about acceptable and unacceptable behaviour. Mourning rituals and contexts channelled this range of expressiveness and created environments in which the sounds, sights, smells and gestures of mourning, extreme and muted, genuine and performed, merged rather than collided. Many of these sounds, sights and smells must have been unforgettable and very specific to funeral rituals, and in consequence would have shaped people's subsequent encounters with mourning across their lifespans and as they fulfilled new and different mourning roles.

Mourning was not the same sensory experience for all, nor a consistent sensory experience for the individual, across different funerals or bereavements. At any death some individuals, whether through instinct, choice, expectation or money, used their bodies as a canvas for expressing or enacting mourning; but for others experiencing mourning may have been more about sensing the changes to other people's bodies than changing their own. All those classed as mourners were not grieving to the same degree. Some were forced to mourn for someone they had never met, and equally those related to the deceased may not have been experiencing any grief at all. To a large extent this was the advantage of mourning rituals, including the organised and performative elements, since these guided people through a difficult time and transition to new roles, by providing an accepted script. Mourning rituals supplied a framework of expected behaviour, which may or may not have reflected emotional reality, and this expected behaviour was characterised by sensory driven cues.

Notes

1 I would like to thank Eleanor Betts and Emma-Jayne Graham for commenting on an earlier draft of this chapter.
2 All translations are from the Loeb Classical Library.
3 For an overview of the distinctions between grief and mourning, see Hope, 2011a, pp. 92–5. Latin vocabulary can distinguish between grief and mourning. Mourning is most often *luctus* (suggesting wailing), and other commonly used words capture the inherent physical manifestations of mourning: lament (*lamentatio*), groaning (*gemitus*) and striking the body (*planctus*), and a dirty and dishevelled appearance (*squalor*). The term employed for grief is most often *maeror*, with the words *dolor* (sorrow) and *tristia* (sadness) also frequently used to express the pain brought by bereavement. However, the fact that *luctus* and *maeror* are used and linked together (for example, Cicero *Philippics* 14.11, *For Milo* 5; Apuleius *Metamorphoses* 1.6) suggests that, as in English, there was no hard and fast dividing line between what was grief and what was mourning.
4 The corpse was probably tended both day and night (Apuleius *Metamorphoses* 2.22–26), although the mourning (especially wailing, lament and gestures) may have reached a crescendo at key points, perhaps when visitors were present and immediately before the body was carried out of the house. So the experience of entering the atrium, where the corpse was displayed, may have differed across the course of the day (and night).
5 Funerals took place in daylight, though precise timings and length are unclear. The funerals of children and infants could be held at night, supposedly a more discrete exit reflecting the lesser social disruption and significance of such deaths (Servius 11.143; Seneca *On the Shortness of Life* 20.5; Tacitus *Annals* 13.17). These funerals lacked pomp, but their torch-lit simplicity may have been striking and poignant nonetheless, and provided an evocative sensory experience.
6 This may have been particularly the case during seasons when mortality rates, and thus the number of funerals, increased (Shaw, 1996). Seasonal and climatic conditions would also have affected the sensory experience; for example, heightening certain odours, changing dress requirements, the distance sounds carried or the availability of certain products, such as flowers.
7 The exact nature of these rituals and where they occurred is unclear. The rite of *os resectum* may have meant that a bone from the deceased was also burned in these rituals, possibly at the house (see Graham, 2011b; Lennon, 2013, p. 145).
8 The formal ending of the mourning period for men did not mean that their grief ended, nor that all mourning (that is public expression of grief) was curtailed. Roman society promoted memories of the dead, and the living were supposed to be active in this memory promotion (such as through publishing eulogies, building monuments, erecting statues). Memory promotion may have merged with, and been the acceptable face of, mourning. Such memory preservation could also have a more subtle, domestic and semi-private side; for example, personal portraits, heirlooms and jewellery which may have acted as tokens of mourning (see Hope, 2011b).
9 Women were expected to mourn for fellow women (mothers, wives and daughters), but not for as long as they could mourn for a husband, and the latter could opt not to mourn for a deceased wife at all. The symbolic significance of female mourning as a reinforcement of male power is illustrated by public mourning, whereby women were obliged to

mourn leading politicians and emperors for a year (for example, Dio Cassius 56.43.1); presumably this entailed wearing dark clothing, thus primarily giving visual representation to the loss.

10 Lucian suggests that mourners might fast for three days (*On Funerals (On Mourning)* 24), although the exact nature and length of any dietary restrictions is unclear (could the fast last longer if the funeral happened more than three days after the death?). It may have been the case that a loss of appetite was an acknowledged (and expected) 'symptom' of grief (Livia was said to have refused food after the death of her son Drusus, Pseudo Ovid *Livia* 416–21) rather than all food being avoided. Fires may not have been lit in houses of mourning (Apuleius *Metamorphoses* 2.24), encouraging a basic diet. Mourners were therefore associated with the absence, or dulling, of the sense of taste.

11 The body may have been moved, at or just before the moment of death, and placed on the ground, perhaps to symbolise that at death man returned to the earth (Artemidorus 1.13). Moving the body in this way, and also positioning it in the atrium, would have required several people, and by necessity may have brought male members of the household into contact with the corpse.

7 Blood, fire and feasting

The role of touch and taste in Graeco-Roman animal sacrifice

Candace Weddle

Come to the chorus, Olympians, and send over it glorious grace, you gods who are coming to the city's crowded, incense-rich navel in holy Athens and to the glorious, richly adorned agora. Receive wreaths of plaited violets, and the songs plucked in springtime. . . . Like a seer, I do not fail to notice the clear signs, when, as the chamber of the purple-robed Horai is opened, the nectar-bearing flowers bring in the sweet-smelling spring. Then, then, upon the immortal earth are cast the lovely tresses of violets, and roses are fitted to hair and voices of songs echo to the accompaniment of pipes, and choruses come to Semele of the circling headband.

(Pindar *Fragment* 75)[1]

In this song fragment written to celebrate the altar of the Twelve Gods in Athens, the sensual elements of ritual are wonderfully muddled: songs are culled like blossoms, the very navel of the city is drenched in the scented smoke of offerings and the Olympians hurry to attend the festivities. The verses celebrate the purpose of Ancient Greek sacrifices: because the people of Athens offer their incense, their flowers and their songs, they will receive the favour of the gods, and communion with their deities is assured. The poet compares himself to a seer who perceives signs of the gods' favour in natural sensory wonders: the sweet scents of spring flowers and the vibrant hues of violets and roses. The passage is evocative of the rich sensual nature of ancient worship and how all the elements combined to create a sensory 'spectacle' appreciated by both people and gods. Although written with a specific Greek celebration in mind, Pindar's description evokes elements not only of other Greek religious events but also of later Roman ritual as well. Although there were differences in specific rites, Roman religious traditions drew heavily on Greek models and shared much in common with them.

Sacrificial rituals were a visceral, aggressively multisensory aspect of ancient life. Based in part on the influence of a Judaeo-Christian religious tradition, which privileges the dichotomy of seen versus unseen as the primary framework for interaction between humans and the divine, and in part on the fact that archaeological evidence is strongly visual in nature, researchers have often approached the sacrifices primarily as visual spectacles. This misrepresents the

Graeco-Roman concept of the rituals in which the smell of the sacrifices was the most ritually important sensory aspect because the smoke produced was considered the vehicle by which the devotion of the people was transported to the gods in the form of the scent of the immolated offerings.[2]

Sound played an important role in sacrifice as well, with music and prayers serving both utilitarian and ritual purposes. Both the olfactory and auditory aspects of the rituals are celebrated by Pindar, and both have recently received increased scholarly attention (On sound, see especially Bremer, 1981; Fless, 1995; Furley and Bremer, 2001; Fless and Moede, 2007. On scent, Harvey, 2006. On both, Weddle, 2011, 2013). The two remaining senses, touch and taste, are less in evidence in both ancient sources and modern scholarship, but allow me to suggest some haptic elements of the sacrificial experience: bodies press against each other in the crowd; a toga drawn over the head is stifling in the heat; the hide of an animal shudders under the touch of its handler. Each of these tactile elements was an aspect of the sensory experience of ancient Graeco-Roman sacrifice. Each is potentially evoked by artistic representations of sacrifice, and we can imagine their effects on the participants, but to what end? As rich as the touch elements of sacrifice were, what is the value of investigating them, beyond an opportunity to more richly – if hypothetically – imagine the experience of an ancient worshipper? The same questions may be asked concerning the sense of taste. In this chapter, I will discuss these two senses and demonstrate the important ritual role they played in the sacrificial process, one that is markedly different from that played by most of the other senses.[3] To state it simply, the sounds of prayers and music called the gods to attend rites where the scents of sacrifices were understood as the primary conduit for communication between gods and men. In contrast, touch and taste, rather than uniting humans with the gods, served as ritual separators between mortal and divine; they were the two senses that clearly set humans and gods apart.

Taste and touch are natural partners in a study of Graeco-Roman sacrifice not only because they served similar ritual purposes (as I will show), but also because these two senses were considered by Graeco-Roman philosophers to be strongly intertwined. For Greek philosophers, beginning with Aristotle, and later for Galen and other Roman thinkers, taste was understood to be a subset of touch and to function through similar physical processes (Siegel, 1970, p. 158). Aristotle pronounced this belief most clearly in *On the Soul* (434b.19): 'This is why taste is a kind of touch; for it relates to food, and food is a tangible body.'[4] Proposing this close sensory relationship was in part a way to address the fact that the five senses did not align in number with the four elements. As noted by Louise Vinge (1975, p. 17), tying touch and taste together allowed Aristotle to assign both to the corresponding element of earth (*On Sense and the Sensible* 439a). His explanation of their interconnectedness also has much to do with the physical properties of things that are tasted and felt, and Aristotle develops a sophisticated argument for their relationship in several passages in different works, notably *On the Soul* and *On Sense and the Sensible*. Later thinkers accepted his theories with some amendments. The ancient understanding of the close relationship between these two senses provides firm footing from which to consider the roles of touch and taste in the process of ancient sacrifice, based on analysis of visual and textual sources.

The role of touch

As with ephemeral scents and sounds, touch is difficult to recover in the literary and archaeological record. Nevertheless, the physicality of the rites ensures that moments of touch are everywhere represented in Graeco-Roman art showing sacrifice. The images provide much more than an index of tactile experience, and I shall not attempt here an exhaustive list of the types of touch represented in sacrificial art. A more fruitful approach is to identify images that portray specific moments of sacrifices proving that tactile elements of the experience of the worshippers and of the animals carried significant ritual import, and to analyse them in light of what we know about the rites and their meaning from literary descriptions. Given the topic of the present volume, I will focus from this point forward primarily on evidence from the Roman world.

A challenge that presents itself in the study of this topic is that touch is addressed in the literary sources for ancient sacrifice less often than sight, hearing and smell. Further, when the sense of touch *is* mentioned, it is rarely analysed in an explicit way, with reference made to the sense of touch itself. To put it another way, there are few moments in accounts of Roman sacrifice in which touch is clearly (or directly) discussed as playing an important role in addressing the gods. By contrast, when the sweet smell of incense or the savour of a sacrifice wafting heavenward are described, we understand that the gods will partake of the smell and be affected in some manner. Likewise, when a hymn is referred to as being sung *to* Apollo, the implication is that he will hear it and therefore that the sense of hearing is ritually important. The implications of moments of ritually important touch are rarely so apparent, but even when it is not specifically identified as such, touch may be the sensory vehicle for accomplishing certain ritual objectives.

The act of sacrifice

This investigation of the tactile elements of sacrifice begins by considering the importance of the physical presence of the victims. The physicality of sacrificial animals is stressed in Roman images of sacrifice. One of the most common means of visually indicating sacrifice in the Roman tradition is to depict the progress of animals to the altar. Indeed, it is enough to depict a procession of animals with human participants conspicuously absent, as in the *suovetaurilia* (sacrificial offering made up of a pig, a sheep and a bull) forming part of the reliefs of the so-called 'Anaglypha Traiani/Hadriani' in the Forum Romanum (Figure 7.1) (Kleiner, 1992, pp. 248–50). This underscores the importance of the animals' bodily presence; they are not included in sacrificial imagery merely as a record of their role, but rather serve as emblems of the act of sacrifice.

Figure 7.1 Suovetaurilia from the so-called 'Anaglypha Traiani/Hadriani' in the Curia Iulia,
    Forum Romanum, Rome. Probably Hadrianic
Source: Photo: Candace Weddle

An emphasis on the physicality of the animals is also evident in written
descriptions of interactions with the victims during the sacrificial process, in
which the most important moments of contact between animal and sacrificant
are those of ritual touching. In both Greek and Roman rites, the animal was
touched in specific ways, using specific instruments. Dionysius of Halicarnassus
outlined the steps of a Roman animal sacrifice he observed in the first century BCE. His description is full of references to actions involving touch:

> After the procession was ended the consuls and the priests whose function
> it was presently sacrificed oxen; and the manner of performing the sacri-
> fices was the same as with us. For after washing their hands they purified
> the victims with clear water and sprinkled corn (Δημητρίους καρποὺς) on
> their heads, after which they prayed and then gave orders to their assistants
> to sacrifice them. Some of these assistants, while the victim was still stand-
> ing, struck it on the temple with a club, and others received it upon the
> sacrificial knives as it fell. After this they flayed it and cut it up, taking off
> a piece from each of the inwards [*sic*] and also from every limb as a first-
> offering, which they sprinkled with grits of spelt and carried in baskets to
> the officiating priests. These placed them on the altars, and making a fire
> under them, poured wine over them while they were burning.
>
> (*Roman Antiquities* 7.72.15)[5]

The elements of Roman sacrificial ritual Dionysius describes were drawn in part from earlier Greek rites, as is clear from the writer's description of the processes as 'the same as with us'. Ritual similarities between the two cultures were intentionally stressed in a specific mode of sacrifice practised by the Romans, known as the *Graecus ritus*.[6] The most distinctive elements of rites carried out in the Greek manner were that they were celebrated *capite aperto* (that is, with uncovered head and sometimes wearing laurel wreaths, in contrast to other Roman rites carried out *capite velato*) and at times involved the substitution of Greek words for certain key terms. Thus, Septimius Severus speaks in a prayer of offering *splanchna* to Jupiter, using the Greek ritual terminology for the animal's internal organs rather than the Latin *exta* (both words meaning 'entrails') (Pighi, 1967, pp. 154–5). In certain cases, the division of the sacrificial animal after slaughter was also carried out according to Greek models (Scheid, 1995, p. 28). In terms of haptic elements present in the *Graecus ritus*, in addition to sprinkling the animal with water and cereal grains, a lock of hair was cut from its forehead and burned, an action described in Homer and therefore a very ancient element of Greek sacrifices (Homer *Iliad* 3.273, *Odyssey* 3.446).

Importantly, in both the Greek and the later Roman form of sacrificial rites, the animal was touched in specific ways in order to signal its designation as an object of sacrifice. Touch, as I have already stated, was a ritual separator of human from god. The division between mortal and divine was manifested both in rituals involving the living animal prior to sacrifice and in the handling of the carcass and meat after its conclusion. Tactile gestures marked important moments at which ancient worshippers defined what was owed to the gods and what fell within the purview of man. As gestures of touch were performed, the animal became sacred and the property of the god.

One of the most important tactile gestures in Roman sacrifices was the application of *mola salsa*. Though the English word 'immolate' has come to mean literal or figurative sacrificial destruction of an object (especially by fire), its linguistic root lies in the Roman tradition of sprinkling a proffered sacrificial animal with *mola salsa*, salted flour (Scheid, 2007, p. 265). It is significant that *mola salsa* was composed of organic and mineral substances taken from the earth, a reference to the fecundity of nature. This symbolism is recorded for us literally in Dionysius who, either unfamiliar with the Roman term *mola salsa* or perhaps choosing to employ a comparable Greek term that would have been meaningful to his readers, calls the mixture Δημητρίος καρποὺς, 'the fruits of Demeter' (7.72.15).

A next tactile step included in many Roman rites was wetting the animal's forehead with wine, an act that further emphasised an appreciation for the plenitude of nature and probably served as a ritual gesture of cleansing as well. The altar shown in Figure 7.2 is almost unique in the body of surviving Roman sacrificial imagery in showing this moment, despite the fact that it was an important part of the sacrificial process (Beard, North and Price, 1998b, p. 149). Were it not for the chance survival of this altar, we would have little evidence in the archaeological record for this moment in which the physical act of touching the animal with a sacred liquid took place. Following the application of wine,

Figure 7.2 Pouring wine on the head of the sacrificial victim. Panel from the 'Altar of Scipio
        Orfitus', Rome, 295 CE. Musei Capitolini, Rome

Source: Photo: John Pollini

the animal was also touched with the sacrificial knife, which was run lightly
down its back (Scheid, 2007, p. 265).

The gestures of touch described here were indispensable aspects of the con-
secration process and preparation for slaughter. With the physical application of
the *mola salsa* and wine, the victim was handed over from human to divine use.
Once the animal was thus sanctified it was time for the slaughter, one of the
most overtly physical aspects of the rites. Ritual actors responsible for handling
the animals (*victimarii*) led them into position, and the *popa* struck large victims
on the head or neck in order to stun them and drop them to their knees before
their throats were slit. Following the killing, the animal was butchered and
divided (more on that division below) and certain entrails (*exta*) were transferred
to the altar for immolation (see Scheid, 2003, pp. 79–110).

During slaughter and butchering, proper tactile interaction between the victim and the ritual actors was vital to successful completion of the rites. I have discussed in detail elsewhere the slaughtering process, as well as the handling of the animals by the *victimarii* both prior to and during sacrifices, with particular attention to the reaction of animals to sensory stimuli (Weddle, 2013). Though not every interaction between the handlers and the animals was ritually significant, they all had important implications because they impacted upon the responses of the animals. The behaviour of animals in the moments leading up to sacrifice was extremely important as any mistake, mishap or unusual event that occurred during sacrifices could result in negative ritual consequences and was understood as an inauspicious portent (Beard, North and Price, 1998a, p. 36; Scheid, 2003, p. 83). The impact of the handling of the victims continued beyond the moment of death. For instance, on several occasions Roman writers note that a victim was seen to move after it had been killed.[7] If we take the reports of these portents at face value and assume that the animals in question did in fact move post-mortem, it could be that this negative outcome was the result of sloppy handling of the animal by the *victimarii*. A mistake in the process of slitting an animal's throat can result in a vigorous reaction of the body that can continue for quite some time. The expertise of the *victimarii* in the tactual skill of cutting the animal was of paramount importance.

Feeling the signs

Even after successful accomplishment of the slaughter, any unusual events that occurred between the death of the animal and the delivery of the god's portion to the altar were also viewed as significant. In some cases, portents noted in Roman records as occurring during this important section of the process bear on the haptic realm. The ritual actors and others present at the rites had to take great care in how they touched the by-products of sacrifice, as inattentiveness in this regard could result in an inauspicious outcome. For example, we read in several sources of the unfortunate incident of an individual slipping in sacrificial blood. Dio Cassius (*Roman History* 46.33) describes how, following a pre-war sacrifice (*profectio*) being performed by the consul C. Vibius Pansa in 43 BCE, a man slipped in the blood of the victim and fell, an ill omen that was compounded when the palm frond he was carrying to Pansa touched the blood of the victim and was defiled.[8] Though sacrificial blood being in contact with the altar, the sanctuary and the sacrificial participants does not seem to have been considered tainting, *improper* physical contact with that blood had negative ritual consequences.

The importance of tactile engagement with the animal did not end after the slaughter. The success of a ritual could not be determined until an inspection of the entrails of the animal(s) had been completed and all were found to be flawless, a process that involved very sustained and invasive physical contact with the victim. In every case, once the animal was opened up, a *haruspex* (diviner) inspected the *exta* closely for any sign of abnormalities, a process now referred to as extispicy (Scheid, 2003, pp. 123–4). If everything was in order, it was assumed that the god accepted the sacrifice and his or her approval (*litatio*) was noted. That approval was not always granted, and the god's displeasure manifested in physical abnormalities in the animal, which in some cases were interpreted as omens. More extensive signs pertaining to the future were sometimes sought in further inspection of the *exta* through the process of haruspicy, but care should be taken to distinguish between haruspicy and the confirmation of *litatio*, which was a required step in every sacrificial rite; examining the entrails to ensure that signs are auspicious is not the same thing as fortune telling.

There were multiple ritual possibilities why abnormalities might be discovered in the organs, and in some cases they were the direct result of mishandling some sensory element of the sacrificial process. For example, Pliny (*Natural History* 28.3.11) notes that the sound of an improperly worded prayer during sacrifice could affect the animal's internal organs, causing them to transform or even disappear. Interestingly, in further confirmation of the importance of the application of *mola salsa* to the victim prior to slaughter, Cicero (*On Divination* 2.16.36) notes (with some scepticism) the apparently common belief that the abnormalities in the *exta* that signalled divine rejection appeared *cum immolare* – that is, at the moment the salted flour was sprinkled on the victim – though the effects could obviously only be detected after the animal had been killed and gutted. That moment of ritual touch somehow activated the appearance of omens in the entrails. This explained why it was possible, for example, for an animal to be alive without a heart (*On Divination* 1.52.118; *Julius Obsequens* 67).[9] A sacrificial victim whose abnormal organs delivered a divine message need only survive for a few moments at the altar afflicted with whatever physical defect later inspection would bring to light.

Despite the ritual importance of confirming *litatio*, our knowledge of the process is limited primarily to written sources. Few representations showing either *litatio* or haruspicy have survived in Roman art. In one of those images (Figure 7.3), we see a *victimarius* bending over the open belly of an ox and pulling its entrails out so that they may be examined by the *haruspex* who stands to the far left of the image and gestures toward the prostrate animal. The *popa* stands behind with his axe thrown over his shoulder. In his left hand, he holds a bucket in which to carry the *exta* to the altar, where they will be converted by fire into a divinely-appreciated savour. A third *victimarius* in the background completes the group. In this case, the specific action being performed is *haustia consultatoria*, the examination of auspices prior to a military undertaking (Giroire and Roger, 2007, p. 232).

Notably absent from the scene is a certain type of touch. If the artist were to represent the event as it truly took place, it would be necessary to indicate one or more of the *victimarii* manhandling the carcass, taking hold of the legs of the creature and stabilising it while the gut is opened. There are several possible reasons for the exclusion of this detail. From an aesthetic standpoint, the composition is more comprehensible to a viewer as is than if a greater number of figures were engaged in more actions in the foreground around the body of

Figure 7.3 A scene of extispicy. Part of a marble relief from Trajan's Forum. Rome, early
second century CE, Louvre, Paris

Source: Illustration by Jasmine Parker

the animal, the focus of the scene. Symbolically speaking, I would also argue
that the absence of men handling the body allows the viewer to appreciate the
physical perfection of the beast, a perfection that was of the utmost importance
in the selection of the sacrificial animal and a prerequisite for its acceptance
by the deity. Depicting the physicality of the animal, and its perfect form even
when dead, was more important than a true representation of the tactile actions
involved in the moment in which the entrails are examined.

As hands-on as the process of investigating the entrails of the animal was,
extispicy and haruspicy were first and foremost rituals of looking. Were the
correct organs present and were they within the range of normality for the type
of animal offered? Were there anomalies that indicated something about the
future? In the next stages of the process, however, the organs moved from being
the focus of visual inspection to being components whose status and suitability
were specifically dependent on how they were touched.

Dividing the body

Perhaps the most important tactile moment in sacrifice was the division of the
body post-slaughter (Beard et al., 1998a, pp. 36–7). The physical perfection
of the parts designated for the gods had to be joined with proper handling as

they were removed from the animal and offered to the god. The *exta* were first prepared as if for eating, being either boiled or roasted on spits. Now called *prosecta*, they were placed on a dish and once again touched in specific, meaningful ways – they were sprinkled with *mola salsa* and wine before being placed on the altar, where they were burned (Rüpke, 2007, p. 88).[10]

The *prosecta* (as well as any other parts reserved for divine use, which varied depending on the specific ritual) represented only a small portion of the body of the victim. The rest was utilised in other ways, but here I am concerned only with the edible portions. Certain parts were, of course, consumed by the attendees, and sometimes the general public, at post-sacrificial banquets. Again, touch played a key role at this stage, because the sacrificant had to once again touch the portions intended for human consumption before they could be prepared and served. This touch cancelled out the prior ritual dedication of the animal and moved the meat from being *sacra* to being *profana* (Rüpke, 2007, p. 144). In a reversal of earlier steps, a haptic gesture indicated that the offering no longer belonged to the god and could now be consumed by humans.

Touch and taste at the sacrificial banquet

A sacrificial banquet followed the dispersal of the body, though often removed by a significant amount of time to allow for the immolation of the god's portions to be completed. Tactility was as important in the consumption of sacrificial products as it was in their preparation. The topic of post-sacrificial feasting in the ancient world is a rich one. Even if I were to confine my consideration solely to Roman evidence, as John Scheid writes, the topic 'presents a complex problem, since there was a vast array of different procedures' (2007, p. 267).[11] For this reason, I shall be concerned here with a few very specific aspects of the sacrificial banquet that have particular bearing on my analysis of the roles of touch and taste in sacrifice.

I have focused so far on the tactility of sacrifice, especially of ritual touching involving the animal and its organs. It was during the feasts that followed that the sense of taste came to play an important ritual role. Like touch, the sense of taste is ephemeral. It is also highly subjective and, as with touch, is rarely explicitly addressed in ancient literature dealing with sacrificial practice. Bearing in mind the ancient understanding (discussed above) of the interplay between the two senses, in which philosophers held taste to be a form of touch, it is nevertheless possible to discuss some important roles the sense of taste played in sacrificial ritual.

Let us begin with an image, the sole surviving representation of a Roman post-sacrificial banquet that can be confidently identified as such (Figure 7.4). This fragmentary relief of the first century CE depicts six women with covered heads, likely Vestal Virgins, reclining around a table.[12]

The head of the woman seated at the right end of the table, whose legs are shown in profile, is broken completely off the relief, leaving only the bottom portion of her veil intact. Two figures stand behind her. One of them, the drape

Figure 7.4 Fragment of a relief showing a post-sacrificial banquet, probably of the Vestal
Virgins. Rome, first century CE, Museo dell'Ara Pacis, Rome

Source: Photo: John Pollini

of whose clothing can be seen to the far right, is represented by the barest trace
of a surviving facial profile and a hand raised toward her chin. Another, whose
head can be seen directly behind the neck of the damaged Vestal, wears her hair
parted down the middle. In addition, three heads in profile are visible behind
the five central figures, their low relief indicating that they occupy a spatial plane
further away than the viewer. Beyond this singular relief, we have no evidence
in Roman art for sacrificial banqueting practice; even if we did, it could not
convey anything about the sense of taste. Nevertheless, when combined with
written and archaeological evidence, it does help set the stage for enquiry into
the details of sacrificial banquets.

In the Roman tradition of post-sacrificial banqueting, there were three standard uses for the flesh of the victims: it could be served at a ritual meal following
the sacrifices, such as that depicted in the relief; it could be passed out to designated recipients for later consumption; or it could be purchased by members
of the public, either at the time of the rites or later in the marketplace (Scheid,
2007, pp. 267–8). In the case of large sacrifices, any or all of these outcomes were

possible. For the purposes of this chapter, I will focus on the sensory experience of a participant in a ritual meal such as took place on temple grounds in a specially constructed dining hall (Rüpke, 2007, p. 142).

Sacrificial banquets were an important moment in which ancient worshippers came together to form and renew contacts. As Figure 7.4 shows, the diners literally and figuratively rubbed shoulders with one another as they shared a space and a table. Communing to share a meal following large public sacrifices symbolised not only mutual devotion to a deity but also the need to honour that deity in appropriate ways on behalf of the community in order to procure blessings for the entire population.

In addition to providing a place for social communion, the banquets also served as symbolic moments of communion with the gods. Analysis of communal feasting and of consumption more broadly considered has played an important role in anthropological studies of sacrifice in most world cultures. The anthropology of eating and its ritual implications is an enormous topic.[13] It will have to suffice to address here only a few seminal theories and to suggest how a more sophisticated analysis of the ritual role of touch and taste in Graeco-Roman practice may suggest new nuances in their application.

For both the Greeks and the Romans, a sacrifice and ensuing banquet were representative of the system of 'reciprocal gift-giving' upon which their relationship with the gods was based (Scheid, 2007, p. 267). When those partaking in a ritual feast made their way into the dining area, they were served at the 'table of the god' (Dittenberger, 1915–24; Yerkes, 1952, p. 108). There is some scholarly disagreement as to whether eating at the 'table of the god' indicated that the feasters had been invited into the presence of the god to partake of the bounty of his or her table or whether, conversely, by providing and preparing a sacrifice and laying it on 'the table of the god' the worshippers had invited the deity to dine with them.[14] In either case, given the societal and ritual importance of group dining in Greek and Roman antiquity, the post-sacrificial banquet shared between gods and men was an important moment of interaction. This commensalism was acknowledged even in the case of non-sacrificial Roman meals: it was common practice during both public and private meals to offer wine, incense and a portion of the food to the domestic gods between the first and second course (Scheid, 2007, p. 268).

Case study: The grove of the Arval brethren

Despite the symbolic importance of sacrificial banquets in acting out the close relationship between the gods and their devotees, the details of the banquets implied not only communion but also division. In its most concrete form, this division was expressed spatially. Archaeologically attested examples are rare, but the sanctuary of the Arval brethen in their sacred grove outside Rome is well recorded, and Scheid has recently discussed it in just these terms (2012, pp. 89–90). The case of the Arval grove is particularly instructive for a consideration of the sensory experience of sacrifice and the accompanying banquets, as associated inscriptions provide confirmation of the layout of the sanctuary as well as details on the use of its various structures and the activities of the ritual participants.

The layout of the Arval grove reflected multiple levels of hierarchy, culminating with the permanent temple and altar of Dea Dia at the highest point. Below were ranged the wooden altars of other gods, who were considered invited guests, a Caesareum (a chapel to the deified emperors), a circus for chariot races, and the mortal area of the Arvals. It was in the Caesareum, in the company of the divine rulers rather than their primary goddess, that the Arval brethen celebrated their banquets following sacrifices to Dea Dia.[15]

The Arval sanctuary is in many ways comparable to an exemplary Greek case study, the sanctuary of Demeter and Kore at Corinth. There the sanctuary was divided into multiple terraces, and the act of sacrificing and offering choice portions to the goddesses was performed on one terrace, following which the sacrificial feast celebrated by attendees took place on a lower terrace (Bookidis, 1997). Thus, in both the Greek and Roman traditions, the topography of ritual served to bring mortals and deities together at a sacrifice and ensuing banquet but, at the same time, to keep them separated. If we understand the process of sacrifice and feasting as a literal (rather than, or in addition to, a symbolic) 'communal banquet' with the deities, we must conclude that the Roman and Corinthian worshippers never actually ate in the same place, nor at the same time, as their gods. The fact that the spatial division of the worshippers from the object of their devotion was in such cases intentional and meaningful is reinforced by the existence, in both the Greek and Roman tradition, of a special, distinct type of cult meal, in which one table was shared by gods and mortals. In the Roman *lectisternium,* which drew on the Greek tradition of the *theoxenia,* the gods were represented either by images or simply by the presence of empty dining couches (in the *sellisternium* for female deities, empty chairs were used).

Although in sensory terms the arrangement of sacred precincts and the constructed environment of the banqueting spaces can be considered to bear on the physical experience of the rites, it is in the moments of consumption that the roles of touch and taste become most key. The divisions inherent in the layout of cult spaces did not end with the seating arrangements but extended to the menu as well. With the human banquet removed both spatially and temporally from the god's meal, the idea of communion, though clearly one of the foundational concepts of Greek and Roman sacrificial practice, is further weakened by the stark differentiation between *what* is to be consumed by humans as opposed to deities, in addition to where and when. In other words, 'Mortals and immortals do not eat the same food at the same table' (Veyne, 2000, p. 6).

Conclusion: The significance of touch and taste in Graeco-Roman sacrifice

The use of ritual touch in designating the god's and mortals' portions is a division that has long been recognised by scholars as key to the hierarchical separation between deities and humans in the Graeco-Roman worldview:

The clear separation of the meat between those parts of the animal offered to the worshippers on the one hand and those offered to the gods on the other . . . [implies] that one of the functions of the ritual was to represent the division between gods and men by means of the rules and codes of eating and consumption – men being prohibited from consuming the parts designated for the gods.

(Beard et al., 1998a, pp. 36–7)

Scheid has also pointed to this meaning of the division of the animal, stressing that the evidence of ancient sources indicates that a sacrifice 'established and represented, through the sharing of food between gods and men, the superiority and immortality of the former and the mortality and pious submission of the latter' (2007, p. 270). These scholars understand the sacrifice and sacrificial banquet as illustrative both of the communion of humans with the gods and of the insurmountable division between mortal and immortal, a chasm they see as symbolised most strongly in the physical division of the *exta* and other pieces reserved for the gods from the other portions of meat. This much has been discussed at length in the scholarship on Graeco-Roman ritual. What has not been considered is the important sensory division acted out during the sacrificial banquets, a division dependent not only on the allocation of the portions but also on the physical relationship *to* those portions. It mattered ritually not just *what* was to be consumed but *how.*

Though sharing a table or an animal created a conceptual link between the worshippers and the object of worship, in that both gods and men were ritually consuming, the gods were consuming a substance more sublime than the meat set aside for the human ritual participants. The Greek and Roman gods were thought of as partaking of the epitome of the sacrifices, an ephemeral sensory representation, the 'savour' of the portions burned in their honour. In contrast, humans had a very physical need for food, a need clearly articulated in certain philosophical schools as a barrier between mortals and their gods. Though it was impossible to overcome altogether the biological need for food, certain ascetics such as (the legendary) Abaris, Epimenides and Pythagoras were said to have developed 'superfoods' (*álima* and *ádipsa* [*sic*]), which probably contained mallow and asphodel (Detienne, 1977, p. 47). These 'superfoods' allowed them to consume very small amounts of wild vegetable matter that required neither cooking nor the use of animal labour for ploughing and cultivation, thus freeing them from exploiting animals while bringing them as close as possible to the sublime form of consumption undertaken by the gods. Epitome of the ascetic ideal, Epimenides was said to take his nourishment in the form of a single daily pill that prevented both hunger and thirst, and consequently the necessity to confirm the distance between himself and the gods through consumption of food (Plutarch *Fragments* 26).

The fundamental difference between mortals and immortals in terms of how nourishment was taken, which Pythagoreans and others struggled to mitigate as far as possible, was exposed at the sacrificial feast. While the gods employed the sense of smell (or a divine form of it) to enjoy their sacrificial offerings, the humans' consumption of the meat of the animals was entirely corporeal. The division between humans and gods that was physically illustrated by the apportioning of the body of the sacrificial animal was further emphasised by the senses used to consume the assigned portions. Though the Greeks and Romans may have been 'dining with the gods' when they enjoyed the commensality of the post-sacrificial banquet, at the same time they were also separate from them and were experiencing a different form of consumption. Even at the shared banqueting table, human and god were confronted with an insurmountable sensory divide, a contrast between divinely ephemeral savour wafting to the heavens and grossly physical meat that had to be touched and tasted. Diners were forced to reach a fundamental ritual conclusion: I touch and I taste, therefore I am not a god.

Vernant (1989) touches on this in his analysis of Greek sacrifice by suggesting that the physical need of man to consume the meat of animals rather than the smoke of sacrifices is symbolically referenced in the myth of Prometheus' trickery in Hesiod's *Theogony* (507–616). I would take his analysis a step further – or, rather, a step back – and note that it is only when we consider the role of the dual (in Graeco-Roman thought) sense touch/taste at the sacrificial feast as an *extension* of the roles of touch in the sacrificial ritual itself that the importance of those two senses as ritual dividers becomes clear. It was about more than the physical need for food consumption. Whilst sounds and smells offered the possibility of communication with the gods, touch and taste guaranteed a certain separation. The primary ritual functions of touch and taste were to divide men from gods, first by designating what was *sacra* and what was *profana* and, ultimately, by determining how those portions were consumed. Therefore, although we often consider ancient sacrifice in terms of spectacle, and the Greeks and Romans themselves probably classified it primarily as an olfactory offering, the senses of touch and taste also served vital functions in the correct accomplishment of ritual and, crucially, in defining the boundaries between humans and gods.

Notes

1   Δεῦτ' ἐν χορόν, Ὀλύμπιοι, ἐπί τε κλυτὰν πέμπετε χάριν, θεοί, πολύβατον οἵ τ' ἄστεος ὀμφαλὸν θυόεντ' ἐν ταῖς ἱεραῖς Ἀθάναις οἰχνεῖτε πανδαίδαλόν τ' εὐκλέ' ἀγοράν. ἰοδέτων λάχετε στεφάνων τᾶν τ' ἐαριδρόπων ἀοιδᾶν. . . . ἐναργέα τ' ἔμ' ὧτε μάντιν οὐ λανθάνει, φοινικοεάνων ὁπότ' οἰχθέντος Ὡρᾶν θαλάμου εὔοδμον ἐπάγοισιν ἔαρ φυτὰ νεκτάρεα. τότε βάλλεται, τότ' ἐπ' ἀμβρόταν χθόν' ἐραταί ἴων φόβαι, ῥόδα τε κόμαισι μείγνυται, ἀχεῖ τ' ὀμφαὶ μελέων σὺν αὐλοῖς, οἰχνεῖ τε Σεμέλαν ἑλικάμπυκα χοροί.
2   See especially Homer *Iliad* 1.317. Some later writers (for example Aelian *Various History* 12.51) considered the savoury smoke to actually feed the gods, but others (for example, Arnobius of Sicca *Against the Pagans* 3) were sceptical of such a simplistic explanation.
3   For the purposes of this chapter I will discuss animal sacrifice, although it was neither the only nor necessarily the most ritually significant type of sacrifice practised by the Greeks and Romans. This choice reflects my interest in the treatment of animals in antiquity and is not meant to suggest the primacy of live victims over, for example, offerings of wine

and incense, which in addition to standing alone as important rituals were also included in most animal sacrifices. For a discussion of the tendency in the last century of scholarship to privilege animal sacrifice over other types, see Faraone and Naiden, 2012.

4 διὸ καὶ ἡ γεῦσίς ἐστιν ὥσπερ ἀφή τις. τροφῆς γάρ ἐστιν, ἡ δὲ τροφὴ τὸ σῶμα τὸ ἁπτόν.

5 Συντελεσθείσης δὲ τῆς πομπῆς ἐβουθύτουν εὐθὺς οἵ τε ὕπατοι καὶ τῶν ἱερέων οἷς ὅσιον, καὶ ὁ τῶν θυηπολιῶν τρόπος ὁ αὐτὸς ἦν τῷ παρ᾽ ἡμῖν. χερνιψάμενοί τε γὰρ αὐτοὶ καὶ τὰ ἱερὰ καθαρῷ περιαγνίσαντες ὕδατι καὶ Δημητρίους καρποὺς ἐπιρράναντες αὐτῶν ταῖς κεφαλαῖς, ἔπειτα κατευξάμενοι, θύειν τότε τοῖς ὑπηρέταις αὐτὰ ἐκέλευον. τῶν δ᾽οἱ μὲν ἑστῶτος ἔτι τοῦ θύματος σκυτάλῃ τοὺς κροτάφους ἔπαιον, οἱ δὲ πίπτοντος ὑπετίθεσαν τὰς σφαγίδας, καὶ μετὰ τοῦτο δείραντές τε καὶ μελίσαντες ἀπαρχὰς ἐλάμβανον ἐξ ἑκάστου σπλάγχου καὶ παντὸς ἄλλου μέλους, ἃς ἀλφίτοις ζέας ἀναδεύσαντες προσέφερον τοῖς θύουσιν ἐπὶ κανῶν. οἱ δ᾽ ἐπὶ τοὺς βωμοὺς ἐπιθέντες ὑφῆπτον καὶ προσέσπενδον οἶνον κατὰ τῶν ἁγνιζομένων.

6 Scheid (1995) has convincingly argued that despite its name, the *Graecus ritus* should be considered a thoroughly Roman ritual.

7 See, for example, Livy 21.62. For a discussion of portents in Republican Rome and the relevant ancient sources, see Rasmussen, 2003.

8 In an interpretation that highlights the civic implications of public ritual, Dio understands the evil omen as applying not to Pansa alone (presaging the fatal wound he would receive in his battle against Antony) but to all Romans, since it occurred during a sacrifice performed in the course of consular duties. The same inauspicious prodigy is reported by *Julius Obsequens* (69), who takes the evil omen as applying specifically to Pansa.

9 This particular defect was discovered and ignored by Julius Caesar while sacrificing an ox the day he first appeared in public in a purple robe seated on a throne. Had he heeded that warning sent by the gods, Cicero says, his impending assassination might have been foreseen, though not averted (*On Divination* 1.52.118).

10 Jörg Rüpke (2007, p. 88) uses the practice of sprinkling *mola salsa* on the animal in preparation for sacrifice as an example of a ritual element that originally served a pragmatic purpose. He understands it as a relic of the culinary preparation of meat and argues that once the application of the salted flour moved from its supposed original place in the sacrificial process (in which it was presumably sprinkled on the butchered meat) to the moment in which it was instead applied to the live animal, it ceased to be pragmatic and became, instead, communicative.

11 See J. Paul Getty Museum, 2004–06, volume 2 and Scheid, 2007 for bibliography on the topic.

12 On which see especially Fless, 1995, p. 107 and plates 19–21, with bibliography.

13 A recent overview of the major voices in this debate and some applications in the field of classical studies and archaeology may be found in Stocking, 2009, pp. 8–66.

14 Rüpke (2007, pp. 143–5) problematises the question within the Roman tradition by considering two types of evidence: examples from ancient literature of instances of divine invitations extended to men, and details of the social mores of the Romans, which stipulated that Romans dined only with social equals. Ultimately, he is unable to answer the question of 'who invites whom', but able only to point out inconsistencies in the sacrificial system that prevent us from formulating a satisfactory answer.

15 Scheid (2007) expands on the implications of this topography for our understanding of the middle ground occupied by the deified emperors (*divi*) as somewhere between mere mortals and actual *dei*; in the same study, he takes up the topic of symbolic hierarchy in ritual in general. See also Iara, 2015, pp. 128–32.

8 Babes in arms?

Sensory dissonance and the ambiguities of votive objects

Emma-Jayne Graham

Visitors to one of the many shrines or sanctuaries of Republican central Italy would have found its sacred spaces littered with objects dedicated to the divine. Amongst them might be seen bronze statuettes of deities and terracotta models of human figures, heads, animals and a host of internal and external body parts – so-called 'anatomical' votives. Within this multitude of offerings the visitor might also recognise a number of representations of swaddled babies (Figure 8.1). Several recent studies have focused on this distinctive type of votive dedication and its conspicuous iconography, offering reevaluations of its role within ancient cult, particularly with regards to ancient ideas concerning fertility, birth and infant health, as well as concepts of the beginnings of life and socio-religious identity (Graham, 2013, 2014; Derks, 2014; also Glinister, 2017). These studies have enriched understandings of infant *ex-votos* whilst simultaneously promoting an interpretation of their significance which is visually oriented. This chapter will investigate for the first time the relationship between votive models of babies and other aspects of the human sensorium.

An enquiry such as this involves a more critical appraisal of the materiality of these objects than has been achieved to date. This is presented here with reference to David Morgan's (2010, p. 12) statement that objects engage people in 'forms of sacred imagination that structure their relations to the divine', as well as David Chidester's (2005, pp. 56–7) view that the kinaesthetic movements of the body should be understood 'not only as types of ritual performance but also as *instruments of knowledge*' (emphasis added). The approach adopted in this chapter therefore emerges from an appreciation of the agency of objects within religious performance, particularly the extent to which religious ideas (and indeed religion itself) are brought into being through interaction with the material world, rather than existing as pre-formed abstract concepts awaiting material expression (Boivin, 2009, p. 274). From this standpoint, objects dedicated to the divine can be understood as active material agents in the complex negotiation of the meanings and knowledge associated with religious practices, making it possible to comprehend how ancient votive ritual could be a profoundly creative process. Consequently, this chapter argues that infant *ex-votos* were objects not only to be observed but through which ancient participants in religious ritual could think, feel and, most importantly, *know*. To reach this conclusion

Figure 8.1 Terracotta votive figurines depicting infants in swaddling bands from Vulci, Porta
　　　　Nord, probably second century BCE. Left: inv. 59759, h. 47.5 cm; right: inv. 59760,
　　　　h. 54 cm

Source: Bridgeman Images

it is necessary to acknowledge, firstly, that the consequences of the full sensory
agency of votive offerings have too frequently been sidelined in favour of their
representational (in other words, visual) characteristics. Secondly, that a range
of sometimes conflicting sensory affordances and embodied memories can be

associated with any artefact. It is undoubtedly valuable to record instances in which the senses work together to perceive objects and engage with the wider world, as recent work on synaesthesia has stressed (Butler and Purves, 2013; Toner, 2014b, pp. 2–4). In contrast, this study of the significance of encounters with infant votives as objects which prompt conflicting sensory experiences emphasises the extent to which occasions on which the senses disagree or offer internally conflicting information might be equally as meaningful. Indeed, as this chapter demonstrates, an appreciation of sensory dissonance can be crucial for understanding the attribution of mutable or multiple possible meanings to an object, with significant consequences for the ritual activities and religious ideas produced by sensorially ambiguous materialities.

Holding the baby?

In autumn 2011 I made the first of several archival visits to study infant *ex-votos*. At the time I was struck by their weight: many are made from thick, unrefined fired clay. I also took note of their life-size dimensions and how impossible it was to hold or manipulate many undamaged examples with one hand. The typical length of a modern newborn baby is 46–56 cm (top-to-toe) (Pillitteri, 2010, p. 450), and the average length of the known (complete) infant votives in this study can be calculated at approximately 48 cm. Many of the best preserved examples are larger than this and fragments which lack heads or lower limbs can also sometimes measure up to 50 cm. Complete examples from the Porta Nord sanctuary of Vulci and the Belvedere sanctuary at Lucera measure 84.5 cm and 85 cm respectively (D'Ercole, 1990, inventory number 295; Pautasso, 1994, p. 36). Indeed, the ten complete (and reconstructed) examples from Vulci range between 47.5 and 84.5 cm (average: 59 cm), suggesting that at some sites the dimensions of these votive models correspond more closely to those of an infant a couple of months old: the age at which swaddling probably ended (see below). Turning one of these relatively heavy, life-sized artefacts over to examine the reverse, or lifting it from, or replacing it on, the surface of a table or into a storage crate, is by necessity a two-handed process.

I interacted with these artefacts with deliberate care, but on reflection began to wonder if there was more to my behaviour than professional concern not to inflict unnecessary damage. Aside from taking measurements, scrutinising their form and examining evidence for their manufacture, I engaged with the models in a manner not completely dissimilar from handling a living baby. This was not only a result of anxieties about their potential fragility, it was also related closely to their materiality. In order to lift a life-sized model and carry it from crate to table, or vice versa, it was necessary to do so in a manner which meant that the object lay across both of my slightly flexed hands. In this way it came to be held across my body: my arms were extended in front of me, bent slightly with the weight, the head of the model in one hand, the lower limbs in the other. It was, in some respects, as if I were holding an infant, supporting its head and about to pass it to someone or place it down safely (compare Figure 8.2).

Figure 8.2 Tufa statue of a woman (possibly the goddess Mater Matuta) holding a baby wrapped in swaddling clothes. Note how the infant extends across her entire lap, its head cradled by her flexed left hand. 2nd–1st century BCE. Museo Provinciale Campano, Capua, Inv. no. 425, h. 1.07 m

Source: German Archaeological Institute (photograph by Hutzel)

This raises a number of questions: to what extent do my experiences parallel those of the ancient parents or cult officials who interacted with these same artefacts? Did making an offering at a sanctuary or shrine feel similar to passing over, or putting down (and leaving behind), a living baby? Was this significant for determining how votive ritual was experienced and understood?

Despite such questions the results of my subsequent research project focused almost exclusively on an account of visual characteristics, emphasising the extent to which the dimensions and bodily features of these votives resemble babies of a certain age, and stressing the importance of swaddling clothes as a visual reference for the successful negotiation of a particular passage of life and the moulding of the infant into a social being (Graham, 2013, 2014). On reflection, this paralleled precisely Constance Classen's observation that scholars all too often focus their attention on what objects look like and 'remain ignorant of the symbolic functions of the other senses' (1993, p. 7). The other 'sensory affordances' (Knappett, 2004; Hunter-Crawley, 2013a, p. 162) of these objects, despite being detected in the course of their study, were disregarded, exemplifying Jo Day's recent comment that although we might 'form emotional connections with "our" material, we tend to dismiss these reactions as unworthy of scholarly mention' (2013c, p. 286).

Iconographic interpretations of infant votives are justified and remain valuable for appreciating their function, but the 'feel' of the terracotta babies has remained with me. When recalling those archival visits my memories are grounded in sensory recollections: the dusty dryness of the terracotta on my hands, under my fingernails and in my nose and throat; the rough edges exposed by breaks in the clay fabric; the different sounds produced by solid and hollow examples when placed on a hard surface; not to mention the varied acoustic and temperature properties of the environments in which I encountered them. Nor have I forgotten how difficult it was to reconcile my sensory engagement with these objects: my senses, and the bodily movements occasioned by the materiality with which I was interacting, made me feel as if I were holding a baby whilst simultaneously conveying that it was a terracotta artefact. If the material properties of these objects can make a lasting, if somewhat contradictory, impression on my sensory memories and experiences within the museum storeroom, they undoubtedly had an impact upon those who dedicated them within the context of a highly charged emotional and mnemonically-laden religious performance.

Infant votives in context

In order to evaluate the significance of these potential sensory experiences it is necessary to establish the context in which infant votives functioned. In ancient Italy the relationship between mortals and deities was reciprocal and based in large part around the concept of *do ut des* ('I give so that you may give'). Hence, divine assistance could be attained by means of a formal request, sealed with a vow (*votum*) that any forthcoming intervention would be acknowledged with a gift (*ex-voto*) once the request had been fulfilled, or after a fixed period of time (Rüpke, 2007, pp. 162–5). Concerns about healing, conception, marriage, safe journeys and even economic productivity were frequently expressed through this votive format. At the same time, the successful negotiation of new stages of life or identity could lead to a similar dedication of items to the gods in both Greek and Italic contexts: dolls, emblematic of the period of childhood, were surrendered by women about to marry, whilst retiring craftsmen, for example, might offer their now redundant tools to signify that this stage of their life was over and their identity had undergone a major change (see *Palatine Anthology* 4.103–4; Van Straten, 1981, pp. 89–96). In these cases objects which had been owned and used by the dedicator were relinquished, but in others a specially made *ex-voto*, designed to represent or embody the request, might be offered instead. Between the fourth and first centuries BCE this type of purpose-made offering was produced most commonly using terracotta and occasionally bronze, although preservation factors mean that offerings of wood, wax, textiles and other perishable materials cannot be entirely discounted. These objects could represent specific requests as well as embody abstract ideas and transitional points in the life-course. Interpreting the precise thought processes and intent which lay behind individual examples remains challenging: a clay model of an ear, for instance, might represent everything from earache or deafness to a plea that the god being petitioned would hear the prayer, or even an acknowledgement that a divine response had been heard and heeded (Hughes, 2017; Turfa, 2006; Recke, 2013; see also papers in Draycott and Graham, 2017).

Votives in the form of terracotta mould-made models of swaddled infants were part of this trend for purpose-made offerings, reaching their peak in the third and second centuries BCE. They are associated ordinarily with two circumstances. The first relates to the realm of female fertility, whereby they are assumed to reflect a request or thank offering for pregnancy or successful childbirth (Baggieri, Margariti and di Giacomo, 1996; Miller Ammerman, 2007, p. 143). The second concerns infant health, in which they are connected either with an expressed hope that a baby would survive the precarious moments of birth and the months that followed, or instances in which young children had recovered from a period of serious illness (De Cazanove, 2008). Neither explanation is entirely satisfactory since both are predicated on an assumption that the figure of a newborn baby was an appropriate generic emblem for everything from potential conception by an adult woman and the safe birth of a healthy baby, to the illnesses of toddlers and older children. Many other votive types, including wombs, pregnant torsos, nursing mothers and sitting toddlers (so-called '*bambini accovacciati*' or '*fanciulli*'), align much more closely with these varied concerns (Graham, 2013). Moreover, despite the many thousands of votives recovered from Italian sanctuaries, there is a complete absence of iconographic representations of very young infants *without* swaddling bands. There are, for example, no known models of naked perinatal newborns or of infants between the ages at which swaddling would have ceased (around two months: Soranus *Gynaecology* 2.42) and that at which a child could sit up and play independently, as exemplified by the *fanciulli*, who are often depicted playing with birds.

With these observations in mind the swaddled nature of infant votives emerges as central to an explanation of this type of offering (Derks, 2014; Graham, 2014). Ancient notions about the significance of the short period of swaddling (up to about two months), particularly the use of textile wrappings to mould and provide firmness to new bodies in preparation for their future (Soranus *Gynaecology*

2.14–15), suggest more persuasively that these offerings were associated with a celebration of thanks for the successful negotiation of this critical life passage. Members of ancient communities with the requisite economic resources may have commissioned or purchased a terracotta model indicative of this period which they could subsequently dedicate at a local shrine or sanctuary in order to acknowledge and give thanks for the fact that this stage of life had been traversed successfully. Cast-off swaddling clothes may also have been offered to mark this event, and in some instances might have been used to 'dress' the terracotta (or indeed wax or wooden) models before they were dedicated (Graham, 2014, p. 41). The dedication of infant *ex-votos* as a celebration of the occasion on which the swaddling clothes were removed and a baby was 'released' as a properly formed body into the social and religious world are therefore bracketed more appropriately with the dolls and clothing of soon-to-be-wed young women, and other items resonant of rites of passage, such as the ritual surrender of the *toga praetexta* when a young man came of age (Foxhall and Stears, 2000; Sebesta, 2005). A similar phenomenon is documented for the modern world in the form of christening robes left by pilgrims at the shrine of Our Lady of Lourdes, France (Notermans and Jansen, 2011, p. 182).

What participants in these ancient ritual acts understood they were doing, and why, can therefore be stated with some degree of cautious confidence. Nonetheless, such explanations continue to operate at arm's length from the corporeal and conceptual realities of participation in the religious performances associated with these offerings. In order to interrogate more thoroughly what these experiences meant to people, how they impacted upon embodied understandings of religious activities, and how, in turn, they produced or reworked this knowledge, it is necessary to move beyond the artificial isolation of their visual and iconographic properties to investigate the broader spectrum of the materialities associated with votive cult. Doing so has the capacity to turn existing interpretive perspectives upside down. To date, votive studies have been largely, if unconsciously, driven by the assumption that it was the ancient gods who required material objects – *ex-votos*, inscriptions and other offerings – as part of the reinforcing of the 'if . . . then' relationship established on the occasion of a vow. Rarely has this notion been examined from the opposite position: why did *human* participants need or choose to mediate their relationship with the divine world through objects, and more importantly for the argument presented here, what role was played by engagement with the material form of offerings in legitimising these acts or producing discrete ritual experiences? These are precisely the questions that must be addressed in order to approach more complex questions about the significance of votive experiences, and a consideration of the sensory interaction between dedicator and dedicated object offers one means by which it might be achieved. As Carl Knappett (2004, p. 46) has observed for objects more generally,

> The situation in which object and agent engage is a dynamic one – and the information specifying where the situation can lead is not entirely within

the agent's head, but is in some way also held within the object (itself within an environment).

It is therefore to the sensory properties of votive objects that we must turn.

The sensory materiality of votive infants

Ancient religion is all too easily taken for granted as a prescribed, formulaic and largely cognitive backdrop against which different types of offering can be set and subsequently 'explained' as votive gifts. Brent S. Plate, writing about the materiality of religion, suggests that more attention should be paid to what 'religion', past and present, actually involves, noting that there can be 'no intellectual religion without felt religion as it is lived in streets and homes, temples and theaters' (2014, p. 7). Accordingly, religion 'is rooted in the body and in its sensual relations with the world' (Plate, 2014, p. 7). One means of achieving a more comprehensive appreciation of the power of materiality within ancient votive cult is therefore to consider the relationship between the material properties of the dedicated object and the human body via the human sensorium. Personal communication with the gods of the Roman world was without question a sensorially complex and emotionally laden event experienced through the body (Harvey, 2014). In the context of personal votive cult, sensitivity to these emotions and sensory experiences may have been particularly heightened as a consequence of what depended upon its success: the health of oneself or a loved one, the success of a marriage, the prospect of economic or domestic stability and security, the future well-being of a very young child. Against this background of mnemonic and emotive intensity, the affective agency of the votive object itself had the capacity to enhance, affirm or complicate further any knowledge associated with, or produced by, these experiences. As David Howes (2011, p. 95) observes,

> Religion has, for example often been defined as 'ideas and practices that postulate reality *beyond* that which is immediately available to the senses' (Bowen, 2002, p. 5; emphasis added). But a more nuanced and fruitful definition would underscore the mediatory role of the senses *in* the production of religious experience. (original emphasis)

In an ancient context, different votive types might therefore not only serve to signal and commemorate different religious requests or concerns but, because of their intrinsically different material form, not to mention the specific nature of the activities in which they were implicated and the hopes and concerns with which they were associated, might also be responsible for producing particular religious experiences and forms of embodied religious knowledge.

It is therefore necessary to consider more thoroughly the potential sensory affordances which might be possessed by these objects. Linda Hurcombe's (2007, p. 539) suggestion that archaeologists 'think through what features would draw attention' and consider 'what might be the sensory perceptions of objects in their past social settings/environments' offers a starting point for such an investigation. Posing these questions for infant votives results in a list of potential sensory affordances, presented here in no particular order and with no intention to privilege any at the expense of others:

> The bare terracotta is relatively cold to the touch
> They are hard, dry and unyielding
> They are static, rigid and unmoving
> They are heavy
> Two hands are needed to lift them because of their length
> They resemble swaddled babies
> They look like *models of* swaddled babies
> They smell like terracotta/clay
> They are silent
> Cloth wrapped around them would diminish the coldness of the terracotta
> Cloth wrapped around them would be soft and gentler to touch
> Cloth wrapped around them would recall the feel of similar fabric in other contexts
> Used swaddling clothes might have a distinctive smell

This list of ways in which a terracotta infant *ex-voto* might impact upon the human sensorium includes both positive and negative sensory experiences, such as the absence of sound or movement. It also includes a number of hypothetical sensory affordances based on the possibility that some models were wrapped in cast-off swaddling clothes. Writing in the second century CE, the medical writer Soranus offers specific advice concerning the nature of the material to be used for swaddling. His description overflows with sensory considerations and expectations, for both infant and carer:

> . . . take soft woollen bandages which are clean and not too worn out, some of them three fingers in breadth, others four fingers. "Woollen," because of the smoothness of the material and because linen ones shrink from the sweat; "soft," so as not to cause bruises when covering the body which is still delicate; "clean," so that they may be light and not heavy, nor of evil smell, nor irritate the surface by containing natron; and "not too worn out": for whereas new ones are heavy, worn out ones are too cold, and sometimes rough as well and very easily torn.
>
> (Soranus *Gynaecology* 2.14)

Soranus wrote of the ideal swaddling material, but even if this was not always readily available the texture and, undoubtedly, the smell of the fabric before, during and after use may have been distinctive and recognisable, even more so if the person handling a wrapped model had spent time interacting with, or caring for, the living baby who had once worn it.

The list of affordances is, however, far from straightforward and contains some apparent contradictions which reflect my own experience as described above: models may resemble a baby, but they do not move or sound like one. Can these conflicts be reconciled and, perhaps more crucially, might these complex affordances have encoded particular ideas about the religious agency of these *ex-votos*? Equally, if someone else (perhaps a contemporary parent, child or cult official) was asked to compile their own list it may be found to contain observations somewhat different from those noted here, not least because the terracotta fabric of the objects will have been fresher. Terracotta was also a material used much more widely in the ancient world than it is today, with ancient people likely to be more familiar with its weight and the way in which it feels against the skin than those of more recent periods who are accustomed to the smooth texture of plastics and other lightweight synthetic materials. Nonetheless, although the list originates from my own, context-specific experience of interacting with the materiality of these objects, it raises a number of questions about the potentially wide-ranging ways in which infant *ex-votos* might be experienced – and the subsequent implications – that are worthy of further exploration in light of recent work concerning the contribution of objects and the senses to the production of religious knowledge.

Religious materialities, memories and the senses

Several different types of potential sensory affordance are included in the above list: those associated with the 'traditional' five senses, as well as others connected with movement (kinaesthesia), emotion, memory and what might be described more generally as 'feeling', something which it has become common practice to subsume into haptic studies (Morgan, 2010). Indeed, David Morgan (2009, p. 141) has observed that the relationship between material culture and religion is one which involves what he terms 'felt-knowledge', meaning that 'images [and objects] and their uses should be examined for the ways in which they help to create forms of sympathy, empathy, and antipathy – feeling with, feeling into or as, and feeling against or other than.' His comment aligns with the much wider discourse concerning the materiality of religion discussed above, in which religious objects are interpreted not as the material expression of pre-existing ideas about what constitutes religion or religious belief, but as the material means through which it exists: 'a materialized study of religion begins with the assumption that things, their use, their valuation, and their appeal are not something added to a religion, but rather inextricable from it' (Meyer, Morgan, Paine and Plate, 2010, p. 209; see also Meyer, Morgan, Paine and Plate, 2011, p. 6). Refining his account of the 'felt life' of objects, Morgan (2010) urges scholars of religion to embed such considerations of materiality into their understandings of the ways in which beliefs and ideas are shared, understood and experienced, focusing particularly on the need to consider what he calls quite simply 'sensation'. According to Morgan, sensation and materiality are inextricably entwined as core elements of religious understandings and practice: religious objects *are* religion.

These observations are particularly pertinent to a study of ancient terracotta votives, which by their very nature were material items produced with the purpose of being manipulated and handled in the context of specific and well-defined ritual practices. Votive models of infants, for instance, were designed to be taken into a sanctuary and physically handed to the divine; they were not, as far as can be determined, used in any other capacity or context (although the possibility of the dedication of the used swaddling bands in conjunction with votive models is discussed further below). Without them the ritual being per-formed, and the relationship established between mortal and divine, would be substantially different: the religious knowledge produced might be predicated on ephemeral words (prayers) and other bodily actions. When participants engaged with votives, however, these objects brought about the production and communication of alternative knowledge and understandings creating a different sort of religious knowledge, effectively a different 'religion'. Indeed, Morgan goes on to include 'handling objects' in the types of activity that 'engage people in the social relations and forms of sacred imagination that structure their relations to the divine' (2010, p. 12). Votive offerings were far more than convenient objects to be observed or appreciated as a visual focal point around which religious ritual and thanksgiving occurred. Instead they were agents of those rituals, objects which would be integral to the perfor-mance and production of discrete religious activities and ideas. Votives such as these can therefore be recognised as the embodiment of the religious ideologies being enacted; they *were* religion.

In a Roman context, then, *ex-votos* were a means through which specific religious acts were performed and the human–divine relationship maintained: they were a material expression of the ideological structures which underpinned ancient cult, at the same time as serving as the agents through which those struc-tures were created. Their role was complicated and multifaceted and, fittingly, the sensory experiences associated with them were equally as complex, comprising an intricate combination of synaesthetic and dissonant affordances. Accordingly, whilst it is crucial to consider not only the immediate tactile feedback between hand and votive – in this instance the dry, coldness of the terracotta as a sign of a human-made, inanimate object – it is essential not to neglect the many differ-ent ways in which these objects were manipulated and moved around during the dedicatory process and how these might conflict with that. Incorporating 'feeling' and the implications of 'felt-knowledge' into a study of votive models therefore serves as a reminder to reflect on the way in which immediate experi-ences took place in conjunction with the emotions and memories evoked by the bodily movements that objects necessitated (holding a baby), as well as the ideological context in which they had meaning (marking the end of swaddling). It was through the combination of these potentially incompatible experiences and the amalgamation of sensory memory and immediate sensory perception that religion was produced and understood.

Writing recently about the tangled relationship between memory and the senses, Yannis Hamilakis (2014, p. 118) has pointed out that 'The materiality of the world is sensorially perceived through all previous mnemonic experiences, not only of that specific materiality but also of all other materialities and all other experiential encounters' (see also Knappett, 2004, p. 48). Memory was an intrinsic component of ancient cult, not least because the votive offering itself was essentially a mnemonic device designed to acknowledge and commemorate a bond between human and divine, or even a specific occasion or personal circumstance (Graham, 2017). The formulaic nature of ancient cult also meant that participants performed the necessary ritual acts in a consistent format which recalled other, similar occasions. Religious practice was deeply embedded within daily actions and ways of thinking about the world, and regularly entailed the giving of offerings of all types. On the occasion of the dedication of a votive infant it is possible that the dedicants recalled visiting the same shrine or sanctuary to make other offerings, perhaps on behalf of the infant's siblings or in relation to previous requests connected with health and other personal concerns. The parents may even have visited the sanctuary in order to seek divine assistance with conception or the safe delivery of their as yet unborn baby. As children they would have witnessed, and as adults they would have participated in, household rites involving the giving of offerings of food, incense and prayers to the divine, perhaps also becoming involved with public religion within the wider community. The dedication of an infant votive was therefore an act embedded within an extensive memory landscape of religious experience. The minds and bodies of participants carried memories of how they had moved, acted, thought and felt in ritual settings. As Hamilakis suggests, 'When human bodies perceive the world, their perception is pregnant with memories which inevitably shape that perception. At the same time, the material world enacts multiple times, and through sensuous actions and effects, it activates mnemonic experiences' (2014, p. 103).

As well as drawing upon and reinforcing these embodied memories, sensory interaction with the materiality of the votive itself had the capacity to distinguish between these different religious experiences, meaning that once again these might fall uneasily between the creation of a sense of familiarity and one of strangeness. In broad terms the formal act of dedicating a model of a terracotta infant might involve essentially the same ritualised process and order of activities (travelling to the sanctuary, prayers or other verbal communication, ritual purification and so on) as those performed when dedicating other votives, such as a terracotta womb. However, what separated these two acts and marked them out as different was the specific materiality with which the dedicant engaged. The subtly distinct sensory affordances of different types of votive offering could imbue the act of dedication with a more precise contextual meaning which went beyond what a person saw in front of them. These objects also *felt* different, involved varied types of bodily movements because of their size, shape and weight, and consequently conjured memories, emotions and understandings which were linked with a range of embodied sensory memories.

Votive cult did not take place in either a sensory or a mnemonic vacuum. Returning to the list of potential sensory affordances for infant *ex-votos* noted above, it might be most appropriate to categorise these offerings as having 'messy sensory stratigraphies' (Hamilakis, 2013, p. 413) or, perhaps better, involving 'intersensoriality, that is the multi-directional interaction of the senses' noted by David Howes (2005b, p. 9). What is more, as the list implies, it is quite possible for sensory experiences to pull in different directions: these votives look like babies but they also look like models of babies. What type of knowledge did this produce and was this conflict intentional? Instead of focusing on how one sensorial experience might trigger another and/or combine with it in order to produce an apparently more profound and multi-layered sensorial experience, exploring the significance of those which offer internally conflicting information – those which are genuinely multi-directional – makes it possible to consider further the significance of the multi-directionality of the senses in the production of religious experience. The apparent discord of affordances could in fact texture the specific agency of religious objects and the resulting ritual performances in a way that was entirely appropriate for that particular votive context.

Touching is believing?

According to De Witte, 'people tend to trust their sense of touch. . . . Of all the senses, we take touch to be the one least prone to trickery, the most direct of all senses, providing us with unmediated access to the real. More than "seeing is believing," touching is believing' (2011, p. 148). What, however, if touch disagrees with other sensory information derived from the same source? Should it be written off as an inconsequential anomaly? As the example of infant *ex-votos* makes plain, elements of the materiality of objects such as these can signal to the dedicant making such an offering that they were interacting with a cold, hard piece of moulded terracotta. In this, their senses were probably in agreement with their cognitive knowledge that the votive was indeed a manufactured and inanimate artefact. Equally, however, there are other affordances which suggest that the bodily responses of the dedicant might cause them to recall sensations associated with a real living baby. The extent to which individuals shared the same responses will have varied widely, depending upon age and gender, whether they were dedicants or cult officials, as well as their relationship with the living infant whose release from swaddling was being marked. Nevertheless, leaving aside the possible use of cloth for the moment, it is evident that, on the one hand, when encountering these votives the majority of the 'traditional' senses (that is, the modern five) would have worked collectively to dispel any idea that this object was anything other than a lifeless piece of moulded terracotta. The item would not move, it was entirely rigid and even the gentle sensation, sound or movement of breathing would be absent. It would not respond to the bearer's voice or touch; there would be no sound of crying, gurgling, wind and other sounds associated with a young baby. Effectively, the senses acted to confirm that this was a substitute, a stand-in for the real infant. In fact, the reception of these material cues may have been essential for understanding the context of this specific dedication. The body being dedicated to the divine was not soft and fluid, but firm, its form now set and its existence unequivocal, with the very hardness and solidity of the terracotta potentially reinforcing the idea that now that the period of swaddling was over the infant's body had been shaped and firmed up adequately (Graham, 2014). Emphasising permanence, solidity and stability, the senses affirmed the underlying purpose of the votive offering. On the one hand, then, sensory perception of the votive as an artificial ritual object was an appropriate 'reading' of its materiality in this dedicatory context.

It is important not to stop there, however, and ignore the other potentially competing or conflicting affordances associated with bodily movement, memory and sensation that these objects might possess simply because they seem to be at odds with the interpretation offered by the traditional sensorium. As my own experiences demonstrated, in order to interact with a life-size model it is necessary to behave as if holding a real baby: bending over in a particular way to lift it or place it down; its weight felt in the shoulders and forearms; the constraints of having to use both arms and its impact on balance and movement. In order to pass one of these objects to someone else (in an ancient context perhaps to the other parent or to a cult official) or to put it down (on or near the altar or within a designated area), the bodily movements involved draw upon the muscle memory and embodied understanding of the sensations connected with the care of a real infant during the first few months of its life. This is exactly what Ruth Tringham describes when she calls attention to the fact that the 'tactile-kinaesthetic sense includes not only the more obvious haptic sensations, such as surface, form, pressure, pain, temperature, and texture, but also those full-body sensations of *balance and the sense of movement in any part of the body*' (2013, p. 178; emphasis added). Of course it is not only babies which might be lifted and carried in this way, but in the context in which these objects were encountered and manipulated – a dedication on behalf of a living infant – these emotional and physical experiences would have been at the forefront of the dedicator's mind and body.

Rather than attempting to identify which of these complex competing experiences was dominant – was it thought of as a baby or not? – incorporating this competition and dissonance as an element in the way in which the materiality of these *ex-votos* was understood makes it possible to acknowledge that it might in fact be entirely unproblematic for these objects to exist simultaneously as both babies and non-babies. Interacting with the ancient gods meant engaging with the liminal world between the community of the living and that of the divine. The sanctuary represented the point at which these two met; it was a special place, a sacred betwixt and between environment. The material and sensory ambiguities of votive offerings such as models of swaddled infants were perfectly suited to both this setting and to a ritual which marked the end of a liminal stage of life between the womb and the social recognition of a child. Furthermore, votive cult which engaged the body in different forms of movement and sensory perception associated with the distinctive materiality of other types of offerings and a range of different circumstances may have facilitated the production of alternative experiences, each embedded in the specific circumstances associated with that offering. Dissonant sensory experiences need not be written off, explained away or even downgraded as unimportant or somehow less powerful. Instead, what this example suggests is that the very ambiguity which they produced could be integral to the meaning of the religious activities in which they were implicated.

These experiences would have been complicated still further if the terracotta model was wrapped with the cast-off swaddling bands. This may have resulted in a votive model which felt and smelled slightly more like the real baby for which it was a substitute. The agency inherent in the swaddling clothes themselves, as agents responsible for actively shaping the body of the infant, may also have been significant. Indeed, it might be suggested that wrapping a clay *ex-voto* in such a way was intended to deceive the senses into believing or 'feeling' that this was, in some way, the same baby as that which had been wrapped and moulded by the swaddling bands over the preceding months, tapping directly into embodied memories of holding that individual swaddled child and its own swaddling clothes. Such an experience had the potential to emphasise a conceptual connection between the agency of the swaddling clothes, the model, the living baby and even the dedication itself. The dissonant sensory experiences involved, however, and the constant reminder that this was *not* that baby, also served to reinforce the nature of the liminal votive process at the heart of these experiences. In other words, incorporating the cast-off swaddling clothes may have heightened the intrinsic ambiguity of these objects, intentionally blurring the sensory boundaries and producing a sense of uncertainty and an object which sat uneasily between worlds. Such ambiguity was entirely appropriate for an act of dedication in a context that was, in many respects, precisely about negotiations involving different worlds (human and divine), states of existence (from womb to socially recognised being) and even bodies of different character ('soft' to 'firm').

A matter of dimensions

The argument presented here relates only to those examples of terracotta infant votives which were life-sized, or near life-sized. Many examples of smaller models are known, including one from Bomarzo measuring just 23 cm (Baglione, 1976, inventory number 97/69), and another from the Campetti sanctuary at Veii of only 13.2 cm (Vagnetti, 1971, inventory number 2609). Dedicating small items which could be grasped easily in one hand will inevitably have entailed entirely different sensory experiences. In such cases none of the sensory affordances associated with these models will have recalled embodied memories connected with the bodies of the real babies they were a terracotta substitute for. Nonetheless, the existence of smaller models, including those which fall between the smallest and largest known examples noted here (the twenty examples known from Bomarzo, for instance, range between 23 and 63 cm in length), does not negate the observations above concerning the sensory experience of votive cult. Instead, they prompt alternative questions.

Like their life-size counterparts, these objects were integral to embodied sensory experiences of votive cult practices just as other types such as heads, half-heads, wombs and small figurines were, even if the sensory experiences they produced differed in subtle ways. The act of dedication, interaction with a material object, and the emotional and mnemonic context in which this took place will have continued to combine in order to produce discrete, personal, context-specific understandings of those acts and the religious knowledge created or negotiated via them. What is more, such material variety hints at an even more complex multiplicity of meanings that might be embedded in the act of dedicating a votive, providing an important reminder of the extent to which these were highly personal occasions. Each occasion may have produced distinct interpretations which enabled participants to position themselves within a much broader religious or cultural framework. Indeed, miniaturisation itself was connected with a complex series of meanings and it was not unusual for earlier Italic votive offerings in particular to take the form of intentionally miniaturised everyday items (Rüpke, 2007, pp. 154–5; examples in Schultz and Harvey, 2006). In the case of an infant *ex-voto* of a mere 13 cm, the unrealistic miniaturisation of the figure – which may have reproduced more readily the 'felt-knowledge' and bodily behaviours associated with dolls than with living babies – may have been equally as resonant, serving to accentuate the ambiguity and 'otherness' of votive cult as well as connecting to a host of other embodied sensory memories. Roman dolls made from wood, ivory, bone or terracotta commonly took the form of adult women rather than babies, although examples of linen rag dolls more akin to young infants are also known (Harlow, 2013, pp. 330–2).

It is therefore possible to speculate about the experience of a new mother, who had previously surrendered her favourite doll to the divine on the occasion of her marriage (see for example *Palatine Anthology* 6.280), as she interacted with yet another model. A small infant votive may have simultaneously recalled and contrasted with the former plaything which had been designed in part to prepare her for her future role as wife and mother – the very role she was now playing. How did this relate to the living baby itself, and how might the texture of cast-off swaddling bands, the firmness of the terracotta beneath and recent experiences of interacting with a newborn infant be reconciled with past haptic and kinaesthetic experiences of a much-loved doll? The full implications of the relative sizes of terracotta baby votives at different sites, as well as within the same assemblage, not to mention of different materials, are yet to be explored in detail, but evidently extend beyond more traditional economic considerations concerning the affordability of larger offerings and the availability of raw materials. Smaller dimensions do not negate the effective power of an object's distinctive materiality.

Conclusion: Blurring sensory boundaries

Through the example of terracotta *ex-votos* of infants in swaddling bands, this chapter has demonstrated how apparently contradictory sensory information might combine with embodied memory in order not just to enact the ideologies associated with ritual activities but to produce discrete religious experiences. This case study of infant votives exemplifies how the relationship between material objects and the human sensorium, in its widest possible definition, can produce ritual performances which serve as 'instruments of knowledge' (Chidester, 2005, pp. 56–7; see also Harvey, 2014, p. 96). Seen in these terms, the sensory ambiguities of infant votives, and their implications for the embodied experience of votive cult, were the material means through which religious knowledge was expressed but also produced, negotiated and understood. In this way different strands of votive ritual, and different types of votive offering, can be understood as discrete 'religions' within a much broader framework of ancient religious activity. Far from involving repeated formulaic acts, religious performance was complex, dynamic, contextual and grounded in the materiality not only of the objects concerned, but the sensing bodies of the participants themselves.

This case study has essentially explored a form of synaesthesia in which the senses can be seen to work together in order to produce understandings not by triggering one another in a mutually supportive manner, but by offering competing, conflicting and potentially confusing information. In isolation these sensory experiences appear to produce an experience which is internally at odds with itself, one that defies categorisation. Seen in its proper context, however, this can be explained as entirely rational. Indeed, it is only when ambiguous sensory affordances such as those described here are contextualised in relation to what is known about votive cult and the role of the specific type of artefact implicated in the act of dedication that it becomes possible to analyse the role of material objects in shaping the religious experiences associated with and produced by them. Sensory dissonance makes perfect sense in this context. It was acceptable, indeed entirely appropriate, for an infant votive to appear to exist as both a real and a representational infant at the same time, and it was sensory dissonance which allowed for this to become a meaningful reality. Senses frequently trigger one another and work together, but as this chapter has demonstrated it is also necessary to acknowledge that 'working together' might also include a more complex process of negotiating competing and conflicting sensory experiences. Allowing for and examining a blurring of sensory boundaries, rather than seeking to make judgements about which experience was most valid or dominant, offers a new and productive means of thinking about the nuanced role of the sensoria of the past.

Plate 1 Painting of fullers working in tubs, *fullonica* (VI.8.20–21.2), Pompeii. The four workers are painted in a different bodily position, highlighting the diversity of movements
 involved

Source: Illustration by Jasmine Parker

Plate 2 Painting of fullers trampling clothes, House of the Vettii (VI.15.1), Pompeii

Source: Illustration by Jasmine Parker

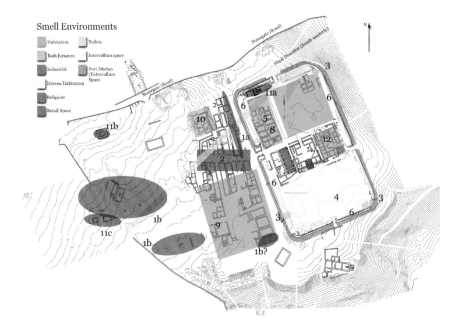

Plate 3 A Vindolanda smellscape

Source: Thomas J. Derrick (image courtesy of Andrew Birley)

Plate 4a Fields of saffron crocuses around the town of Krokos, northern Greece

Source: Photo: J. Day

Plate 4b Separating the crocus stamens from stigmas, which will then be dried to make saffron

Source: Photo: J. Day

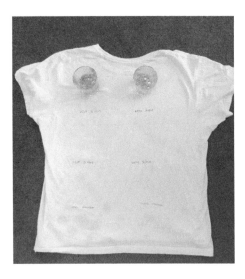

Plate 4c Saffron sprinkles on a white t-shirt. Saffron diluted in wine is on the left, in water on the right. Three measurements were taken: after 30 minutes, after 90 minutes and after eight hours

Source: Photo: J. Day

9 All that glitters

Roman signet rings, the senses and the self

Ian J. Marshman

The study of signet rings has traditionally been a niche pursuit within the field of Roman archaeology, restricted to specialists in glyptics (gemstone engraving). The majority of scholarship considering these objects has also been undertaken from a narrow art historical perspective, interested primarily in studying iconography (such as Richter, 1971). Such studies have often been undertaken on large collections with little or no provenance (for example, New York (Richter, 1956), Munich (Brandt, 1968), Fitzwilliam Museum, Cambridge (Henig, 1994), Carnuntum (Dembski, 2005, p. 18); compare Vindolanda (Greene, 2006)), meaning that the contexts of these objects are rarely considered. This approach views signet rings simply as a 'minor art' and obscures their potential to inform on wider social issues around status, dress and identity. This chapter demonstrates how a sensory approach to signet rings can help develop a better understanding of their use and significance in Roman society.

As with many artefacts, it is difficult to get much of a sensory appreciation of a Roman signet ring from the typical published catalogue or excavation report (compare Graham, this volume, with respect to terracotta votives). This situation is made worse in the case of signet rings because attention is mainly focused on one element, the intaglio. The most common type of signet rings used during the Roman period had its motif engraved in intaglio on a gemstone or moulded in glass paste. Most of the space in catalogues is devoted to describing these engraved images, and in citing parallels, with little interest in the ring, even where one survives (for example Krug, 1981). Illustrations distort the matter further, with the convention being to publish photographs of plaster impressions of the engraved gemstones, and include only a few token photographs of the artefacts themselves, which may or may not show part of the ring (for example, Guiraud, 2008, plates). This publication style surely influences how readers perceive these objects. They are presented with row upon row of black and white images arranged by subject, emphasising similarity and obscuring their diversity. Publication in this form prioritises the iconography of signet rings above all other aspects of their materiality, and reinforces the interpretation of them as *objets d'art*, rather than as functional objects of personal adornment.

New technologies are beginning to enable more realistic renderings of artefacts that provide viewers with the potential for greater sensory appreciation.

Increasingly, catalogues of signet rings and intaglios are beginning to incorporate colour photography, as it decreases in cost due to the switch to digital printing (see Nestorovič, 2005), thus allowing the vibrancy of these objects to be more readily experienced. Laser scanning means it is now possible to make three-dimensional models of artefacts available online (De Montfort University, 2013), and the move to open access online publishing of complete datasets (Nagy, 2013) makes these objects more accessible than is possible with the traditional catalogues found only in specialist libraries. There is of course no substitute for the sensation of studying an artefact first-hand in a museum (compare Graham, this volume), but due to pressures on staff time, security and conservation this will always remain a privilege for the few. I decided to try to examine as many examples as possible during my research on the signet rings of Roman Britain, and doing so has certainly informed my sensory appreciation of these objects.

The materiality of Roman signet rings has rarely been discussed, but as relatively expensive objects of personal adornment worn directly upon the body, this must have been of interest to their wearers. Whilst the choice of image engraved upon a signet ring would have been an important decision, it would not have been a wearer's only concern. Two of the senses would have been foremost in the minds of those purchasing and using a signet ring: what does it *look* like, and what does it *feel* like. These are still the most important questions when buying a ring today, with its form, material and size still taking precedence. This chapter will consider these visual and tactile aspects, and also explore how the function of Roman signet rings gave these objects a special relationship with an individual's sense of self. Finally, it considers how sensory studies can increase our understanding of how signet rings contributed to the way an individual's identity was perceived by others.

Sight: Visual complexity and the brilliance of colour

It is often noted that the sense of sight dominates sensory studies in archaeology, and material culture more generally (Elkins, 1997; Gosden, 2001, p. 165; Fahlander and Kjellström, 2010a; Hamilakis, 2014, pp. 76–80). Whilst this is rightly viewed as a shortcoming of these studies, it can be easy to overlook how complex our sense of sight is and just how significant it would have been for people in ancient societies for comprehending the material world around them. Sight is also the sensible place to start this study, as it would have been by sight that a purchaser would have first experienced a signet ring in a workshop or worn by somebody else (in most cases at least).

We do not simply *see* objects; both their materiality and the context in which we view them influence our experience of looking at them. Peter Wells (2008) suggests seven elements that can affect how we see an object, and how attractive or 'visually complex' it is to our eyes. These are the object's surfaces, its edges, its texture, how it is decorated, its glitter, what colour it is, and the type and movement of the light in which we see it (Wells, 2008, pp. 42–8). Wells explains that objects with more visual complexity can 'powerfully, even emotionally, engage or . . . enchant the viewer' (2008, p. 52). Thus a drab courseware jar when viewed in a dark cupboard would be less engaging to the eye than a shiny red Samian cup at a dinner party, decorated in relief with figures that seem to dance around its surface by the flickering light of the oil lamps. This disparity in visual complexity is the same today as it was in antiquity, although how we interpret it (as beautiful or garish, extraordinary or ordinary) is unique to each individual and is conditioned by the sensorium with which they are familiar.

Roman signet rings are particularly visually complex objects. By including an engraved gemstone they were already more interesting to look at than a plain metal ring, or a signet with its motif engraved directly onto the bezel. Many of the intaglios used had convex surfaces but even those that were flat often had bevelled sides which, together with their contrast in colour and texture with the metal ring, served to draw the eye to the engraving. Images engraved using the negative intaglio technique may not be as visible as the positive reliefs of cameos, but the presence of an image on such gems is identifiable when close at hand, and so subconsciously they invite your mind to try to decipher them. The glitter and gleam of both gem and metal ring would have helped attract attention to the wearer at a distance, especially in bright sunlight, or when caught shimmering in flickering artificial light. The visual complexity of Roman signet rings draws you in, and the nearer you get to the wearer the more your eyes are made to focus on the motif engraved on the glittering stone.

The small size of Roman signet rings and their physical attachment to the wearer's body restricts access to their images, making viewing such objects an intimate sensory experience. Thus it would have been those who came within the wearer's personal space and were able to linger there who would be best placed to view such images. As anyone who has ever tried to study these objects in a museum display can testify, this distance is not enough, and the best way to really appreciate a signet ring is to hold it yourself. In antiquity it would have been a risky thing to pass your signet ring to another person, given their material value and necessity in daily life. Consequently, the experience of seeing a signet ring would probably have been primarily the luxury of the wearer, and a privilege for their closest clients, friends and family, as well as the slaves or freedmen who may have been authorised to seal documents on their behalf. The highly personal experience of viewing someone's signet ring contrasts with the wider circulation of the same imagery on the sealings produced using them, which would have been seen by all who had dealings with the wearer. The images used on the seals of famous men appear to have been well known (Sulla, Pliny *Natural History* 36.4; Pompey, Plutarch *Pompey* 80.5; Commodus, *Historia Augusta Commodus* 11) and we may suppose that the same was also true of those of ordinary people within their own social circles.

The attractive visual complexity of Roman signet rings would have varied according to status. The right to wear a gold ring was an important mark of rank in Roman society, at first restricted to senators and magistrates, then granted to all who were of equestrian status (Livy 9.7, 23.12; Florus 2.6; Pliny *Natural History* 33.8). Much later the privilege was also bestowed upon soldiers, by Septimius Severus (Herodian 3.8). The gleaming vibrant yellow of gold rings would have had greater power to draw the eye than the dull iron rings worn by those of lower status. The curious Roman practice of using iron for signet rings is all the more interesting when we consider that bronze rings would have been easier to produce, and provided a shine and colour much closer to gold. It may be that the use of iron for signet rings reflects an attempt to restrict, or to reject, the 'bling' worn by the social elite. Those who could not afford to purchase a genuine gemstone for their rings had to make do with glass pastes which were mass produced in moulds and so also afforded their wearers less choice over imagery than those who could commission engraved gems. These glass pastes were often polished but could not rival the gleam of the real thing. A brilliant glittering shine was certainly a desirable characteristic when purchasing a gem, as is evidenced by the best preserved examples and by the polish that usually survives on the rear of loose intaglios. Over time the polish of gems used in signet rings wears away and whilst this is helpful to archaeologists, as it gives an indication of how long an object may have been used, the lack of shine could have marked out someone wearing a hand-me-down.

Styles of Roman signet rings changed over time, with an ever increasing emphasis on achieving visual complexity and successfully catching the eye. In the late Republican period signet rings were plain bands of metal, which conveniently strapped the necessary gemstone to the wearer's finger. Under the Empire the forms of rings became more varied and complex, often becoming chunkier and wider at the shoulders, meaning more shiny metal was on show across the knuckles. Second- and third-century CE rings often have gems mounted ostentatiously to stick out above the bezel. In Britain, from the mid-second century CE onwards, people seem to have increasingly exploited loopholes in the sumptuary laws, swapping iron for silver against which there was no proscription, and tinning and gilding even cheap bronze rings. Later signets frequently include decoration on the rings themselves, often concentrated on the shoulders where it would have been most visible and effective for catching the eye of both viewer and wearer.[1] This increasing visual complexity of signet rings was not an isolated phenomenon; it can be seen as one element of a wider trend for flamboyancy which reached throughout the arts and across various classes of material culture, and went on to typify the sensorium of Late Antiquity (Roberts, 1989, pp. 116–18).

The sense of sight was also important for differentiating between the different types of gemstones used in signet rings. In an age before the concept of geology or of mechanical methods of testing, people had to rely on their own senses rather than those of machines. Many of the stones used in Roman signet rings are defined by geologists today as varieties of the gemstone chalcedony, which is a cryptochristoline form of quartz. In the absence of such scientific ontologies, a great range of names were used to categorise these stones, based almost exclusively on factors perceptible to the human eye, such as colour, banding, inclusions and translucency (compare Pliny *Natural History* 37). The varieties of gemstones as understood by the Romans were also seen to possess a range of supernatural properties (Pliny *Natural History* 37) which, in addition to their visual appearance, influenced how these gemstones were perceived; and consequently the ways in which they were used. Whilst scientific analyses are of increasing importance for how we interpret artefacts in an etic sense (for gems see Insoll, Polya, Bhan, Irving and Jarvis, 2004; Gliozzo, Grassi, Bonanni, Meneghini and Tomei, 2010; Hatipoğlu and Güney, 2013), to approach an emic understanding of objects it is useful to include a sensory perspective alongside our readings of the historical sources.

As we have already seen, colour was an important factor influencing how the gemstones worn in Roman signet rings were viewed. The role of colour as an aspect of materiality is increasingly discussed by archaeologists and classicists (such as Jones, 1999; Allison, 2002; Freestone, Meeks, Sax and Higgitt, 2007; Bradley, 2009, 2013; Jones and MacGregor, 2002), but its role in relation to the value of gems was particularly significant. It is easy to forget, in our modern world of plasma screens, billboard advertising and tablet computers, just how rare the vibrant brilliant colour of precious stones would have been before the modern period, and consequently the extent to which this was valued and invested with powerful symbolism (Finlay, 2007, pp. 398–401; Rapp, 2009, pp. 91–2). The rich deep purple of amethyst was said to be the benchmark against which dyers tried to match their purple cloth, but it was also thought to be reminiscent of wine, leading some to believe that it could give the wearer the power to prevent drunkenness (Pliny *Natural History* 37.40). It is, therefore, perhaps not surprising that Bacchic imagery is encountered engraved on this material. Gems with green hues were frequently used to bring to life the pastoral scenes that were popular amongst elite purchasers. A signet ring with a similar scene on green jasper may have inspired the epigram:

> The little jasper stone holds a seal of seven cows as though they were one, and all looking as though they were alive. Perhaps the cows would have wandered off; but as it is the little herd is confined in the golden pen.
>
> (*Palatine Anthology* 9.746)

As well as mirroring the subject of their engravings, the colour of the gems used in signets may also have been influenced by the personal preferences of the wearer. An interesting example of this has been suggested by Savay-Guerraz and Sas (2002) whose research has produced evidence that intaglios depicting chariots frequently appear in the colours of the four circus *factiones*. Even in Britain, the gems used in signet rings cover the full spectrum from black and white to red, brown, orange, yellow, green, blue and purple. That such diverse gems were traded the length and breadth of the empire is testament to the desire of wealthy individuals to have and to be seen to have stones of certain colours.

Touch: The feeling of sealing

After sight, touch was likely the most important sense by which individuals encountered a signet ring. It is interesting to note that in most seal-using societies they were worn close to, if not touching, the body. In Mesopotamia cylinder seals were worn on a chord around the neck where they could be clearly seen (Collon, 1997, pp. 19–20), whilst in the Mycenaean polities seals were sometimes strung around the neck or wrists, and also worn as signet rings (Flouda, 2010, pp. 61–2). In medieval Europe seals were worn on the body as signets and as pendants (Henig, 2008), although larger official seal matrices were delegated to chancelleries (Steane, 1993, pp. 22–4). In the seventeenth to early nineteenth century fob seals became popular, in addition to signet rings (Daybell, 2009, p. 660). These could be attached to ribbons for easy retrieval from a gentleman's pocket. Having a seal pressing against or touching your body would mean it was always at your fingertips, but it would also provide added security, since it is unlikely that you would not feel its removal by a thief. Wearing your seal also reinforced the symbolic link between object and user, emphasising the personal nature of the seal by its restrictive physical proximity to the body.

Although signet rings are worn upon the body, it is interesting how the feeling of wearing a ring is a sensation that we quickly grow accustomed to and no longer notice. Often we are only reminded of a ring's presence by the jarring pain when it becomes caught on something, or when it is removed and the change in pressure means we suddenly begin to feel its absence. This phenomenon means that over time it can feel almost as if a finger ring becomes a part of the wearer's body (see also Aglioti, Smania, Manfredi and Berlucchi, 1996).

Today, almost everyone who wears a finger ring has access to one made from smooth precious metal. However, in the Roman period wearing gold was a privilege restricted by sumptuary laws (see earlier discussion). It can of course be argued that we do not know the extent to which these laws were followed, but the fact that they were reissued, and that the right to wear a gold ring continued to be granted, suggests that wearing a gold ring remained a prestigious status symbol. This was especially the case amongst men, for whom the signet ring was the only item of jewellery that was traditionally considered socially acceptable (Croom, 2000, p. 71). For much of the Roman period, those who could not wear gold wore rings made from iron. This peculiar practice is often taken at face value and has rarely been discussed (Manning, 1976, p. 36; Henig, 2007, p. 12). It may have been inspired by the myth of Prometheus who reminded himself of his torment by wearing an iron ring set with a fragment of the stone to which he had been shackled (Pliny *Natural History* 37.1). Yet iron is not suited for use as jewellery, being difficult to work into smooth intricate shapes and prone to staining the wearer's skin and clothes. It seems likely, therefore, that the feeling of wearing iron was rather more uncomfortable and messy than wearing a ring of precious metal.

The Roman tradition of wearing iron rings may have developed in response to concerns about the corrupting effect of luxury. Looking back to a more noble and frugal past, Pliny the Elder suggested that once even senators had worn iron rings, with gold rings given only to ambassadors visiting peoples whose elite were marked out by such rings (*Natural History* 33.4). Nevertheless, in the late Republic and early Empire wearing iron was confusingly both a mark of humility in the eyes of moralists like Pliny, and also a mark of second-class status. Whether individuals wore iron out of choice or because they were restricted from wearing gold, the fact that a distinction existed and had to be enshrined in law suggests compulsion and a desire to restrict wearing gold to the social elite. Unlike smooth precious metal rings, the uncomfortable feeling of wearing iron would have been a constant reminder of lower status. Rather like wearing a hair shirt, for those who chose to wear one this feeling of flagellation might have been a mark of pride, but for those who *had* to wear iron it is unlikely to have been something they relished. In Roman Britain, iron continued to be used for signet rings well into the second century CE, but it was increasingly replaced by silver or bronze, both of which would have been more comfortable on the wearer's hands. This peculiar Roman use of iron for signet rings requires further study and as they are often poorly preserved our understanding of the phenomenon could benefit from experimentation with producing and wearing recreated examples.

Signet rings were not only worn for decoration, so it is also worth considering how it might have felt to use one for sealing. First of all, you would need to prepare the wax or clay that would be used to produce the sealing (see surviving sealed documents in Thompson, 1895; Gesztelyi, 2000, Appendix II). In the case of the former this would have required melting the wax, and it is possible that this task had a particular smell associated with it since Roman sealing wax has been found to have been coloured red with lead oxide (Furger, 2009; Spangenberg, 2009). The process of dripping the molten wax to make an impression required skill as the wearer risked the stinging sensation of burning themselves and the danger of making a mess by applying too much, which in some later seal-using societies was seen as careless and unsightly (Favret, 1993, p. 135). We know that the next part of the process usually involved the wearer pressing their signet to their lips to moisten it. In Pompeii flirtatious graffiti attests the practice: 'Primigeniae Nucer[inae], greetings! Oh how I wish I could be your gemstone for just one hour, so that I could give you kisses when you impress your seal' (*CIL* IV.10427; see also Ovid, *Amores* 2.15 where the poet imagines himself as his lover's signet ring). Although the taste was probably not a memorable sensation, the routine ritual of 'kissing' your ring would have reinforced its intimate nature, and emphasised the close relationship between object and wearer (see also Weddle, this volume, on the Aristotelian relationship of taste and touch). The final act of pressing your ring into the hot wax and imprinting your mark was a curiously forceful yet delicate procedure, requiring accuracy and just enough pressure. It is interesting to note how much more personal, sensual and embodied the experience of sealing a document would have been in the Roman period, when compared with the modern, arm's length actions of simply signing off a printed document, folding it and tucking it inside a self-adhesive envelope.

The self: Between brains, bodies and things

An individual's sense of self and how they perceive their identity is not defined purely by their biological body but also includes their relationships with objects (Gardner, 2002; Gosden, 2005; Hodder, 2012). As Hodder puts it, 'sentient beings depend on things to bring their sentience into being' (2012, p. 9). Whilst Roman signet rings cannot claim a unique significance in this regard, as we have already seen they had a particularly personal relationship with the body of the wearer. The sensation of sealing a wine vat, purse or strongbox also physically imprinted it as belonging to you, and when you sealed a contract, letter or will, these sealings continued to function as a symbol of your agency within the world, beyond the bounds of your body's senses. The signet ring can thus form part of what Malafouris terms 'the extended self' (2008). This concept, he suggests, places the self not within or without the body, but constantly enacted by relationships between brains, bodies and things (2008, p. 1997). Thus, through wearing a ring as a mark of your identity, and using it for sealing, it becomes increasingly a part of the way you conceive of yourself and likewise how others perceive you.

It could be argued that such a relationship is purely an abstract theoretical concept, alien to the way Roman individuals conceived their sense of self, but there is some evidence to suggest that this is not the case. Historical sources give us numerous references to the use of signet rings, and indeed Platt has suggested that ancient authors may have viewed them as objects that were particularly 'good to think with', because of their links to individuals and their relationship with the world (2006, pp. 241–2). The most insightful reference occurs in a letter written by Cicero to his brother Quintus, advising him on his new position as Governor of Asia: 'Don't let your signet ring be a mere implement, but, as it were, *your second self*: not the minister of another's will, but a witness of your own' (*Letters to His Brother Quintus* 1.1.4; my emphasis). With this Cicero seems to remind Quintus of the importance of his signet ring as a way by which to enact his agency throughout his new dominion, and cautions him against letting it become a 'rubber stamp' to the ideas of others on his staff. We also get a sense of how Quintus' ring forms part of his sense of self, and that it will be integral to the way he is perceived in the new province. It is clear that Cicero also believes that the way Quintus chooses to use his seal will change the way he is perceived, which will have repercussions for his self-image. Whilst Cicero saw the signet ring as a second self beyond the confines of the body (a 'sensory artefact', Betts, this volume), his conception fits well with the idea of an extended self formed from the relationship between an individual and objects.

For signet rings to have a function they require their images to be invested with the identity of their wearers, and for this to be recognised by others. Sealing a purse of coins, for instance, provides no defence against theft in and of itself; it is merely a symbolic barrier, created by conditioning in the mind of the viewer that breaking the seal will have consequences. Similarly, a seal on a contract is no guarantee that the individual who placed it there will abide by its terms; it requires all involved to place trust in the system. In both cases the power of the seal depends on recognising its relationship with a known individual, and will be influenced by the viewer's perception of that person. Thus, not only is the signet ring part of an individual's extended self, the sealings produced using it can be seen to imprint their identity and carry it out into world, where it can influence the lives of others even without the wearer's presence.

The power of the images used on signet rings to represent a person's identity can be found in literature. In Plautus' play *Curculio* a signet ring is used to great effect as a plot device, specifically because of its power to identify individuals. The story revolves around the escapades of the slave Curculio trying to buy the freedom of his master's lover, the slave girl Planesium. To do this Curculio cheats a soldier at dice to win his signet ring, and uses it to fraudulently take out a loan in his name (*Curculio* 2.3, 3.1). When Planesium is finally set free she recognises the ring's image (a man spearing an elephant) as belonging to her father, and it is revealed that she is in fact the long-lost sister of the cheated soldier and so was freeborn after all (*Curculio* 5.2). Whilst these events are contrived for dramatic effect, they rely on the audiences' acceptance that people would identify a seal image as belonging to a particular individual.

As with any image, the motifs used for sealing could be interpreted differently by different people, challenging the expression of identity intended by the wearer. This problem befell the young Octavian, who chose an image of a sphinx for his first seal but had to replace it when he was later ridiculed that recipients feared the sphinx-like trickery contained in the letters that bore it (Pliny *Natural History* 33.6). So strong was the relationship between a signet ring's image and an individual that, as in the case of Planesium, it could invoke memories and emotions even without the presence of its wearer. In Plutarch's account of the death of Pompey he describes how Caesar was said to have turned away at the sight of his adversary's severed head, but burst helplessly into tears when presented with his signet ring (*Pompey* 80.5). To Caesar it was not the lifeless, decaying head but the sight of the ring that stirred his feelings, encapsulating the essence of the life he had taken. For Pompey, the relationship with his signet ring transcended his own existence; it had gone from an object that expressed his identity, to an object that identified his body.

Conclusion

Issues of preservation, collection and publication have meant that all too often the materiality and function of Roman signet rings has been overlooked in favour of their beauty as *objets d'art*. In this chapter I have demonstrated that a sensory approach to these objects, when considered alongside archaeological and written evidence, can help us move beyond the traditional interpretation of these objects. Many classes of Roman material culture would benefit from such attention, not least those which are generally considered only in terms of their function as art.

Roman signet rings were paradoxically both particularly personal objects and an important element of an individual's public persona. The brilliant colours of their intaglio gemstones would have provided attractive flashes of colour, and their gleaming rings could catch the eye even at a distance. Yet, because of their small size, being able to view their iconography properly would have been an intimate sensual experience, restricted, because of proximity, primarily to the wearer. Just as the image on a signet ring is intimate and attached to the body, so the images they produce on sealings are common and dispersed, taking the agency and identity of the wearer beyond the bounds of their senses and engaging their recipients in their own sensory experiences. Through such use signet rings would become increasingly a part of their wearer's extended self. Over time a ring and an individual's sense of self could become indistinguishable, in both their own mind and in terms of how others perceived them.

For Roman men in particular, who traditionally wore less jewellery than women, signet rings offered an important vehicle for displaying status. It is perhaps because of this that sumptuary laws were used to restrict the right to wear gold rings, not only to those who had enough wealth, but also to those who possessed the correct social status. To some extent signet rings can be seen as objects of the social elite, who would have had access to the most flamboyant materials and the best craftsmanship. Those lower down the social ladder often had to settle for rings that were less comfortable, less shiny and often with motifs that were less personal to them. The use of iron for signet rings has particular implications for the sensory experience of these objects and warrants further study.

Despite their small size, signet rings offer us a disproportionately significant insight into Roman society. Their production in such numbers and with so much variety required trade on a global scale, which was only made possible by the connectivity of the empire. Yet, as objects, each was closely tied to an individual's sense of self and reflects their desires about how they wanted to present themselves to others. Today, as in antiquity, signet rings and their engraved gemstone settings possess a remarkable potential to excite the senses.

Note

1 See http://www.britishmuseum.org/research/collection_online/collection_object_details.aspx?objectId=1362221&partId=1 and http://www.britishmuseum.org/research/collection_online/collection_object_details/collection_image_gallery.aspx?assetId=1549633001&objectId=1362221&partId=1#more-views.

10 Tuning into the past

Methodological perspectives in the contextualised study of the sounds of Roman antiquity

Alexandre Vincent

In 1942, in a work crucial to what was destined to become the new genre of the history of mentalities, *Le problème de l'incroyance au XVIe siècle,* Lucien Febvre sketched in a few lines what was to become one of the most promising research avenues of the future: '*Ne craignons pas d'insister sur tout ceci. Il y aurait une suite d'études captivantes à entreprendre sur le support sensible de la pensée aux diverses époques*' (Febvre, 1942, p. 471).[1] In these terms the father of the *Annales* pointed out to historians a whole new object of study, as vast as it was primary, namely the material transmitted by perception: smells, tastes, sounds, tactile or visual experiences; in other words, the complete sensory framework that surrounds a human life in its daily context.

Although Febvre's call went largely unanswered at the time, seventy years later these studies are numerous. Strengthened by anthropological thinking on the senses, historians today are not far from having completed the *sensual revolution* for which David Howes pleaded so passionately (Howes, 2005b, p. 4). When leaving the well-trodden paths of institutional, economic or cultural history, it is no longer a question of claiming without qualification the discovery of some sensorial *terra incognita*, since an abundant bibliography exists to unmask so-called inventions.[2] Despite recognition of the necessity in taking a multisensory approach to historical phenomena, that is, taking into account all the senses in play during any given historical moment, the bibliographical explosion has pushed researchers to specialise in just one particular sense. Only a larger collective team effort could hope to attempt a synthesis which is far beyond the powers of the single researcher.[3]

The present contribution is no exception to this general rule and proposes to focus solely on sound and its perception in the Roman period. Such a limited objective might seem less surprising, perhaps, with respect to the single type of perception chosen than the chronology. Does antiquity, whether Egyptian, Greek or Roman, not warrant to be treated as one whole? Is the sound of a trumpet played by an Athenian companion of Pericles not the same as that emitted by a soldier in one of Trajan's legions? In truth, the ineluctable difference between perceiver and perceived requires a strictly contextualised approach: even if the sound produced by the Athenian and Roman trumpet was the same (and it may not have been), we cannot be sure that it was interpreted in the same way by the players and listeners in these different temporal, geographical and cultural contexts.

One of the principal contributions of the anthropology of the senses is to have underscored the extent to which sensory perceptions of social phenomena are anchored in the space and time that presided over their genesis. Beyond the givens of physiology, which can be measured, quantified and even qualified if one has a willing subject, but which are irrevocably lost to the historian, the issue is one of the interpretation of these givens by contemporaries rooted in their specific social context. Many anthropological studies have as an aim the progressive documentation of the diversity found in the relationship different societies have with sound. It is principally ethnomusicologists who have contributed to the general picture by extending the boundaries of their discipline to include 'non-musical' sounds (Zerouali, 2015). The seminal work of Steven Feld (1982) opened the way by revealing the capital importance of auditory perceptions in understanding their environment in the case of the Kaluli of New-Guinea. The sheer abundance of scientific output today allows whoever has the will and strength to do it to study acoustic ways of understanding the world on five continents. From the Bororos of the Brazilian Mato Grosso to the perception of the bells of Kanda cathedral in Tokyo (Torigoe, 2002, pp. 39–57), many areas and aspects of sound have been analysed, all isolated elements of a vast, planetary sonorous landscape.[4]

The challenge for these studies stems from the necessity on the part of the external observers to abandon their own sensory categories in order to limit distorting the perceptions of their subjects of study as much as possible (the *emic/etic* dichotomy). In other words, it is a question for the researcher of 'learning to listen', to borrow a phrase brought back by Paul Stoller from an interview with one of those practitioners of exorcism rituals that he studied in the Songhai of Niger (Stoller, 1984, pp. 559–70). Theorised by anthropologists and ethnomusicologists as being part of the methodological prerequisites for the proper practice of the discipline, this problematic goes largely unrecognised by ancient historians for whom the relation to sound is not evident. If one cannot pretend that sound is absent from historiography, the field of history should be approached with caution as not all scholars of all periods have launched themselves into the *sensual turn* with the same alacrity. Alain Corbin deserves credit for the growing awareness among historians of the interest in considering sounds as markers of social identity in a given territory. His study of the sound-scapes of the French countryside in the nineteenth century has indeed found great acclaim since its publication in 1994, in France as well as abroad (see also Laurence, this volume). Ari Kelman has recently shown the extent of the debt (2010, pp. 212–34). However, there is a noticeable gap between work done on antiquity and other historical periods. Where medievalists, modernists or contemporary historians have taken full possession of their field of study, classicists have left theirs virtually untouched, something clearly shown by the timeframe chosen for the title of a recent work, *Les cinq sens de la ville du Moyen Âge à nos jours* (Beck, Krampl and Retaillaud-Bajac, 2013).

Did the people of the ancient past not feel anything then? This line of questioning, which seems purely rhetorical at first sight, has no other aim than to highlight an absence, one stemming as much from the *habitus* of scholarly practices as from the *a priori* fact that ancient sources are not adapted to this kind of questioning (Bettini, 2008). As the contributions gathered in this volume show, however, there is no doubt that ancient sources permit one to envisage the construction of a history of perceptions in antiquity. The sources for classical Rome ring, rustle, hum, explode with references to sounds and perceptions, and it is up to historians to interpret them with the help of a suitably adapted methodology. This latter cannot but be inspired by the theoretical advance made by anthropologists on this point which, as it happens, leads historians back to the very foundation of their discipline, namely interpretation in context. Since auditory perceptions are social phenomena determined by the space-time framework of their production, just as it would not occur to anyone to examine the sound productions of the Quechua in Peru by using the framework deployed by Indians in Kerala, so it is clear that the right understanding of acoustic perceptions of antiquity can only be effected by taking context into account in the most detailed and robust manner possible. If further proof of the necessity of contextualisation were still needed, it would be enough to recall the demonstration of Peter Coates regarding the perception of noise pollution on the part of the English bourgeoisie of the second half of the nineteenth century (Coates, 2005, pp. 636–65). The sources of the Victorian era clearly distinguish the street organ players, Italian immigrants trying their luck in the cities and suburbs of the Industrial Revolution, on the one hand, and factory noise on the other. The former were considered exceedingly annoying by the bourgeoisie, whereas the latter, the source of their wealth, did not disturb them in the least. This reversal of *a priori* expectations which would have thought music to be a sound preferable to that of roaring furnaces, clearly shows the methodological imperative of anchoring as precisely as possible the sounds of the past in the social reality of their time.

Sounds and perceptions: *La chose et les mots*

The distinction between a sound and its perception is a fundamental one: they are two subjects of study which are often confused even though they derive from different levels of analysis and even types of source (see also Veitch, this volume). It is the written, literary sources that constitute the richest depository of sounds of the past. However, they only give access to acoustic perception, that is, the relationship between the emitter of the sound (such as a trumpet – or a person blowing a trumpet) and its sensory reception, in these cases, by the author of the source or their literary persona. The sounds of the past, in literary sources, only exist insofar as they have been perceived and re-transcribed by a subject.[5] The real thing has been filtered by the perception particular to an author, his interpretation of sensory givens. In other words, the sounds of the *Annals* and *Histories* are a characteristic of Tacitus' perception of the world, which is no more universal than it is socially objective.

The way the real is used in literary creations can radically distance the facts described from their transposition into a narrative whose primary objective is not veracity. Anyone interested in the sensory perceptions in Seneca's work, for example, should especially be aware of this. Certain passages in his work, such as *Letters* 56, are thus regularly cited to illustrate the sounds of the city (Betts, 2011; Betts and Veitch, this volume). Seneca there deploys a veritable lexical arsenal related to the sounds of the voice, of cries and also the noises of water in the context of the surrounding baths, none of which succeed in disturbing him in his reflection. Yet one cannot understand this text correctly if one does not take account of the Stoic background of Seneca's thought.[6] If the sensory apparatus, including the ear, are often marshalled in Seneca, it is in order to demonstrate that any idea of 'neutrality' in relation to the real is illusory. As for the poetic texts, they pose the problem of a purely literary or sonorous use of words, and the relationship between literature and reality. And what of the sonorities of elegiac poetry? Can they teach anything to a reader seeking to escape from literature as the art of arranging words and breaths? The historian of sounds is thus in a similar position with the textual sources as the historian of emotions who has to definitively renounce the hope of getting to the emotions of the past and make do with a history of the construction of emotive perceptions, since this latter is all that the texts have preserved (Boquet and Nagy, 2011, pp. 8–9).

A change in the type of evidence nevertheless allows some hope that the methodological blockage induced by textual sources can be circumvented. For example, certain fragments of artefacts pertaining to the sonorous world have survived and allow one to imagine it is possible to hear real sounds from the past. In this chapter, I refer to musical instruments, objects whose very existence is justified by the making of sound. Whilst their individual states of conservation are not optimum, the remains of musical instruments which survive in several museums give the hope that the sound of the past can be heard again.[7] The importance of these remains and the hopes they inspire have led to real excitement over the last decades, both among scholars and a wider public (Bélis and Homo-Lechner, 1994; Buckley, 1998; Homo–Lechner and Vendries, 1999). A special sub-discipline has arisen, musical archaeology, with its own academic networks and channels of transmission. Scholarly associations, such as *MOISA International Society for the Study of Greek and Roman Music and Its Cultural Heritage* and the *International Study Group on Music Archaeology* (ISGMA), have made this an international discussion. ISGMA regularly publishes the results of its encounters in *Studien zur Musikarchäologie*.[8] *MOISA International Society* for its part has its own journal (*Greek and Roman Musical Studies*) and annually updates the growing bibliography on its Internet site. It is a meritorious effort given the bibliographical explosion produced by the 'sound fever' whose methodological coherence, as with all new domains of research, is sometimes difficult to discern.[9] The end result of many studies in musical archaeology is the reconstruction of musical instruments 'in the antique manner'. Playing them would then resuscitate the sounds of the past.[10] Though this hope is understandable, it is also dangerous: just because an instrument physically resembles what is found in the sources does not mean it will produce the same sound. Materials and construction techniques are crucial elements in sound production, without even mentioning playing conventions and body postures (compare Slaney, this volume). It is thus only precise data on the fragments of instruments, resulting from minute observation and from sustained analyses to which rigorous standards are applied, that one can reduce to their bare bones the hypotheses and fantasies contemporaries project onto antique instruments. Such studies have already been conducted, or are in progress, and allow the hope that such 'acoustic capsules' from ancient times can increase in the future. Musical instruments thus offer the chance to break through the time barrier by reviving sound *emissions*, but these reconstructions cannot tell us unequivocally how their sounds were perceived by their ancient users and audiences.

Nevertheless, it is precisely in the juncture between the emission and the perception of sound that the study of musical artefacts has unexploited potential. Comparison of the data of perception, as described in the literary sources, with that of emission allows one to attenuate the subjectivity of the perception reported by linking the word(s) used by an author with the empirical evidence from sonorous material. Inversely, it allows one to describe the sounds produced by ancient artefacts with the words belonging to the same world. It is therefore a question of initiating a methodological movement in the application of lexicography to a very circumscribed domain: how did the authors of literary sources perceive? In other words, how did they qualify in their writing the acoustic reality that a detailed musical archaeology will allow us to resurrect from the past? We are still far from possessing all the elements that can allow such a novel crossover to occur, but in this chapter I propose the first steps for this kind of study, to be conducted on a small scale. I take as a focus the Roman *tuba*, a bronze instrument which has the advantage of having been the object of some of the most advanced analyses done to date and which offers at the same time a sufficiently large number of literary references to make a useful contribution.[11]

Qualifying the Roman *tuba*: Emissions and perceptions

During a show at the Musée historique et archéologique d'Orléans organised in 2007, a team of academics took an interest in a *tuba* discovered in 1861 at Neuvy-en-Sullias (Loiret, France) together with a quite exceptional set of bronzes (Gorget, 2007). The instrument, the best preserved of the western Roman empire, became the object of a multidisciplinary study that combined the approaches of historians and metal experts. The results were published in two articles which constitute the most complete study of this type of instrument to date (Mille, 2007, pp. 146–55; Vendries, 2007, pp. 120–44). The *tuba* was situated in the context of its discovery and then compared with artefacts of the same type in order to determine its mode of construction. Parts of very fine layers of beaten metal alternated with cast sleeves, the whole flaring outwards in a continuous manner from mouthpiece to bell. The piece was X-rayed and then analysed by means of the particle accelerator of the Centre de Recherche et de

Restauration des Musées de France, which yielded a complete metallographic analysis. The hammered pieces were made of brass containing a high zinc content, whereas the cast pieces used a lead alloy that was easier to mould in liquid state. The X-ray showed the way the different parts of the instrument had been put together, including earlier restorations. Placing each piece back in its original position revealed that the *tuba* had been longer than the instrument now on display in the museum in Orléans by 40 cm (a total of 180 rather than 140 cm). This precision is far from incidental since the length of the *tuba* has a direct impact on its acoustic capacity, as Vendries has reminded us (2007, pp. 133–7). The longer the instrument the greater the number of notes a musician can derive from it. Taking this longer dimension of the instrument into account, a replica was made by artisans of the artistic foundry Courbertin (Saint-Rémy-lès-Chevreuse, France), using metals with the same chemical properties. The final instrument, the result of a detailed and scientific reconstruction, was subsequently played by a professional trumpet player. The sound was described as 'strident', a logical result when one considers the morphology of the instrument and the mouthpiece, with its wide and shallow cup.[12]

The adjective is important because it inaugurates a change in the object of analysis: it is no longer a question of the sound as such, definable by mathematical data (see Veitch, this volume), but of the way it was apprehended by listeners. Still, according to Vendries, the perceptions of those contemporaneous with the instrument and those of the twenty-first century seem to converge: '*Les observations des acousticiens et des spécialistes des "cuivres" recoupent la plupart des descriptions de la sonorité de la tuba dans la littérature gréco-romaine qui insistent sur l'aspect strident de cet instrument à vent*' (Vendries, 2007, p. 135).[13] This is interesting as it suggests a lack of evolution over time of auditory perception with regard to a specific sound, in this case that from the *tuba*. Yet this assertion, made in a single paragraph, does not seem to be based on a proper lexicographical examination. If we carry out that examination, the terms 'clamour' and 'din' used by Pollux the grammarian, and two quotes from the Latin poets Virgil (*At tuba terribilem sonitum procul aere canoro increpuit . . .* , *Aeneid* 9.503) and Ennius (*At tuba terribili sonitu taratantara dixit*, *Annales*, fragment 140) are the only instances in which the sound of the *tuba* is described. The latter gives an idea of the kind of rhythmic sequence that could be played on a *tuba*. The closeness of the two lines lends credibility to the idea that Virgil reused Ennius here. The two poets associate the sound of the *tuba* with the qualification *terribilis*.[14] This is an interesting adjective because it does not correspond to language describing a specific sound: *terribilis* is an adjective describing the quality of any fearsome reality, which is only marginally acoustic. The question which then arises is about the equivalence of stridency and fear: is a strident sound always fear-inspiring or is a fearsome sound always strident?

In order to enrich our knowledge of how the ancients perceived the sound of the *tuba*, the most pertinent method, in my view, is a systematic review of all the adjectives qualifying it in the written sources. A full literature survey reveals that the occurrences of the term *tuba*, or its derivative *tubicen*, the one playing a *tuba*, are numerous, close to a thousand, but not all of those references describe an aspect of sound. If we isolate the passages where there is an adjective relating to the sound, we find that only fifty or so describe the sound of the instrument, using around thirty different adjectives or expressions.[15] The adjective *terribilis* is indeed the most widespread: it is used nine times to describe the sound of the *tuba* or the instrument itself. This purely statistical approach needs to be nuanced, however, by considering the character of the texts envisaged. When Servius comments on the form of line 503 of *Aeneid* book 9 (*At tuba terribilem sonitum procul aere canoro increpuit . . .*), he repeats it without adding any new qualification to our knowledge on the sound of the *tuba* (Servius 9.501). The play of quotation and repetition on the part of ancient authors therefore means the epithet *terribilis* is falsely classed as top of the list. If one excludes these, only three authors qualify the sound of the *tuba* as *terribilis*, Ennius, Virgil and Ovid (*Metamorphoses* 15.784), relegating it to second position.[16]

Occurring five times, it is the adjective *raucus* that is actually most often used to describe the *tuba*. Ennius uses it, but also Lucretius, Propertius, Lucan and Statius (Ennius *Annals* 485; Lucretius 4.544; Propertius *Elegies* 4.3.20; Lucan *Pharsalia* 1.238; Statius *Thebaid* 3.709). The diversity of contexts, in elegiac poetry as well as a treatise, strengthens the idea that this perception is not relative to a single author or a particular context. Contrary to *terribilis*, *raucus* is also a term proper to acoustic perception. These two terms are not on the same level. Where *terribilis* can be called an adjective of impression, *raucus* is an acoustic qualification. This duality runs right through the sources under consideration.

The information given by adjectives of impression must be gathered in order to study the connotations of the sound: what did the sound of the *tuba* evoke for the Romans? The list of these adjectives of impression is longer than that of the acoustic ones, probably a sign of the value given to the acoustic properties of bronze instruments in the collective Roman imagination. The overwhelming majority of terms refer to the fear or horror inspired by the sound of the *tuba*. To Ovid and Martial the *tuba* is *fera* (Ovid *Fasti* 1.716; Martial *Epigrams* 10.64). It is *saeua* for Silius Italicus (*Punic Wars* 11.290, 12.210), *torua* for Apuleius (*Florida* 17.33), or again *trux* for Seneca and Tacitus (Seneca *Octavia* 400; Tacitus *Annals* 4.25.6), which are so many ways of signifying its savage or ferocious quality. The written sources confer great emotional power on the *tuba*. It stimulates its hearers, arousing disturbing emotions, at least in the accounts given by the authors. The *tuba* brings terror (*terrificus*) or sorrow (*luctificus*) but never leaves one indifferent.[17] Seneca characteristically pretends to ask himself, 'Who would ignore the fact that *litui* and *tubae* are stimulants?' (Seneca *On Anger* 3.9).[18] The *tuba* is, in essence, the instrument of the Roman legions. Its notes resounded on the battlefields as a signal to attack or retreat, to excite the troops and to silence them (Alexandrescu, 2010, pp. 33–45; Vincent, 2016). It thus incarnated the sound of war, of bloody conflicts (it is the *tuba sanguinea* of Valerius Flaccus)[19] and as a result the sound of loss and mourning too (see also Hope and Laurence, this volume).[20] Metonymically the instrument therefore became the incarnation of affliction: the *tuba* is sad.[21]

The most common acoustic adjective is *raucus*, followed by *clarus*, which is used three times.[22] The other adjectives are all unique and can be grouped into three categories: those characterising the qualities of the sound (*grauus, acer*),[23] those relative to its power (*clangente, canorus*)[24] and lastly the expressions characterising the signals played on these instruments (*lentus murmur, fractus sonitus*).[25] The term *stridentus*, corresponding to the English 'strident', only appears once in the body of texts and is excluded from the study: although the term *tuba* is used (*Sarmata, bracis Vangiones, Batauique truces, quos aere recuruo stridentes acuere tubas*: Lucan *Pharsalia* 1.430–2), it is in its generic form of 'tube', the curved bronze instrument in question being most likely the *lituus*. How can we understand this absence? In truth it is only surprising if one starts from the premise that the acoustic qualifier 'strident' *ought* to occur because that is how a modern person would qualify it. If one accepts, however, that one should listen to the sources 'with new ears', that is, devoid of contemporary *a priori* assumptions, there would be no need for surprise: if one chooses to believe classical authors, the *tuba* was *not* perceived as strident by its contemporaries. If it were to end here the study would risk leaving the reader rather dissatisfied: the *tuba* was not a 'strident' instrument but a 'raucous' or 'hoarse' (*raucus*) one. This merely shifts the problem: what did *raucus* actually mean to a Latin speaker? This requires a new lexicographical study and gives an appreciation of the work still to be done to gain a better understanding of the perceptions of the ancients.

A survey reveals close to 200 occurrences of *raucus* in the literary sources, covering a relatively restricted number of themes. Musical instruments, and particularly bronze ones,[26] are amongst the objects most frequently described as *raucus*. Thus it is not the exclusive property of the *tuba* to be *rauca*: it is a quality it shares especially with another bronze instrument used in the Roman army, the *cornu*. Even if other musical instruments are designated as *rauci*, *tuba* and *cornu* constitute the lion's share of occurrences. The link between the two should probably be sought in the material of its composition, bronze, as cymbals, percussion instruments of the same metal, also receive this acoustic qualification in Propertius when he describes a Bacchic procession (Propertius *Elegies* 3.17.36). Over and above musical instruments, it is door hinges (Propertius *Elegies* 4.8.49; Ovid *Loves* 1.6.50) and even shields clashing (Virgil *Aeneid* 2.545; Ovid *Fasti* 4.212; Silius Italicus *Punic Wars* 2.245) that give raucous sounds, thus confirming the link made by the ancients between a metallic sound and raucousness.

It is not musical instruments that provoke the use of this acoustic epithet above all, however. The voice, whether human (in the majority of cases by far), animal or divine, is the object most often described by authors as *raucus*.[27] The human voice goes hoarse from talking, whether one is a lawyer or in love (Plautus *Epidicus* 200; Cicero *On Oratory* 1.259; Propertius *Elegies* 1.16.39; Apuleius *Metamorphoses* 8.3.20; Martial *Epigrams* 4.8.2). Hoarseness is therefore a default, the symptom of an illness one can treat (Celsus *On Medicine* 2.1.15; Pliny *Natural History* 20.53, 20.87, 22.104; Scribonius Largus *Compositions* 74.1, 185.3), unless it is the indelible social marker of inferiority: the voice of a pleb or a woman of ill repute (Ovid *The Art of Love* 3.289; Horace *Letters* 1.17.62;

Apuleius *Metamorphoses* 8.26.2; Juvenal *Satires* 11.156; Martial *Epigrams* 1.42.9, 10.5.4). The harsh voice is not the pure human voice in its most beautiful state. It is a transformed voice and it is no accident that among the first signs of the metamorphosis of a person into an animal both Ovid and Apuleius single out hoarseness, an acoustic defect that signals the crossing from the human to the animal world.[28] In fact, in the overwhelming majority of occurrences of the epithet it is brought into relation with nature. Certain animals such as bears, wild boars, donkeys, horses, elephants and bulls emit harsh sounds, something a modern person will understand without any difficulty.[29] It is, however, more disconcerting to find that the cries of birds,[30] the song of cicadas (Virgil *Eclogues* 2.12) or even the hum of bees (Virgil *Georgics* 4.71; Columella *On Agriculture* 9.9.4; Silius Italicus *Punic Wars* 2.221) are also described as *raucus*.

It is easier to understand that bees and cicadas produce a *raucus* sound when one considers the most common association of this word in the literature: the sound of water.[31] The stagnant water of swamps (Fronto 3.1.11), the voice of the running water of the river (Apuleius *Metamorphoses* 6.13.4; Virgil *Aeneid* 9.125; Ovid *Loves* 3.6.52; Ovid *Fasti* 5.638) or the sea itself (Propertius *Elegies* 2.30.20; Ovid *Letters* 18.29), the aquatic element is simply 'hoarse' (*raucus*) to Latin authors. More than the water itself it is the lapping, rustling or backwash that merit this qualification: wine fermenting in the vat or boiling lava are also 'hoarse' sounds (Calpurnius Siculus *Eclogues* 1.3; Virgil *Appendix Vergiliana: Etna* 3). The raucous sound par excellence is that of minerals rolled by moving water: rocks moved by a river or the waves on the shingle. 'The stream falling onto a bed of smooth pebbles' (Virgil *Georgics* 1.109)[32] thus produces a hoarse murmur in Virgil's poem; in Ovid it becomes *raucus* when crashing on the rocks of the Black Sea shore (Ovid *Metamorphoses* 11.783).[33] The sounds in question are powerful, rich and complex. The human ear hears them as one without being able to differentiate the acoustic units they are made up of; what Leibniz called the '*petites perceptions insensibles*' (1886, pp. 41–5).[34] The hum of a swarm of bees, the song of the cicadas or the wash of the surf have this same powerful acoustic complexity based on the combination of sonorous micro-events that are repeated *ad libitum* and continuously renewed.

Is this how the sound of the *tuba* was perceived? We can only put this hypothesis forward with great caution but the frequent use of the epithet *raucus* to qualify it allows us to do so. A powerful instrument – Pollux noted (*Onomasticon* 4.88) that one could hear it from 50 *stadia* away, that is, 10 kilometres in all directions – the *tuba* had a very limited tonal repertoire, which presupposes that the sounds played on it were characterised by repetitiveness. Powerful, emitting a complex sound, vibrant and repetitive, the *tuba* was a harsh rather than strident instrument for the Romans.

Conclusion

As always in a historical discipline, the combining of sources and methods seems to be the best way to extract the maximum of information. This is particularly true of subjects such as sound, whose traces are fragile. We are fortunate to have the remains of Roman period musical instruments, which enable work to be carried out on both the emission of their particular sounds and the perception of those sounds by Roman authors. The work recently undertaken on the *tuba* of Neuvy-en-Sullias was the starting point for the present enquiry. In this chapter I have aimed to demonstrate the value of using a wide array of techniques, from X-ray to lexicography, thus combining novel approaches with more traditional forms of historical analysis. The conclusion is that, for the Romans, the *tuba* was less a strident instrument than a *raucus* one, an adjective which has also needed its own enquiry.

Does the method proposed here for the study of the perceptions of the past make sense, based, as it is, on a strictly analytical approach to lexicography? The most obvious risk is that of a forward flight into the illusory quest of thinking 'like a Roman'. In order to understand the sound of the *tuba* one has to understand the term *raucus*, to understand *raucus* one has to understand the verb *spumo*, to understand *spumo* . . . the risk of lexicographical regression is real. Yet, all the same, the methodological contribution should not be neglected. The historian of the twenty-first century will never be able to think – or feel – like a first-century Roman. At the very least, however, we can be aware of it and try, by contextualising the categories of perception, to open our ears and not forcefully project our own cultural frameworks onto the sounds of the past.

Notes

1 'Let us not be afraid to insist on all this. There is a whole series of fascinating research studies to be done on material support in different epochs.'

2 A very recent and efficient entry into the English- and French-speaking bibliography can be found in the work of Palazzo (2014), one whose methodological interest far exceeds the chronological span of its title. For a synthesis of the methodology adopted by Palazzo, see Palazzo, 2012, pp. 339–66. There is another useful bibliographic synthesis by Krampl and Beck, 2013, pp. 13–25.

3 Regarding these collective works, see, for example, Classen, 2014.

4 For further reflection on the notion of 'sonorous landscape' or 'soundscape' and its use in the social sciences, see Vincent, 2015a.

5 One finds here the formulation of the question as posed by Berkeley, considered as paradigmatic of empirical philosophy: if a tree falls in the forest but there is no-one to hear it, does it make a sound in falling? According to Berkeley (1710, section 45), *esse est percipi (aut percipere)*, to be is to be perceived (or to perceive). This is a field that has mainly been worked on by psychologists and ethnomusicologists.

6 For acoustic perceptions in Seneca, see André, 1994, pp. 145–54; Vincent, 2015b.

7 For bronze instruments of the Roman period the standard work is Alexandrescu, 2010; for string instruments, Vendries, 1999; for instruments of the *tibia* family, a survey still has to be conducted, while the thesis of Péché (1998) remains unpublished.

8 The collection currently consists of eight volumes, published between 2000 and 2012.

9 The variety of articles gathered in *Studien zur Musikarchäologie* is a good reflection of this sometimes disordered richness characterising musical archaeology.

10 This is what provokes the passion of the general public, as seen by the success of recordings that give an immediate appreciation of the sounds of the past, such as the CD by Synaulia and the Kérylos Ensemble or the concert of 'Paleomusic' given by the very serious *Orchestre national de France* on 22 March 2014.

11 Studies associating precise organological with lexicographical analyses should be conducted for all instruments for which we possess sufficient information: *cornu, tibia, cithara* and so on.

12 Elsewhere in Vendries' paper (2007, p. 135) there is mention of '*clairs*' ('clear') and '*brillants*' ('brilliant') sounds, terms borrowed from aspects of nineteenth-century instruments to which the *tuba* of Neuvy had been compared. It is a pity that the publication did not give rise to precise and coded acoustic transcriptions of the sounds derived from the response. It is the only shortcoming of an otherwise exemplary study.

13 'The observations of acousticians and copper instrument experts concur with the greatest number of descriptions of the sound of the *tuba* in Graeco-Roman literature which insist on the strident nature of this wind instrument.'

14 It should be noted that Ennius indeed uses the epithet *terribilis* and not *horribilis* as Vendries stated (2007, p. 135), an understandable error given the lexical field surrounding the *tuba*.

15 There are 52 qualified situations, with 34 different modes of expression, according to my examination. I think, however, that the relative numbers matter less than the overall tenor.

16 Besides the passages from Ennius and Virgil mentioned earlier, Ovid *Metamorphoses* 15.784. The repetitions of these three passages are Terentianus Maurus *On Letters, Syllables and Metre* 1854, 1858 and 1912; Servius Honoratus *On Different Metres* 462.23; Zeno of Verona *Tractatus* 1.15.3.

17 *terrificus*: Silius Italicus *Punic Wars* 5.189; Seneca *Letters to Lucilius* 102.29.5; *luctificus*: Statiaus *Thebaid* 10.552; Valerius Flaccus *Argonautica* 3.349.

18 *quis autem ignorat lituos et tubas concitamenta esse . . .*

19 *Bistonas in medios ceu Martius exsilit astris currus, ubi ingentes animae clamorque tubaeque sanguineae iuuere deum, non segnius ille occupat arua furens . . .* (Valerius Flaccus *Argonautica* 3.84).

20 A rare exception to this univocal connotation of the *tuba*, the *placida tuba* of Statius *Silvae* 3.1.139, where the adjective serves to signify the return of peace through an effect of opposition.

21 *triste*: Silius Italicus *Punic Wars* 15.460; *tristior*: Propertius *Elegies* 2.7.1; *maesta*: Propertius *Elegies* 4.11.9; *ferialis*: Quintilian 9.6.12.

22 Virgil *Aeneid* 5.139; Seneca *Agamemnon* 428. One has to add the comparative *clarior* in Seneca *Letters* 108.10.2.

23 *grauus*: Lucretius 4.543; *acer*: Statius *Silvae* 5.3.193.

24 *clangente*: Valerius Flaccus *Argonautica* 3.349; *canorus*: Ovid *Metamorphoses* 3.705. The power of the *tuba* and bronze instruments in general is a recurrent theme in the literature. One is reminded for example of the acoustic ambiance for waking the dead created by the bronze players during the funeral procession of Claudius as described by Seneca in the *Apocolocyntosis* 12.

25 *lentus murmur*: Propertius *Elegies* 4.4.9; *fractus sonitus*: Virgil *Georgics* 4.72, quoted by Columella *On Agriculture* 9.9.4 and Servius 3.556.

26 Bronze instruments: besides the *tuba*, the *cornu* above all (Lucilius *Satires* frag. 26.605; Catullus 64.263; Lucretius 2.619; Propertius *Elegies* 3.3.41; Virgil *Aeneid* 7.615, 8.2; Lucan *Pharsalia* 1.238; Valerius Flaccus *Argonautica* 6.92; Silius Italicus *Punic Wars* 12.182; see also the epitaph *CLE* 2121). One also encounters the sound of the *classicum*, played by the bronze instrumentalists of the army (Caesius Bassus *On Metre* fragment 6.69) and the *bucina*, a military instrument of uncertain nature (Virgil *Aeneid* 11.474; on the *bucina* see the first chapter of Vincent, 2016). Other instruments are the *tympanon*: Ovid *Metamorphoses* 4.391; Ovid *Isis* 456; Silius Italicus *Punic Wars* 17.19; the *tibia*: Propertius *Elegies* 3.10.23; and the *barbitos*: Lucretius 4.544.

27 The voice is hoarse in 46 passages of Latin literature, according to my counting.

28 Ovid, *Metamorphoses* 2.484 (transformation into a bear), 6.377 (frog), 8.287 (wild boar), 14.280 (horse); Apuleius *Metamorphoses* 1.9.3 (frog).

29 Donkey: Ovid *Fasti* 1.433. Horse: Lucan *Pharsalia* 4.756. Elephant: Pliny *Natural History* 11.269.3 (comparison between trumpeting and a *tuba*). Bull: Seneca *Natural Questions*

2.27.2; Silius Italicus *Punic Wars* 5.63. For the bear and wild boar, see the preceding note on the transformation of human into animal, and also Statius *Thebaid* 11.29.

30 Owl: Seneca *Medea* 733; Ovid *Loves* 1.12.19. Crows and jackdaws: Lucretius 5.1084, 6.751; Persius *Satires* 5.11. Swans: Virgil *Aeneid* 11.458. Magpies: Ovid *Metamorphoses* 5.678. Cranes: Statius *Thebaid* 5.12. Geese: Serenus Sammonicus *Book on Medicine* 12.172. Farmyard fowl: Martial *Epigrams* 7.31.1. Unspecified birds: Virgil *Aeneid* 7.705; Ovid *Poems from Exile: Ex Ponto* 3.1.22.

31 Note, for example, Virgil *Aeneid* 6.32; Horace *Odes* 2.14.14; Ovid *Letters* 10.26; Apuleius *Metamorphoses* 6.13.4.

32 No doubt one can find an echo in Calpurnius Siculus *Eclogues* 6.63. See also the *rauca saxa* battered by masses of salty seawater in *Aeneid* 5.866 or the elegy *CLE* 273.

33 Also Silius Italicus *Punic Wars* 4.657: the rocks render the hoarse sound of the river.

34 'little imperceptible perceptions'.

11 Motion sensors

Perceiving movement in Roman pantomime

Helen Slaney

Think of Roman theatre and we think of spectacle, the imperium of the gaze. The implication is that the typical perspective adopted was that of an observer, either sitting in the crowd looking down at the stage, or zooming out for a bird's-eye view of the theatre so as to better examine its social stratification or its architectural design. A recent Bryn Mawr reviewer commented that 'trying to figure out Greek and Roman performance is like watching a fast-paced play from the restricted-view seats' (Polt, 2013). This perspective puts us in a particular relationship to the performance activity taking place in our imaginative reconstruction: we are its consumers, its voyeurs, watching the show from a privileged (or for Polt, a not so privileged) vantage point. The performers' bodies appear in this vision as pictorial elements, insubstantial and two-dimensional as the figures on a painted *scaenae frons*.

To regard ancient theatre from the performer's point of view involves making some changes to our epistemology and our language. 'Regarding' assumes a visual paradigm, and taking a 'point of view' yields only partial information. But developing a multisensory mode of engagement dissolves the paralysis of vision. Instead of looking on like spectators, we might practise a kinaesthetic mode of historical enquiry. Kinaesthesia, or our own sense of movement, enables us to represent to ourselves the corporeal experience of others (Foster, 2008). This adjustment is particularly important when considering ancient dance, in this instance *tragoedia saltata*, otherwise known as Graeco-Roman tragic pantomime, or simply *orchēsis*. Dance is notoriously difficult to pin down and is resistant to verbal description. One strategy for overcoming, or perhaps evading, this difficulty is to reconfigure *tragoedia saltata* as something you would *do* rather than watch. In this chapter traditional analysis will alternate with instructional exercises designed to prompt you to relate to *orchēsis* as a practitioner rather than as a reader-spectator.[1]

In addition to the five generally acknowledged exterior senses, the human organism constantly monitors its own internal condition via its somatosensory system, which processes information about movement, orientation, balance and exertion (see for example Damasio, 1999, especially pp. 145–61; Berthoz, 2000; Berthoz and Petit, 2008; Millar, 2008). While the operation of this system is largely automatic, conscious interpretation of the signals it circulates depends on the way we have come to experience our body interacting with the world (Damasio, 1999). Dance, for the dancer, involves a continuous stream of sense impressions other than sight. In conjunction with haptic information such as pressure or tension, the faculties of balance, spatial awareness, kinaesthetic judgement, muscular endurance and nervous responsiveness all come into play. Susan Leigh Foster describes what occurs in sensory terms as a dancer moves:

> Dancers see large portions of their own bodies, a vista that changes as they move. They hear the sounds produced by locomotion. . . . They feel the body's contact with the ground, with objects or persons, and with parts of itself, and they sense its temperature and sweat. . . . They sense kinaesthetic indications of the tension or relaxation, tautness or laxness, and degree of exertion for every muscle.
>
> (Foster, 1997, p. 237)

For the practitioner, dance consists of a constant synthesis of environmental information with feedback received from within his or her own body. For example, some kinds of pain experienced by the dancer during performance, such as muscle fatigue, simply fade into the background. Other kinds might signal that the desired limit of a stretch has been achieved; conversely, they could signal over-extension or damage. Physiologically, the dancing body of 2016 depends on the same faculties and metabolic functions as the dancing bodies of second-century CE Rome, but the individual's experience of living in this body is saturated in cultural specifics.[2] Kinaesthesia, like other senses, is conditioned by custom, habitus and the meanings attached to certain sensations. In the effort to recover this most elusive of historical sense experiences, it may be helpful for us to move (quite literally) beyond a visual and linguistic *modus cogitandi*. Although the experience itself cannot in any way be replicated, we can nevertheless process the information we possess about *orchēsis* using our own corresponding sense of kinaesthesia.

Imagining or anticipating movement does not involve creating a separate 'mental image' of that movement. Rather, the same neural apparatus used in the execution of actual, realised (overt) movements is also used when we represent unexecuted (covert) movements to ourselves (Jeannerod, 1994, 2001; Gallese and Lakoff, 2005; Berthoz and Petit, 2008, pp. 43–58). Although we can form a rough, analogical simulation of movements we have never performed ourselves (Gallese and Lakoff, 2005, p. 461), it has been shown that embodied expertise significantly affects our perception of skilled activities such as dance (Calvo-Merino, Glaser, Grèzes, Passingham and Haggard, 2005). That is, your ability to imagine (i.e. covertly simulate) movement is enhanced by performance and practice. With this in mind, you are invited here to flesh out the idea of ancient pantomime by committing some of its components to motor memory.

The sensational body

Graeco-Roman tragic pantomime was an enormously successful and highly developed art-form popular between the first and fifth centuries CE. It was essentially a form of solo ballet in which tragic or erotic scenarios drawn from classical mythology were danced by a masked performer who played each role in turn. The dancer's extraordinary polymorphism, his ability to embody a vast gallery of characters, emotions and nonhuman entities, was a skill that verged on the magical (*thelxis*), something *thaumastos*, a wonder.[3] His sensational gyrations were accompanied by musicians, a percussionist who kept time with a *scabellum* (a foot-clapper) and either a solo *cantor* or a whole chorus who sang the libretto of the piece alongside. No designated libretti or *fabulae salticae* have survived, but various extant candidates have been conjectured including Ovid's *Metamorphoses*, to which we will return below.[4] Many pantomime dancers were highly skilled professionals and some of them attained top celebrity status. The form reputedly originated in Augustan Rome but rapidly spread throughout the empire, remaining a prevalent performance medium throughout the Second Sophistic and into Late Antiquity.

Our knowledge of pantomime's choreographic content comes almost entirely from textual sources, the foremost of which is the dialogue by second-century satirist Lucian entitled *The Dance* (*peri Orchēseōs*). Lucian purports to defend pantomime against detractors who would condemn it as frivolous by treating the dancer's craft in a framework borrowed from contemporary handbooks of rhetorical training. One copious section catalogues the roles that successful dancers supposedly ought to have memorised, from 'Chaos and the creation of the world' down to historical figures such as Cleopatra (*The Dance* 37). Lucian's ideal dancer, like the ideal orator, is learned and eloquent, with a prodigious memory. His eloquence resides not in his use of language – the dancer's mask with its closed mouth attests to his muteness – but in the elaborate vocabulary of hand gestures, codified poses (*eikones*) and figures of movement incorporating the whole body (*schēmata*) that convey his narrative.[5] As Lada-Richards has shown in her study of Lucian's dialogue, professional dancers were embroiled with professional sophists in an ideological conflict over the possession and location of knowledge, specifically knowledge of classical Greece and the appropriate transmission of its legacy (2007). For the orators and grammarians, Greek culture inhered in *paideia*, the formal education program based on a canon of authors and the principle of *imitatio*.[6] It was an elite prerogative. For the dancers and their fans, meanwhile, classical Greek culture inhered in the myths of passion and pain embodied by the voluble limbs of the *pantomimos*, theoretically accessible to all.[7] This rhetorical polarisation inevitably overstates the contrast, since orators also relied on popular followings while pantomime had its connoisseurs, the *orchēstomanēsontes* (*The Dance* 85), which might translate into 'balletomanes',[8] but it is this enduring perception of theatrical dance as the disreputable *alter ego* of clean-cut masculine oratory which gives Lucian's satire its edge.[9]

The issue of how we know what we think we know about ancient culture, particularly embodied aspects such as dance, lies at the heart of this chapter. To reiterate, our ancient sources are in the main textual, albeit supplemented on occasion by iconographic analogues from the visual arts (Slaney, forthcoming; Lada-Richards, 2004). The impressions we receive, although rich in detail, are therefore necessarily disjointed, fragmentary and displaced, requiring reassembly for coherent patterns to emerge. Over the past decade a number of excellent studies have reformulated pantomime into academic prose.[10] Vital though these studies have been for rehabilitating the previously marginal phenomenon of Graeco-Roman dance and granting it the same critical rigour afforded to any other ancient performance activity, there remains a gap at the centre of our discursive scrutiny: the dancer's absent body. This absence acquires particular prominence when our subject is an archaeology of the senses. Evidently, the experiential gap can be neither ignored nor overcome. We cannot perceive the ancient dancer's own sensory world nor occupy his body, since our senses are differently attuned by cultural conditioning. Rather, this chapter proposes that alongside the translation of ancient dance into language, we might practise translating it into movement; that alternative points of sensory access to the representation of ancient culture might provide us with a notional affinity neither more nor less imaginary than that facilitated by a rendition of bodily experience circulated in printed prose.[11]

Sensory insights into pantomime are made tantalisingly immediate by both ancient authors and their modern interpreters, especially Webb's evocative portrayal of pantomime as a synthesis of visual, sonic and kinaesthetic elements (2008b). To begin with the primary articulation of muscles and joints, Galen explains that it is the dancer's training that develops his body type: 'graceful and muscular and sturdy and compact and toned' (*De Sanitate Tuenda* 2.11).[12] Although Galen's perspective is that of a physician assessing the dancer's body from the outside, we might also infer from this how it felt to inhabit and mobilise such a body. Pantomime dancers were capable of extraordinary feats: *thaumata* such as long-distance leaps, high kicks, spinning and tumbling. Their acrobatic or gymnastic abilities were likewise the product of intensive training, particularly in early childhood. The fourth-century orator Libanius describes a training regime in which the instructor, the *paidotribēs*, forcibly twists and stretches the apprentice dancer's limbs until he is able to produce fabulous contortions. The dancer's body thus becomes 'as impressionable as wax' (*Orations* 64.104). It developed pliancy and plasticity, simultaneously developing the stamina necessary to sustain a demanding physical performance. Performances may have varied in length, but a full-scale tragedy with multiple character changes could easily involve an hour or more of non-stop dynamic activity. Even if overlaid by wood,[13] his stage was certainly not the sprung floor to which modern dancers are accustomed. Its hard surface, unforgiving not only to falls but to any kind of impact, including the steps and leaps and backflips involved in pantomime, meant that a dancer's hips and knees had to absorb considerable shock.

Several other haptic and aural factors might also be considered. *Pantomimoi* wore long, diaphanous robes and a versatile silk cape called a *pallium*. Moving in a swirl of fabric that must be coordinated with the choreography so as not to impede its execution, the dancer temporarily absorbed both *pallium* and mask into his body schema.[14] Rhythm was provided by a musician wearing a *scabellum*, a metal-soled shoe that drummed against the stage platform. Other musical accompaniment included the syrinx and aulos, and possibly stringed instruments such as the cithara. The pantomime libretto was sung either by a soloist, a *cantor*, or by a chorus of voices. The dancer had to coordinate his movement to this soundtrack, embodying both the content of the lyrics and the more abstract rhythmic and melodic elements. In synchronising movement with music and lyrics, the dancer had to integrate haptic, aural and kinaesthetic information, and it was this synthesis that enabled him to generate appropriate responses, moment to moment, as his field of sensory input changed. Thus, a great deal can be ascertained in theory about the ancient dancer's sensorium; but it is now time to switch your own sensory attention away from the visual, moving into the kinaesthetic and consciously proprioceptive.

Exercise 1: Choreographic pick-'n'-mix

a) Below is a list of terms used by ancient authors to refer to a range of steps performed by *pantomimoi*, and their approximate English translations.[15] These terms represent a pitiful fraction of the choreography available to a *pantomimos*, and they are derived moreover from the non-specialist observations of spectators; we cannot know to what extent an ancient performer would conceive of his work as broken down into discrete units like this. Based on accounts of the dancer's training,[16] and by analogy with the practice of epic rhapsodes, it is more likely that dance pieces could be fashioned to suit the moment out of a repertoire of somatic formulae. This list is merely a starting point for training your own kinaesthetic imagination. Experiment with different ways of representing each movement.

pēdēmata – leaps[17]
periagōgē – spin, revolve (pirouette?)[18]
huptiasmos – back-bend / turning upside down[19]
fluctuans spinula – bending spine[20]
exapinēs epesēs – suddenly falling down[21]
oklasantes exanistanai – squat down and rise up again[22]
prossurousi ta skelē – sweep the leg/s forward (a type of kick?)[23]
diasurousi ta skelē – sweep the leg/s to the side[24]
katanankazein – to forcibly contort[25]
exaiphnēs pagios stasis – sudden rigid stillness, posing *graphikōs* (like a picture)[26]
helissein – to coil, to twist[27]
seiein – to shake, gyrate[28]
homozugoi tarsoi – soles of the feet clapped (literally 'yoked') together.[29]

Now try combining them into short, purely technical sequences (for example, *periagōgē* [1] + *oklasantes exanistanai* + *helissein* + *periagoge* [2] + *exapinēs epesēs*).

b) Next, try colouring your sequences with some of the terms for emotions or *pathē* represented in pantomime, as identified by Lucian:

> *orgē*, 'anger, rage'
> *thrēnousai, lupē, penthos*, 'to grieve', 'pain', 'sorrow'
> *zēlotupia*, 'jealousy'
> *phobos*, 'terror'
> *aidōs*, 'shame'
> *erōs*, 'love, lust'
> *mania*, 'psychosis, delusion'.[30]

Do certain emotions seem consonant with certain movements? What happens when you use the tension between apparently mismatched terms? Perhaps you find that you now want to adjust your sequences of steps, or build up some new ones.

c) Finally, using your emotionally charged sequence, imagine you are portraying one of the characters appearing in pantomime scenarios. According to Lucian, the entirety of Greek mythology is your palette, but you might like to start by contrasting a pair of figures. How would Venus perform the sequence, as opposed to Hercules; Hecuba, as opposed to Medea; or Vulcan, as opposed to Io?

Experiment with unlikely combinations. What happens when Io is jealous or Hecuba in love? Do you find it easier to match new steps to these given conditions or to flesh out a pre-existing sequence with different personae?

d) As a further extension, you may wish to incorporate the two accoutrements essential to pantomime performance: the mask and the *pallium* or cape. A plain full-face mask is best, and any large piece of fabric will do (at least 1 m²). Do you find these elements easy to integrate or do they prompt you to adjust your movement vocabulary to accommodate them? Do they augment or impede your movements?

The sensing body

How you imagine, and hence relate to, the invisible, necessarily inaccessible interior of your own body is determined by various factors: the impersonal understanding of anatomy you have gained from diagrams or other depictions, supplemented by messier visual images of surgery, wounds or autopsies; hands-on first-aid training, perhaps, or even experience of its application; you may have suffered injury or illness yourself, acute or chronic, that focused your attention on the painful (mal)functioning of an organ or a limb. More benignly, you may have disciplined your body for the performance of specific motor activities: playing a sport, playing an instrument, martial arts, yoga, dancing. The specialised coordination of movements involved in performing such activities requires deliberate training and practice. This premise might appear superficially facile, but provides an essential foundation for the exercises included in this chapter.

Methods for teaching movement vary, but most involve a visual component (observation and imitation of the instructor), a tactile component (the instructor physically manipulates or adjusts the student's posture) and an aural component (the instructor describes verbally the sensations that ought to be occurring in the student's body).[31] Practice, meanwhile, or the deliberate repetition of these learned sequences, is almost wholly proprioceptive, fostering the reflexive reproduction of these sensations in the absence of external correction. We are mainly concerned in these exercises with finding appropriate verbal stimuli for movement. In teaching dance, the instructor relies on a range of metaphors to convey an ideal version of their own musculoskeletal condition to the student and develop a mutually comprehensible vocabulary for referring to internal processes. This may not be physiologically technical, as 'produce an elongation of the fibres in your *vastus lateralis* muscle by contracting your *biceps femoralis*' may be less effective, for example, than 'demi-plié, third position' or 'place your right heel in your left instep and bend your knees'. At the same time, more figuratively, your posture might be modified by notions of squeezing your shoulder blades together or imagining yourself suspended from the ceiling by a silver thread running through your spine. Insofar as any of these directives furnishes a linguistic reference point for physical action, they are all metaphorical, as they all require translation into a somatic medium before their literal, performative meanings take shape.

With reference to the physiology of the senses that Roman pantomime stimulates, we can envisage the dancer's activity as the skilled interpretation of sensorimotor feedback. The language used by ancient authors to convey the idea of a dancing body encodes not only their spectatorial perceptions but also the performer's experience. For example, the leap (the *pēdēma*) has to begin with a preparatory contraction and end in the foot's sudden jolt of contact with the stage. The *periagōgē* ('spin') destabilises the fluid in the dancer's vestibular canals and results in temporary dizziness as his eyes and inner ear resolve their disparity. As he *prossurei* or *diasurei ta skele* (sweeps the leg/s forward or to the side), the motor neurons in the sartorius muscle that flexes his thigh monitor the rate of stretch being exerted. When he freezes in a fixed, iconic pose his acute proprioceptive faculties allow him to recognise when the familiar position has been attained. His hands are notably articulate, but he does not have to watch them to know what shapes they are forming, as his motor neurons will readily fire in patterns established by constant repetition.

Graeco-Roman dancers, however, did not conceive of their bodies as motivated by neuronal activity. Their experience of somatic functioning was conditioned (as is ours) by contemporary medical discourse. Although medicine in the early Empire comprised eclectic approaches, it was generally agreed that mind and body were interdependent: physical disease could be treated behaviourally and malaise of the spirit alleviated with medication or dietary adjustments.[32] Balance was a crucial concept and medical knowledge consisted of determining which interventions would compensate for imbalances elsewhere. Brooke Holmes observes that 'Physicians were inviting people to see themselves first and foremost as composite, labile, and often disordered physical bodies', diagnosing these bodies in accordance with 'a humoral, primarily fluid model' (Holmes, 2010, p. 90). As an ancient dance practitioner you would have been aware that your body contained bones and cartilage, muscles and tendons, and other soft tissues, but you would also have been aware that these components were all formed of basic elemental and humoral compounds in various ratios. Your mental and physical health depended on maintaining the ideal homeostatic ratio of qualities – hot and cold, wet and dry – appropriate to each component.[33] In this way your body formed a chemical microcosm of the universe around you, whose relative concentration of different elements or qualities likewise performed more or less tolerable fluctuations, forcing you to be constantly vigilant about adjusting your internal levels accordingly.[34] The following exercise invites you to conceptualise your body in humoral and elemental terms.

Exercise 2: Constituent elements

Begin by standing in a neutral position. Close your eyes. Notice how your feet are placed on the ground, where your weight is gathered, how your breath moves in and out. Become aware of your fingers. Now imagine each joint in your fingers is filling with water. Let your hand move in its new watery state and notice how this feels. Now gradually let the water move into your wrist, your elbow, your shoulder, across your shoulder blades, down your other arm; then gradually down each vertebra in your spine, through your pelvis, your knees, your ankles, your toes. Each articulation is now liquid. Move around the space. How does water travel? How does a body animated by water travel?[35]

Come to stillness. Now repeat the exercise using the following substances:

ELEMENTS: water; fire; earth; air
QUALITIES: sweet; bitter; sour; salt.[36]

Once you have established the sense of each of these constituents flooding your body in turn, you can combine them. Is salt air different from bitter air or bitter water? You can experiment with whole-body blends, infusing salt/earth or sweet/air throughout, for example; or you might place different elements in different parts of your body: can you have airy feet but watery arms? A rogue fiery elbow?

The social body

As well as formulating a sense of interior functioning founded on concepts like humoral dispersal, the *pantomimos* developed his body schema or perception of physical self in accordance with the socio-cultural discourses impinging on his praxis. The significance assigned to his body's public display in the context of performance ranged from celebrity notoriety, enviable virtuosity and erotic cynosure to servile degradation and the vulnerability of *infamia*.[37] Both of these states constitute extremes of objectification, the former reifying the dancer's glamour into an alienated professional persona and the latter reducing him to dehumanised matter by depriving him of a citizen's integrated selfhood. The paradox affecting a dancer's overall relationship to his body was the contempt associated with all types of Roman performance that coexisted with an equally fervent admiration. In the early Empire actors of all kinds were subject to *infamia*, or loss of citizen rights. Their bodies, like those of prostitutes or gladiators, were treated as commodities, even when the actors in question were not themselves slaves.[38] Later, the disapproval of Christian authorities constructed another negative psychosomatic framework. Discussing the physical impact of hate-speech, Judith Butler observes:

> One need only consider the way in which the history of having been called an injurious name is embodied, how the words enter the limbs, craft the gesture, bend the spine . . . and how these slurs accumulate over time, dissimulating their history, taking on the semblance of the natural, configuring and restricting the doxa that counts as 'reality'.
>
> (Butler, 1997, p. 159)

Imagine, then, the strain of resisting (for example) some of Tertullian's choice language as he denounces your idolatrous, *diaboli* works of pagan lust as *exsecranda* and *spurcitia*, perversions to be reviled (*On the Spectacle* 17). 'As a Christian,' he advises, 'you will despise those responsible for these despicable acts' (*Oderis, Christiane, quorum auctores non potes non odisse, On the Spectacle* 10).

The performer's transgression of gender norms as he embodied both male and female roles likewise provoked divergent responses, regarded in some quarters with disgust or suspicion, while others found his assumption of androgyny appealing, even alluring.[39] To know that your body is capable of performing at will these shifts in gender and status, recognising and eliminating the habits of movement imposed and ingrained by everyday life, is inherently empowering; but at the same time it can signal a disturbing disconnect between outer body and inner self, or raises the even more troubling concern that alterations in external form entail unavoidable repercussions in the psyche.[40] The author of the pseudo-Aristotelian *Physiognomica*, a treatise purporting to demonstrate how the nature (*physis*) of various types of people can be inferred from their appearance, certainly detects this reciprocity at work:

> It seems to me that the mind (*psychē*) and the body (*sōma*) are synchronised with each other. Changing the state of the mind alters the shape of the body, and vice versa: altering the shape of the body changes the state of the mind.
>
> (808b 12–15)[41]

A professional dancer, it is true, need not subscribe to this perception when it came to his personal identity, but his art-form dealt nevertheless in the recognisability of character types, communicated not (just) through spoken text but primarily through the disposition of his physicality.

Like elite athletes, pantomime dancers were encouraged to measure their bodies against a standard of perfection: medium height, lean build but not too thin, limber and flexible or what Galen calls *suntonos*, toned and muscular (*De Sanitate Tuenda* 2.11). Dancers who did not match this ideal could be jeered offstage. Lucian relates a succession of anecdotes in which dancers are verbally abused by spectators for their stature and weight, mocked for attempting to play characters who do not correspond to their body type, for lankiness or landing too heavily or appearing cadaverous (*The Dance* 76). Unlike ballet, pantomime did not necessarily exert pressure on dancers to lose weight, but rather to achieve a physique like that of Polykleitan sculpture (*The Dance* 75).[42] Nevertheless, the self-consciousness engendered by deliberately cultivating such an appearance – not to mention the public embarrassment of failing to conform – affected the dancer's relationship to his body in that he was constantly prompted to assess its exterior aesthetic impact as well as its interior athletic function.

Exercise 3: Physiognomies (caricatures)

This exercise allows you to experience how status and identity were imprinted on the body, according to ancient perceptions of posture. It may be useful to work with a partner so that you can juxtapose contrasting attitudes. Once you have established each posture, take time to move around inside this body; note how changing one part of your anatomy activates changes elsewhere. You may wish to interact non-verbally with your partner and see how your respective states affect one another.

1a) Servility. Elevate and contract the shoulders, hunching your back. According to Quintilian, this will produce a stance 'somewhat ingratiating and servile and rather deceitful, in which fear shapes itself into the guise of admiration' (*Institutes of Oratory* 11.3.83).

1b) *Eleutheria* (freedom). If, on the other hand, the shoulders are *eulutoi*, loose and supple, this indicates freedom in the soul (Pseudo-Aristotle *Physiognomics* 811). Allow your shoulders to drop, and feel a corresponding sense of expansion across your collarbone: releasing your clavicles permits the free circulation of sensations (*aisthēseai*), keeping you alert and presenting an open front to the world.

2a) *Andreia* (masculine bravery). The carriage is upright (*orthos*).[43] Think Polykleitos' 'Doryphoros'.

2b) *Deileia* (cowardice). Note that this need not be the same as fear. These states are *dianoiai*, underlying dispositions, rather than *pathē*, transient responses to stimuli. The body of a coward is typically *sungkekathikos* or stooping, perhaps with bent knees (*Physiognomics* 807b).

3) Femininity. The *Physiognomics* suggests a mincing gait, walking with the feet *exestrammenois*, 'turned out' (813a). Davies shows how sculptural representations of men typically adopt a dominant 'macho sprawl' – compare our stances for *andreia* and *eleutheria*, above – while women typically attempt to reduce the space they take up, folding their arms across their bodies, lowering their gaze and possibly walking on tiptoe (Davies, 2005; see also Llewellyn Jones, 2005 on feminine body language in ancient Greek theatre).

4) Evil. A bent back and stooped shoulders indicates malignance (*kakoētheia*) because it hides from view the front parts of the body that ought to be fully and honestly visible, implying you have something to hide (*Physiognomics* 810).

5) *Anaideia* (impudence). The schema, the position of the body, is upright, *orthos*, but inclined rather forward, the shoulders sloping or drooping, *propetesteros*, a word which can also refer to flowing rhythms in music (*Physiognomics* 807b). If *anaideia* is interpreted as sexually provocative, this could be combined with an undulating motion of the hips and/or torso, *kallabis*,[44] and a coquettish inclination of the head to one side. Alternatively, the head thrown back reads as arrogance (Quintilian *Institutes of Oratory* 11.3.69). Pseudo-Aristotle also specifies that shameless movements are quick or sharp, *oxus*.

6) Depression. Again, like cowardice, this is an underlying *dianoia* rather than an acute attack of grief. The body's schema is *tapeinos*, low or abjected, and the movements you perform should be *apēgoreukōs*, weary or worn out (*Physiognomics* 808a).

The protean body

By all accounts, one of the most thrilling and unsettling properties of pantomime was the dancer's apparent capacity for transformation, not merely in assuming the body-types of other human beings but even more radically compromising his very identity as human. For Lucian, this provides a rationalising explanation for the myth of Proteus:

> The ancient myth, it seems to me, says that Egyptian Proteus was none other than a mortal mimetic dancer (*orchestēn mimētikon*) who presented all kinds of figures and had such power of transformation that he could imitate the liquidity (*hygrotēta*) of water, the rapidity (*oxytēta*) of fire with the vigour of his movements, the ferocity (*agriotēta*) of the lion and boldness (*thumon*) of the panther and the wavering (*donēma*) of leaves – in short, whatever he likes. And the myth takes up his physical nature and describes it as something supernatural, saying that he truly became that which he imitated. This persists even among dancers today, and you might on occasion see them performing swift transitions in imitation of Proteus himself.
>
> (Lucian, *The Dance* 19)[45]

This passage suggests that inanimate elements joined animals and gods in the dancer's repertoire, and that their embodiment was predicated upon characteristic qualities of *kinēsis*: fluid and flowing for water, sharp and staccato for flames, and animals identified by typical rhythmic or energetic essences rather than attempting to distinguish between (say) breeds of big cats on the basis of documentary observation. Instead of presenting the visual appearance of a lion, the dancer connects kinaesthetically with the associated attribute of *agriotēs*, thereby enabling himself to assume a more polysemous and hence more evocative or resonant corporeal state.

Ovid's *Metamorphoses* stands out as a potential source for pantomime libretti, displaying considerable overlap with the catalogue of metamorphic plots supplied by Lucian (Garelli, 2007). Ovid himself writes that his *poemata* were being 'danced' in Roman public theatres around the time of his exile (c. 8–9 CE) (*Tristia* 2.519, 5.7.25).[46] A century of so later, Lucian attests to the preoccupation of pantomime with 'the amours of the gods, above all those of Zeus' (*The Dance* 59) and, more tellingly, with 'all the mythic metamorphoses, those who were changed into trees and beasts and birds, and women who became men' (*The Dance* 57).[47] Even if the lyrics of the accompanying libretti were adapted, the interests of pantomime converged substantially with the content of Ovid's text.[48]

Instances of transformation, and the physical processes of change involved, place particular emphasis on the *pantomimos*' subversive condition of somatic instability. Even within a role he hovers on the edge of morphic collapse, scrupulously maintaining the lineaments of character and the illusion that his body is something other than itself. Or is it so illusory? Held in a temporary alterity sustained by concrete musculoskeletal effort, the *pantomimos*, for the duration of performance, reshapes and resculpts himself.[49] The proprioceptive feedback he receives informs him not that his body is simply moving neutrally in space but that its singular organisation moment to moment, its shifting organic geometry, make it constantly capable of and vulnerable to change. Pantomime fosters a sense that the body is unstable, that the skin does not quite contain its potential configurations, that at any moment the bounded self might dissolve and slip into something more comfortable. The dancer's corporeal identity, the selfhood that is coextensive with his kinaesphere, is at once more firmly defined and more malleable than most of ours. It is more defined because the dancer's training has produced a keener awareness of his physical potential and its limitations; more malleable, because it transforms as he dances, when he infuses himself with the grace of Aphrodite, the brawn of Hercules, the frenzy and horror of Agave, Callisto becoming a bear, Alcyon a bird and Niobe indistinguishable from stone. The dancer's mutability, paradoxically, is essential to his identity, implicated as he is in the professional manufacture of sensations.

Exercise 4: Metamorphosis

'I'm in the mood for singing of physical forms reshaped into new / bodies.'[50] Here are five metamorphoses to try out. You can draw on previous exercises or simply attempt to capture the various sensations of water, bark, smoke, wings and bestial ferocity.

9.649–65

Exhausted by running,
you gave up and lay with your hair spread out on the hard earth,
Byblis, pressing your lips to the fallen leaves.
Silent she lay, pulling up the green plants with her fingernails,

Byblis, and flooded the grass with a river of tears.
After a while, like droplets of pine resin out of cut bark
or viscous bitumen seeping thickly from the earth,
or waves which had been frozen solid softened, melted
by the gentle sun and the return of the west wind's breath,
consumed by her own tears, Apollonian Byblis
turned into a fountain. Even now it bears her name
as it flows through those valleys under the black shade of holm-oaks.

1.232–39

Terrified, he fled, and having reached the silence of the countryside,
he howled aloud and tried in vain to speak.
From his mouth came slaver. With his usual love of slaughter
he turned on the flocks and rejoiced in their blood.
His clothes disappeared into fur, his forearms into shinbones:
he became a wolf, but still retained traces of his former self.
His grizzled hair and savage demeanour were the same,
the same light glinted in his eyes, and he gave the same impression of ferocity.

10.488–98

Her prayers in extremis
must have reached the gods. For as she spoke,
the earth crept up over her legs, and out from under her torn-off fingernails
roots came twisting, propping up her elongated trunk;
her bones became wood, but their core of marrow remained;
her blood became sap, her arms great branches,
her fingers twigs, skin hardening to bark.
Now the rising tree constricts her burdened womb,
swallows her breast, and prepares to encase her neck.
She couldn't bear to wait for it. Into the rising tide of wood
she dived, submerging herself in the bark closing over her face.

13.600–611

With an updraft of flame
Memnon's steep pyre collapsed, and a plume of dark smoke
tinged the daylight, as when rivers exhale
floating mists that the sun cannot penetrate.
The black ashes flew. Coalescing, they condensed into a single
body, taking on form and heat
and spirit from the fire. Weightlessness made it feathery.
First like a bird, then as a bird in truth,
it beat its wings. And with it beat countless sister-birds,
all born from the same source.

Three times over they circled the funeral pyre, and into the air
rose their harmonious keening, three times over.

14.59–67

Scylla walked into the trap. She'd immersed herself up to the waist [in the pool]
when suddenly her lower half became a foul mass of barking monsters.
When she saw them, she could not believe they were part
of her body, and fled and tried in her terror to drive them away,
the upturned muzzles of dogs; but as she ran, she dragged them with her.
Seeking her own limbs among them, in place of her thighs and calves and feet
she found the jaws of hell-hounds.
She stood on a pack of slavering dogs, conjoined to the backs of the beasts,
her groin and trunk and belly emerging, surrounded.

Some conclusions

No two sensory experiences are the same. This need not, however, lead us
away from investigating lived experience in favour of its more accessible textual
constructions. The point of the exercises offered in this chapter is not the creation of some fallacious trans-temporal rapport, however powerfully they may
appear to lure the imagination towards seizing on psychophysical correspon-
dences. Rather, I hope to have shown that antiquity can be mediated through
something other than reportage. Embodied mediation does not concentrate on
developing a more accurate verbal discourse, but instead attempts to develop a
different attitude or mode of relating in ourselves to the mute fact that dance
once occurred. As a thought experiment, this approach prompts us to question our own sensory and somatic relationships to classical antiquity, and hence
our cognitive relationship to its residue. An ephemeral act like *tragoedia saltata*
can never be reconstituted in its entirety as all we have access to is a handful of
arbitrary encounters relayed through the textual record. Nevertheless, we can
select a perspective from which these sense impressions might be reintegrated,
and if that perspective includes a visual dimension (which it invariably does),
can it not also legitimately include an embodied or a proprioceptive dimension?
James Porter proposes that

> Our viewpoint on antiquity today may be in some sense theoretical, in the
> radical sense of being spectatorial and removed from the scene. . . . But it
> is impossible to reach back without reaching within, by way of our own
> bodies . . . into the dark matter of the body within.
>
> (1999, p. 14)

It is unavoidably within our own bodies, our own somatically embedded neural
systems, that knowledge of ancient dance (whatever that may consist of) is to be
found. When analysing the Roman world we have the option of occupying not
only an imagined vantage point, but also an imagined body.

Notes

1 The instructional approach is derived from Turocy (2013), who applies it to reconstructions of baroque dance. The exercises in this chapter have been developed over the course of the practice-based research project Ancient Dance in Modern Dancers (University of Oxford, 2013–16).

2 On the principle that sense experience is culturally embedded, see for example Classen 1993, 2012; Smith, 2007; and articles collected in Classen, 2005 and Howes, 2005a.

3 Lucian *The Dance* 85 on *thelxis*; on amazement, Libanius *Orations* 64.104 (θαυμασιωτέρας καμπὰς) and Aristaenetus *Epistles*1.26 (τίς οὐ τεθαύμακεν ὀρχουμένην).

4 On Ovid see Lada-Richards, 2013. Other possibilities are Seneca's tragedies (Slaney, 2013; Dodson-Robinson, 2011, building on Zimmermann, 2008 and Zanobi, 2008, 2013) and the anonymous 'Barcelona *Alcestis*' (Hall, 2008).

5 μετὰ δὲ τῆς στάσεως ἡ εἰκὼν ἀπαντᾷ (Libanius *Orations* 64.118); Plutarch *Moralia* 747B-E distinguishes between *schēmata* – iconic poses which start and finish a sequence of movement – and *phora*, the movement sequences which represent actions, emotions or possibilities, but Lawler compares the word's usage in other sources and defines *schemata* on this basis as 'brief, distinctive patterns which were visible in the course of a dance, some of them lasting but a few seconds, others longer' (1964, p. 25).

6 For the context of *paideia*, see Whitmarsh, 2005.

7 'While he [the sophist], the proud guardian of Hellenic heritage, sweats out his linguistic skills in order to bring forth a verbal pageant of past glories, the pantomime lives the past *within and through his body*: silencing its distinctive Attic voice, the dancer acts out a classical inheritance 'made carnal', an image of Greekness reduced to flesh.'
(Lada-Richards, 2007, p. 109, emphasis original)
Lucian's anecdotes suggest that anyone can understand pantomime language but this may not in fact be the case; Augustine's remarks in *On Christian Doctrine* 2.25.38 imply that interpreting the form does seem to require a certain level of 'literacy'.

8 Lada-Richards (2013, p. 115) glosses *orchēstomanēsontes* as 'pantomaniacs'.

9 On oratory's use of theatricality as a foil in order to police its masculinity see Gleason, 1995; Gunderson, 2000; Fantham, 2002.

10 The comprehensive historical account of the art-form's development by Garelli (2007) is offset by Webb (2008a), who stresses the volatility of mime and pantomime as sites where everyday customs of movement could be transgressed. Molloy's (1996) commentary on Libanius' *Oration* 64 (another rather tongue-in-cheek tribute to pantomime's moral merit) pays particular attention to issues of sexuality. The contributions collected in Hall and Wyles (2008) address diverse aspects of praxis, social significance and conceptual application; another recent compilation, Macintosh (2010) examines pantomime's reception from baroque ballet through Emma Hamilton's 'Grecian Attitudes' to Isadora Duncan.

11 In this respect, my approach here differs fundamentally from that of Webb (2008b). Phenomenological treatments of performing ancient drama from a modern practitioner's perspective include Harrop (2010) and Montgomery Griffiths (2010).

12 λεπτὸν καὶ μυῶδες καὶ σκληρὸν καὶ πυκνὸν ἔτι τε σύντονον ἀποτελοῦσι τὸ σῶμα.

13 Libanius' opponent is concerned about the stage's 'wooden boards' (ὑπὲρ τῶν ξύλων, *Orations* 64.96); but Wyles (2008, p. 67) cites Syriac author Jacob of Sarugh describing the stage floor as 'marble' or 'stone'.

14 Wyles discusses the 'sense of unity between the performer's body and costume' operating in pantomime (2008, p. 81).

15 This list is by no means exhaustive, but gives some of the more precise and/or evocative terms. A much more extensive list may be found in Naerebout, 1997, pp. 280–9, but it covers all types of Greek dance and only a few of its terms pertain to pantomime.

16 On which see Webb, 2008a, pp. 91–3.

17 Lucian *The Dance* 71. Compare *hallonesthai megista*, 'perform great leaps/jumps' (Galen *De Sanitate Tuenda* 2.11).

18 Lucian, *The Dance* 71. Compare *periphora*, 'whirling, spinning' (Libanius *Orations* 64.118); *peridinēsi*, 'spin, rotation' (Galen *De Sanitate Tuenda* 2.11).

19 Lucian *The Dance* 71; compare Nonnus *Dionysiaca* 19.277–9.

20 Apuleius *Metamorphoses* 10.32. Compare *declinans pectora*, 'bending the torso' (*Latin Anthology* 20.1).

21 *Greek Anthology* 11.254.4.

22 Galen *De Sanitate Tuenda* 2.11.

23 Galen *De Sanitate Tuenda* 2.11.

24 Galen *De Sanitate Tuenda* 2.11.

25 Libanius *Orations* 64.104. Compare *intorta gesticulatio*, 'convulsive/convoluted gesture' (Apuleius, *Metamorphoses* 10.31).

26 Libanius *Orations* 64.118. Compare *adstare*, 'to freeze' (*Latin Anthology* 100.7). *Graphikōs*: Plutarch *Moralia* 747C; Libanius also compares the dancer to a *graphē* (*Orations* 64.116).

27 Nonnus *Dionysiaca* 19.269. Compare *strophē*, 'twist, turn, change of direction' (Lucian *The Dance* 71).

28 Nonnus *Dionysiaca* 19.269.

29 Nonnus *Dionysiaca* 19.269.

30 All citations from Lucian *The Dance*: ὀργὴ: 46 and 67; πένθος: 41 and 58; θρηνοῦσαι: 55; λύπη: 67; ζηλοτυπία: 50; φοβουμένη: 67; αἰδουμένη: 63; ἐρῶντα: 67; μεμηνότα: 67.

31 In the case of body awareness training techniques such as Feldenkreis, the verbal prompts take the form of questions that draw the student's attention to particular motor-neuronal pathways.

32 On medical eclecticism, see Garrison, 2010, pp. 17–18. Aelius Aristides' *Hieroi Logoi / Sacred Tales* bear contemporary witness to the variety of approaches to healing.

33 Galen's *De Temperamentis* discusses *passim* the need to maintain appropriate concentrations of heat, cold, dryness and moisture in different parts of the body (see McFarlane, 2010). On the later development of a precise correlation between humours and temperaments, see Bos, 2009, especially pp. 35–7.

34 The Hippocratic writings stress the balance of humoral components (*On the Nature of Human Beings* 29.4–1–7) and environmental factors in illness (*Airs, Waters, Places*).

35 This exercise is based on Butoh principles.

36 γλυκύς, πικρός, ὀξύς, ἅλς respectively (Hippocrates *On the Nature of Human Beings* 29–30).

37 Edwards (1997) shows *infamia* applying to all types of performing artists, including dancers. Members of the equestrian and senatorial orders were barred from pantomime performance (see Slater, 1994).

38 On the social status of dancers see Webb, 2008b, pp. 50–7; Molloy, 1996, pp. 70–1.

39 See especially Juvenal *Satires* 6.63–5; on the erotic attraction of dancers more generally: Galen *On Prognosis* 14.500–715; Apuleius, *Metamorphoses* 10.31. Webb conjectures that 'the language of sexuality and the demonic [in relation to dance] is . . . a means of talking about other things' (2008a, pp. 142–3), such as the physical magnetism of a dancing body and the dangerous appeal of mimesis.

40 The *locus classicus* for this view is Plato's *Republic*, but see Webb, 2008a, pp. 151–90 on its contribution to early Christian mistrust of pantomime.

41 Δοκεῖ δέ μοι ἡ ψυχὴ καὶ τὸ σῶμα συμπαθεῖν ἀλλήλοις· καὶ ἡ τῆς ψυχῆς ἕξις ἀλλοιουμένη συναλλοιοῖ τὴν τοῦ σώματος μορφήν, πάλιν τε ἡ τοῦ σώματος μορφὴ ἀλλοιουμένη συναλλοιοῖ τὴν τῆς ψυχῆς ἕξιν.

42 Although compare Libanius *Orations* 64.103–6.

43 τὸ σχῆμα τοῦ σώματος ὀρθόν (*Physiognomics* 807a).

44 Lawler lists the *kallabis* along with several other (comic) movements, 'the essential characteristic of which was a rotation of the hips and abdomen' (1964, p. 133).

45 δοκεῖ γάρ μοι ὁ παλαιὸς μῦθος καὶ Πρωτέα τὸν Αἰγύπτιον οὐκ ἄλλο τι ἢ ὀρχηστήν τινα γενέσθαι λέγειν, μιμητικὸν ἄνθρωπον καὶ πρὸς πάντα σχηματίζεσθαι καὶ μεταβάλλεσθαι δυνάμενον, ὡς καὶ ὕδατος *ὑγρότητα* μιμεῖσθαι καὶ πυρὸς *ὀξύτητα* ἐν τῇ τῆς κινήσεως σφοδρότητι καὶ λέοντος *ἀγριότητα* καὶ παρδάλεως *θυμὸν* καὶ δένδρου *δόνημα*, καὶ ὅλως ὅ τι καὶ θελήσειεν. ὁ δὲ μῦθος παραλαβὼν πρὸς τὸ παραδοξότερον τὴν φύσιν αὐτοῦ διηγήσατο, ὡς γιγνομένου ταῦτα ἅπερ ἐμιμεῖτο. ὅπερ δὴ καὶ τοῖς νῦν ὀρχουμένοις πρόσεστιν, ἴδοις τ᾿ ἂν οὖν αὐτοὺς πρὸς τὸν καιρὸν ὠκέως διαλλαττομένους καὶ αὐτὸν μιμουμένους τὸν Πρωτέα.

46 *mea sunt populo saltata poemata saepe* (*Tristia* 2.519); *carmina quod pleno saltari nostra theatro* (*Tristia* 5.7.25).

47 Lucian makes specific reference to Tiresias (Ovid *Metamorphoses* 3.314–36) and Caenis (*Metamorphoses* 12.171–209).

48 Ingleheart argues for the *Metamorphoses* as a 'natural source for pantomime libretti' and examines the pantomimic potential of episodes such as Daphne, Iphis and Althaea (2008, p. 209). Lada-Richards argues conversely that Ovid and other authors 'appropriated the hugely popular corporeal idioms of the pantomime stage' (2013, p. 133). For Murray, Ovid provides 'the ultimate in anthropo-metamorphosis' (1998, p. 80).

49 Lada-Richards (2004) examines instances of the *pantomimos*' comparison to painting and sculpture.

50 *In nova fert animus mutatas dicere formas/corpora* (Ovid *Metamorphoses* 1.1–2). Translations of these passages are my own.

12 Scents of place and colours of smell

Fragranced entertainment in ancient Rome

Jo Day[1]

Roland Auguet, an early scholar of the Roman games, describes the practice that we know by the Latin term *sparsiones*:

> Spectators were revived with perfumed water with which the whole enclosure was sprayed and which was even supplied to the upper tiers through a system of pipes. The air was stuffy and saturated with dust. . . . The freshness of the droplets loosened throats and once more the trumpets sounded.
>
> (Auguet, 1972, p. 55)

Mentioned in numerous literary sources and usually translated as 'sprinklings', *sparsiones* refers to perfumed liquids that were somehow sprayed over the audience in amphitheatres and theatres. This idea of simultaneously refreshing the crowd and covering up the stench of people, animals, blood and death has been reiterated by other scholars. Mahoney explains the practice as 'sprinkling of scented water on the sand and on the crowd, to make people cooler and to cover up the smell of blood' (2001, p. 107), while to Jacobelli it was 'to mitigate heat and lessen odours of beasts and crowd' (2003, p. 36). Cooling, fragranced sprinklings have become intertwined with how we think about entertainment in the Roman world, but the concept needs to be more closely examined, both in terms of what actually happened, and also because thinking about *sparsiones* within the theoretical framework of sensory studies can shed new light on the practice.

Scholarship on the Roman games is now extensive and covers all aspects of the spectacles, from general sourcebooks and surveys (Futrell, 2006; Christensen and Kyle, 2013) to specific elements, such as gladiatorial combat or *munera* (Wiedemann, 1992; Jacobelli, 2003), animal hunts or *venationes* (Lindstrøm, 2010; Epplett, 2013), criminal executions (Coleman, 1990), aquatic displays (Coleman, 1993), amphitheatres (Bomgardner, 2000; Welch, 2007) and psychology (Fagan, 2011). The importance of the gaze and vision at Roman spectacles has been explored by Parker (1999), Hekster (2005) and Bergmann (2008). This richness of scholarship can at least partly be explained by the wide range of sources that can be employed in investigating *ludi* and *munera*, including literature, inscriptions, architecture, mosaics, wall paintings, tombstones, weapons and osteology. Nibley (1945) and Simon (2008) both explored the wider practice of distributing gifts at Roman entertainments (*sparsio missilium*) but, apart from the entry in the venerable Daremberg and Saglio (1873–1919, pp. 1418–19), only Fleury (2008) has focused on the liquid sprinklings. *Sparsiones*, therefore, have not received attention comparable to other aspects of the games, and have not been considered in the context of sensory studies. The time is ripe to look more closely at these fragranced and colourful sprinklings.

This chapter will focus on olfaction in particular, as well as vision, exploring *sparsiones* as delivering both colour and smell to a performance and its audience, and as a way of making scents visible. It is not suggested here that olfactory ways of knowing were dominant in the Roman period (although cultures have been known to privilege osmologies; see Almagor, 1987); rather, that the combination of the scent and visual effects of the *sparsiones* defined their significance at the games.

Sparsiones

Missilia

The terminology requires some clarification as two types of *sparsiones* are referred to in Latin texts and inscriptions. The first is the *sparsio missilium* (or *missilia*). These were small gifts or tokens to be exchanged for gifts that were scattered amongst the crowd at circuses, theatres and amphitheatres. For example, Statius refers at length to treats such as nuts and pastries raining down on spectators at the December kalends (*Silvae* 1.6.9–24). When Nero hosted the Ludi Maximi, he provided a wide range of *missilia*, from birds to food to vouchers for clothes, gold, and even ships and farms (Suetonius *Nero* 11). The delivery system for the gifts appears to have been a system of ropes, pulleys and nets or baskets that ran across the *cavea*, opening to dispense *sparsiones* onto the crowd below (Killeen, 1959). Martial mentions this *linea dives*:

> Each day has its gifts. The wealthy cord takes no holiday and ample plunder falls into the crowd. Now come sportive tokens in sudden showers, now the lavish coupon bestows the animals they have been watching, now birds are happy to fill safe laps and find masters in absence by lot, lest they'll be torn apart.
>
> (*Epigrams* 8.78)

This elaborate mechanical system has been tentatively identified in a mid-first-century CE wall painting from Pompeii (Killeen, 1959) (Figure 12.1). Maiuri suggested it represented fruit and flowers that might fall from the ceiling onto guests at a *convivium* (Maiuri, 1953, p. 126 and p. 130), although Killeen prefers to see it as the *linea dives*. Simon notes another Pompeian depiction of this in the *tablinum* of the *Casa della Caccia Antica*, where its association with scenes relating to the theatre and amphitheatre strengthens her proposal (Simon, 2008,

Figure 12.1 Wall painting of *linea dives* from Pompeii
Source: Drawing by Ella Hassett, after Maiuri, 1953, p. 126

p. 777). *Missilia* are also referred to in inscriptions advertising forthcoming entertainments, such as the day of games '*cum missilibus*' promised by a magistrate at Rusicada in Numidia (*CIL* VIII.7960). These acts of largesse by the emperor or magistrate contributed to an appearance of a munificent ruler bestowing the riches of empire upon the crowd, while the random nature of their distribution alludes to the role of Fortuna in life (Simon, 2008). Undoubtedly, whatever gifts rained down from on high added to the smells, sounds, colours and tastes of the shows, but the focus of this chapter is the less well-studied liquid *sparsiones*.

Liquid sparsiones

References to liquid *sparsiones* occur in a wide range of literary sources, from poetry to letters to histories, but always in relation to events in Rome. Chronologically, they span the first century BCE to the early second century CE, although there are infrequent later references also, such as in the *Historia Augusta*. Unsurprisingly, this timeframe parallels the development of permanent buildings for dramatic productions and gladiatorial games in Rome, as well as the increasing prominence of *munera* and *venationes* amongst the city's entertainments. The first permanent stone theatre in Rome was that of Pompey, inaugurated in 55 BCE, while the Flavian amphitheatre (better known now as the Colosseum) was opened during the reign of Titus in 80 CE. Temporary wooden buildings continued to be used for *ludi scaenici* and *spectacula* into the second century CE. Two characteristics of liquid *sparsiones* are continually highlighted by the ancient sources: their colour and their fragrance, both of which seem to have been provided by saffron (*crocus, crocum* or plural *croci*). Pliny the Elder writes, 'But with wine, especially with sweet wine, powdered saffron makes a wonderful mixture to spray the theatre' (*Natural History* 21.17). These traits will be explored in detail below, as well as the reasons why saffron in particular was deemed appropriate.

Sparsiones delivery systems

Mechanical distribution

Before focusing on the multisensory effects of *sparsiones*, the potential delivery systems must be examined, as spraying a theatre or amphitheatre with liquid requires some ingenious engineering. Fronto notes that 'saffron-water is sprinkled broadcast and high in the theatre' (*On Eloquence* 1.12). This brief description offers no clues as to how this might have been done, although saying that the water goes 'high' suggests some kind of force propelling it upwards and/or outwards. Seneca refers to 'a process for spraying saffron perfumes to a tremendous height from hidden pipes' (*Letters* 90.15), as well as providing a more detailed description of the mechanism used to pump these fragrant and coloured liquids around buildings:

> Take the jet of water that grows from the bottom of the centre of the arena and goes all the way to the top of the amphitheatre – do you think this happens without air tension? Yet neither the hand nor any sort of mechanical device can emit or force water out the way air can. The water responds to the air. It is raised up by the air, which is inserted in the pipe and forces it up.
>
> (*Natural Questions* 2.9.2)

Seneca is probably referring to what is called a force pump, siphon or Ctesibian machine, named after its Hellenistic inventor (Figure 12.2). Vitruvius provides valuable detail on this device, saying it is for raising water to great heights and explaining how it works through a system of pipes, valves and pistons (*On Architecture* 10.7.1–3).[2] Siphons such as these are thought to have been used by the *vigiles* in Rome (Oleson, 1984, p. 323; Fleury and Madeleine, 2010, p. 73), although problems with both their portability and the relatively poor water pressure have led to doubts about their usefulness for fire-fighting (Daremberg and Saglio, 1873–1919, p. 1352). Neither of these would have been a problem, however, if lightly sprinkling a crowd or stage was all that was required.

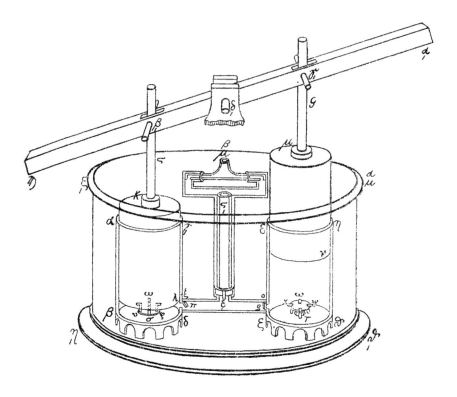

Figure 12.2 Force pump

Source: Schmidt, W., 1899. *Herons von Alexandria: Druckwerke und Automatentheater*, Leipzig: B.G. Teubner. Fig. 29

Other mechanical devices played important roles at entertainments, such as the hoists for lifting animals and scenery into the arena (Wilson, 2008, p. 361) and the *hydraulis* or water organ, also credited to Ctesibius and evident in depictions of the games, such as the gladiator mosaic from Zliten (Dunbabin, 1978, Pl. XX). The *sparsiones* systems are not depicted in iconography. The fresco showing the riot in the amphitheatre at Pompeii shows no such pumps, and coins featuring amphitheatres likewise do not depict any such systems, but the small scale of these images would surely have prohibited any such representation. Archaeology has not identified, to date, any definite *in situ* remains of pumps in entertainment buildings either. One reported example, that has since disintegrated, came from the subterranean level of the Trier amphitheatre, but was probably used to keep the chambers below ground dry (Oleson, 1984, pp. 275–6) rather than for dispensing *sparsiones*. Wooden and bronze remains of force pumps are more commonly recovered from wells, mines and drains (Oleson, 1984, p. 303; Stein, 2004), which is unsurprising as anything that was part of the superstructure of a wooden building rather than a stone one is unlikely to have survived.

This lack of definitive evidence is exacerbated by the fact that water had a range of other uses in amphitheatres and theatres. It was essential for quenching the thirst of the crowds and animals, and supplying latrines, as well as cleaning up after *venationes* or *munera*, never mind any kind of actual aquatic games or fountain displays. The archaeological remains of the systems that provided this essential water include reservoirs, channels and basins, features that could also have supplied a *sparsiones* system, thus making certain identification more difficult. For example, the excavator of the theatre at Corinth reported a first-century CE 'long shallow basin which extended across the entire orchestra a little distance in front of the *pulpitum*. That this served as a reservoir for *sparsiones* . . . may hardly be doubted' (Stillwell, 1952, pp. 41–2). His certainty notwithstanding, there is no explanation for how liquid got into this basin, nor how it was dispersed from there into the crowd. While we might imagine a series of pumps manned by slaves stationed along its 20 m length, it could just as easily have been related to drainage or drinking water. A similar basin in the orchestra of the large theatre at Pompeii, fed by a tank located between the theatre and the Triangular Forum, has been suggested for *sparsiones*, but again proof is lacking (Mau, 1899, p. 146; Sear, 2006, p. 130).

The reservoirs at the top of the four distinctive exterior staircases of the amphitheatre in Pula, Croatia, have been suggested '*à fournir l'eau nécessaire à des sparsiones*' (Golvin, 1988, p. 172). The amphitheatre at Verona, one of only two known to have had basins for water in the arena, features conduits that may in some way have fed a *sparsiones* system (Golvin, 1988, p. 169, n. 96; Dodge, 2011, p. 67). It is tempting to wonder about the network that brought water to the upper levels of the *cavea* of many other amphitheatres. In the Colosseum lead pipes were built into spaces below stairs and recesses in walls in order to carry water up through the structure (Lombardi, 2001, p. 238), emerging as fountains or latrines on the various upper levels. Did any of this piped water spray down over the spectators? The upper stories of most amphitheatres do not survive, and lead pipes or other mechanical devices have been looted or destroyed. For now, it has to be concluded that there is no definite archaeological evidence anywhere of any kind of mechanical *sparsiones* distribution system.

Manual distribution

An alternative, simpler solution to mechanical systems is that liquid sprinklings were dispensed manually. At the circus, *spartores* or 'sprinklers' dispersed liquids by hand. This job title is known from two inscriptions recording the various members of a *familia quadrigaria*, one from the Augustan era (*CIL* VI.10046), the other Domitianic in date (*ILS* 5313). These figures can be recognised in mosaics of the circus, where men holding amphorae, jugs or basins stand at the edge of the track, usually wearing short tunics in their faction's colours (Nelis-Clément, 2002, pp. 278–81). The small circus mosaic from Piazza Armerina and several examples from Carthage feature these *spartores* (Dunbabin, 1978, pp. 89–95). Figures interpreted as *spartores* have also been identified on children's circus sarcophagi from the second century CE onwards (D'Ambra, 2007), where they lie entangled beneath horses' hooves, indicating the dangerous nature of their job. A statue from Carthage of a man carrying an amphora and wearing a short, belted tunic is also most likely a *spartor* (Thuillier, 1999).

What was the role of these 'sprinklers'? One suggestion is that their water sprays were aimed at the chariots to reduce the risk of fire from friction or to keep the wheel spokes tight (Harris, 1974, pp. 34–5). Others suggest their job was to refresh the horses or to remove the breath-inhibiting dusty foam that would build up in their mouths after the requisite seven laps of the track (Humphrey, 1986, p. 393; Nelis-Clément, 2002, p. 280). *Spartores* are not visible in iconography of other forms of entertainment, nor mentioned in relevant texts, but it has been suggested that slaves carrying flagons of scented liquids might have passed through the *cavea*, filling the building with fragrance (Coleman, 2006, p. 47).

Multisensory sprinklings

Cooling

Whilst we may not understand fully the delivery system of the *sparsiones*, implicit in many academic references to them is the idea that they served to cool the air inside a building, akin to the modern outdoor air conditioning systems that work by misting the atmosphere. Ancient sources, however, never actually specify air cooling as a primary goal or even side-effect of *sparsiones*. This mistaken belief probably derives from a passage in Valerius Maximus describing luxurious additions to entertainments in Rome: 'Cn. Pompeius led the way in tempering summer heat with water flowing in channels' (2.4.6). There are two problems with relating this passage to *sparsiones*. Firstly, commentators assume this must refer to a system inside Pompey's theatre in the Campus Martius, but Valerius Maximus does not specify this location. Madeleine (2007) suggests it is more likely that the water channels were to be found outside the theatre, in the associated Porticus Pompeiana behind the stage building.[3] The second problem is a more practical one: is it possible to provide flowing water in channels inside a theatre so that it can refresh spectators without making too much noise or wetting everyone (Madeleine, 2007, pp. 84–5)? Pumps and other machinery would be necessary to make the water circulate, producing noise and possibly being rather unsightly in so beautiful a building. Not only does it seem unlikely that Pompey would have included such a disruptive system, but no archaeological traces of it have been discovered within the theatre.

A second source for this idea of refreshing *sparsiones* comes from *edicta munera*, the painted advertisements for forthcoming spectacles, in which the delights awaiting the crowd are highlighted, such as the number of gladiators or beasts. Philippe Fleury (2008) examined this epigraphic evidence, almost all of it from Pompeii, and found four certain references to *sparsiones* and four other probable references. For example, in *CIL* IV.1177 *sparsiones* accompany *venatio*, *athletae* and *vela*, and so were a feature of the show worth mentioning to a prospective audience. The pairing of *vela*, the awnings, with *sparsiones* undoubtedly plays a role in our understanding of the sprinklings as 'most refreshing to a sweaty audience on a warm Mediterranean day' (Futrell, 2006, p. 111), with both providing relief from the hot sun. One only has to look at the dates that some of these games were held, however, to agree with Fleury (2008, p. 106) that being sprayed with wet saffron in February in Campania might not be a crowd-pleaser. On the other hand, at *munera* held in May (*CIL* IV.1184) and June (*CIL* IV.3883) (Tuck, 2008–9, Table 1), a refreshing spray might have been welcomed. It seems prudent to conclude that at least some of these advertisements referred to *sparsio missilia*, the scattered gifts, rather than scented liquids.

If any liquid *sparsiones* were sprayed in theatres and amphitheatres, they would have contributed to a slight lowering of temperature and/or a moistening of atmosphere inside the structures. Work on haptic geographies has drawn attention to the fact that touching can involve the entire body and its movements in any given space (Rodaway, 1994, pp. 41–2). To that end, the passive global touch of the liquid sprinklings on the crowd and the momentarily damp or humid air should be seen as combining with the active reach-touch of every individual, thus contributing to the multisensory creation of place, event and memory.[4]

Olfaction

Propertius writing of the stage smelling of 'ceremonial saffron' (4.1.15–16) is one of several classical authors who refer to the odour of *sparsiones*. The *Historia Augusta* tells us that Hadrian 'gave spices to the people in honour of his mother-in-law, and in honour of Trajan he caused essences of balsam and saffron to be poured over the seats of the theatre' (*Hadrian* 19.5). This passage does not explicitly refer to the aromas of these products, but we can extrapolate that scent is inferred balsam (Balsam of Mecca or *Commiphora opobalsamum*) was a prized aromatic resin from Arabia and saffron is invariably linked with a sweet smell. Indeed, saffron was a valued ingredient in perfumes (see Propertius 3.10), notably *crocinum* from Cilicia and Rhodes (Pliny *Natural History* 13.2). The saffron crocus, however, does not have a strong smell and we can conclude therefore that literary references are to the spice and not the flower. When Lucretius discusses the nature of good and bad smells, he contrasts a stage freshly sprinkled with 'Cilician saffron' with the stench of burning corpses (2.416; compare Hope, this volume). Apuleius describes an elaborate and aromatic special effect in an arena:

> Then, from a hidden pipe at the very peak of the mountain, saffron dissolved in wine came spurting up into the air and rained down in a fragrant shower. . . . Finally, when the theatre was filled with the delightful fragrance, a chasm in the earth opened and swallowed up the wooden mountain.
>
> (*Metamorphoses* 10.34)

It can be concluded, therefore, that a pleasant fragrance was one of the desired results of sprinkling saffron in theatres and amphitheatres.[5] This is not merely a literary trope; both kinds of venue would have been relatively smelly at times (Koloski-Ostrow, 2015, pp. 104–5), and saffron has a very distinctive and quite pungent odour that could help to mask less pleasant aromas. For example, the town of Krokos in northern Greece is the centre of a modern saffron industry, and during the harvest, a heavy scent of the spice hangs over the entire vicinity (Day, 2005, 2007) (Colour Plate 4a). This is due to the aromatic compounds picrocrocin and safranal, which are enhanced during the drying process that turns the fresh crocus stigmas into saffron (Basker and Negbi, 1983, pp. 230–1). Adding saffron to water or wine to make a liquid suited for sprinkling changes this aroma, making it less acrid, although the extent of the dilution would have impacted upon the strength of the fragrance. No matter how strong the scent was initially, the smell would have been temporary, lasting from only a matter of minutes within the building to more persistent odoriferous traces clinging to the clothing of spectators long into the evening, as personal observation on saffron-stained cloth suggests (compare Colour Plate 4c).[6]

Transience is a key characteristic of scents which, combined with their generally uncontrollable nature, makes them somewhat unreliable elements in planned entertainment, as the short-lived experiments with Smell-O-Vision and AromaRama in twentieth-century cinemas attest. Nevertheless, fragranced atmospheres were essential in Roman entertainment, and at private dinner parties they were provided partly by aromatic chaplets worn by diners (see Pliny *Natural History* 21 for information on chaplets; Jashemski, 1979; Draycott, 2015, p. 70 on commercial flower gardens). On a larger scale, imperial dining rooms could be fitted with mechanisms to add a sudden influx of scent to an already lavish *convivium*. Nero's banqueting rooms purportedly showered flowers onto the guests below and were fitted with pipes for sprinkling perfumes (Suetonius *Nero* 31). If we are to believe Plutarch, Otho surprised Nero when entertaining him when he 'suddenly brought into play gold and silver pipes on all sides of the room, out of which the ointment gushed freely, like so much water' (*Galba* 19.3). The fictional *triclinium* of Trimalchio undoubtedly mimics these (also fictional?) imperial ones, with its ceiling that parted to lower alabaster jars of perfume for the astounded diners (Petronius *Satyricon* 60).

Colour

Colour is the other characteristic of saffron *sparsiones* mentioned by ancient sources. Ovid noted, 'No awnings then hung o'er a marble theatre, nor was the platform ruddy with crocus-spray (*rubra croco*)' (*The Art of Love* 1.104–5). The erupting mountain described above by Apuleius ended up 'sprinkling the goats that were grazing all round, until, dyed to a greater beauty, they exchanged their natural whiteness for a yellow hue (*luteo colore*)' (*Metamorphoses* 10.34). Lucan compared red poison spurting from Tullus to saffron liquid flowing from a statue: 'And as Corycian saffron, when turned on, is wont to spout from every part of a statue at once, so all his limbs discharged red poison together instead of blood' (9.808). Automata including singing birds and crawling snails were devised by experts in mechanics such as Hero of Alexandria (Humphrey, Oleson and Sherwood, 1998, pp. 61–8), and there is no reason to doubt that animated statues could be made to spray liquids. A somewhat similar spurting occurs at Trimalchio's feast where cakes ejaculate saffron liquid when touched, perhaps a nod to the statue of Priapus who stands in the same dish (Petronius *Satyricon* 60).

The colourant power of saffron is undoubted. It is renowned as a dyestuff, and although now mainly used in food it has been used in the past to dye cloth, skin and hair (see Tertullian *On Female Fashion* 2.6.1–2; see also Bender-Weber, 2014, pp. 132–3). Crocin is the carotenoid colourant in the spice and it is extremely powerful, able to dye up to 150,000 times its own weight when diluted in liquid (Humphries, 1996, p. 15). While the strands of the dried spice are red, the colour of a saffron solution tends to be a yellow–orange–red range (*rubro* or *luteo* in the sources). The more saffron is added to a liquid, and the longer it soaks, the deeper hue it will attain. A red appearance could be obtained by sprinkling dry threads or saffron powder too, a practice also attested in the sources. This colourful powder was spread at Trimalchio's feast: 'the slaves took away all the tables, brought in others, and sprinkled about sawdust coloured with saffron and vermilion (*minio*), and, what I had never seen before, powdered mica' (Petronius *Satyricon* 68). The aromatic red of saffron and the vivid cinnabar or red lead (*minium*) mingling with the sparkling mica must have created quite a feast for the eyes and noses of the diners. Saffron was not the only coloured powder available. Both Caligula and Nero supposedly used coloured sands to turn the circus red and green: Caligula employed minium and chrysocolla (Suetonius *Gaius* 18), and Nero had 'the sand of the Circus sprinkled with chrysocolla', and even wore a matching outfit (Pliny *Natural History* 33.27). Elagabalus was more extravagant: 'He would strew gold and silver dust about a portico and then lament that he could not strew the dust of amber also' (*Historia Augusta, Heliogabulus* 31.8).

Multisensory interpretations of *sparsiones*

Effects and emotions

Having examined the literary, archaeological and epigraphic evidence for *sparsiones*, a re-evaluation of this practice is required. While cooling the air or the crowd does not seem to have been a primary concern, adding colour or perfume to a performance was crucial. Whether it was sprinklings of polychrome powders or colourful liquid showers, the *cavea*, arena, orchestra, stage, *pulpitum*, and perhaps some of the audience, would have been speckled a red-orange-yellow hue. This golden colour added another layer of sensory stimulation to an already rich visual spectacle that could include elaborately painted *scaenae frons*, multicoloured marble orchestra floors and bright plasterwork. Calpurnius's Corydon describes the visual splendour of his visit to the games: 'So dazzling was the glitter everywhere . . . the *balteus* begemmed and the gilded arcade vie in brilliance . . . bright too is the gleam from the nets of gold wire which project into the arena' (*Eclogues* 7.37–55). There is little doubt that a trip to the theatre or amphitheatre was an intense visual experience, not just in terms of hues but also through other aspects of colour like shimmer, reflection, brilliance and contrasts of shadows and light.[7] The very air inside one of these buildings could seem to be stained with colour:

> For assuredly we see many things cast off particles with lavish bounty, not only from the depths and from within (as we said before) but from the outermost surface, amongst others colour not seldom. This is often done by yellow and red and dark purple awnings, when outspread in the public view over a great theatre upon posts and beams they tremble and flutter; for then they dye, and force to flutter in their own colour, the assembly in the great hollow below, and all the display of the stage . . . and the more the walls of the theatre are enclosed all round, the more all within laughs in the flood of beauty when the light of day is thus confined.
>
> (Lucretius 4.72–83)[8]

Rather than considering colours and their related properties as something 'to be seen', it is helpful to think of them as having a materiality that could be experienced and contrasted to that of everyday life (see also Marshman, this volume). Controlling colour and light provides the means 'to alter human experiences of space, and to define sensations of intimacy and exclusion' (Bille and Sørensen, 2007, p. 274).[9] Emperors and magistrates were not only providing entertainment for the Roman populace; they were demonstrating their power by creating a particular embodied experience for the audience. It was not just visual spectacle that they presented. The fragrant nature of the *sparsiones* meant that colour had smell, something that Romans would have been used to and maybe even expected, as many perfumes were dyed (Pliny *Natural History* 13.2). Moreover, if the theory of extramission is applicable to a Roman understanding of how vision worked (Darrigol, 2012, pp. 1–15), experiencing colour and light was not merely a passive act but was the eye actively sending out rays to perceive the surroundings, and so was a tactile form of perception akin to the other haptic encounters of the event. Unsurprisingly, the whole experience also had a significant auditory component, ranging from the noise of the crowd to the words of the actors, the sounds of animals and gladiators, to the trumpets of heralds. Even though St Augustine's Alypius closed his eyes, it was the sounds of the amphitheatre that ultimately lured him to enjoy the spectacle (*Confessions* 6.8.13). Hammer makes the important point that 'Bloodlust alone was not sufficient to make a spectacle successful' (2010, p. 69), and technologies like *sparsiones* that combined smell, colour and perhaps surprise were a valuable element in the sensory and emotional extravaganza collectively experienced by the audience at theatres and amphitheatres.

Wealth

In all cases where a colourant or scent for *sparsiones* is mentioned, it is saffron. Yet any of the numerous other products associated with perfumes and garlands in ancient literature could have provided a pleasant smell.[10] Similarly, saffron is certainly not the only substance to provide a yellow-orange dye; for example, pomegranates and onions can provide yellows at a lower cost (Day, 2011, p. 365, note 203), although, unlike saffron-dyed cloth, they do not produce a water-fast colour.[11] One reason for the preference of saffron for *sparsiones* most likely relates to its cost (see, for example, Martial *Epigrams* 5.25). Even today, saffron remains the most expensive spice in the world, with recent prices cited at £6000 a kilogram (Hickman, 2011). This high price is due to that fact that its production cannot be mechanised. Red saffron threads are the dried stigmas of the saffron crocus (*Crocus sativus* L.), and each flower possesses only three stigmas. Every flower must be picked by hand during the brief autumnal flowering season and the stigmas separated from the petals and stamens that same day (Day, 2005, pp. 49–50, 2011, pp. 339–40) (Colour Plate 4b). It takes around 160,000 flowers to produce five kilograms of wet saffron, which then becomes one kilogram of the spice once dried (Humphries, 1996, p. 83), a ratio that probably has remained roughly the same since antiquity. In the Roman era, the best saffron apparently was cultivated in the area of Mount Corycus in Cilicia, followed by Mount Olympus in Lycia, then Centuripa in Sicily, as well as Cyrenae and Thera (Pliny *Natural History* 21.17). In the same chapter Pliny refers to a species of saffron crocus which grows wild, but the yield from uncultivated plants is much lower due to their shorter stigmas.

The amount of saffron required to either fragrance a public building or dye liquids a yellow strong enough to be visible to a crowd would have been quite substantial and of necessity imported, and therefore very expensive.[12] As games and spectacles were provided initially by magistrates who wished to gain public favour for their political careers, and later by emperors who were also striving to gain or keep public support, such lavish expenditure was the norm. For example, according to Dio Cassius (66.25), 9,000 animals were killed over the course of the inaugural games for the Colosseum. Extravagant use of scented substances was not restricted to the world of entertainment; funerals of public figures were characterised by the vast quantities of incense and perfume consumed (see also Hope, this volume). Two hundred and ten litters were needed to transport the spices for Sulla's funeral (Plutarch *Sulla* 38.2). Using precious saffron for *sparsiones* can be linked to this excessive expenditure. It brought a deeper layer of meaning to games and shows, where its scent and colour were redolent of wealth and access to the resources of the wider Roman empire. This high price has meant that throughout time saffron has been adulterated for profit, or other cheaper products passed off as the spice (such as safflower or turmeric), but we do not know whether pseudo-saffron *sparsiones* were ever used as a cost-cutting measure.

Hierarchies

Seating for the games and theatre in Rome was hierarchical, with emperors, senators and their guests seated in the orchestra of theatres or the podium level at the amphitheatre, while the *maenianum primum* seated equestrians and the *maenianum secundum* held the citizens. Slaves and women were right at the back, *maenianum secundum in ligneis* (Connolly, 2003, pp. 52–9) (Figure 12.3). This ordered space defined the social relations of the audience, a community united in spectacle but divided by status and gender.[13] Sitting in or accessing the wrong section of the building could cause uproar, as happened when Caligula deliberately scattered *missilia* for the plebs in the equestrian seats (Suetonius *Gaius* 26). This division of seating reinforced the fact that it was not only important to be able to see the shows, but also to be seen, and this was crucial for the elite (Parker, 1999; Rose, 2005, p. 102; Bergmann, 2008). Tradition determined what should be worn at the events: togas for citizens (whilst women would have worn tunics and veils of other colours too). Calpurnius Siculus describes the dingy garments of those seated towards the top of Nero's temporary amphitheatre, looking down on 'white-robed tribunes' (*Eclogues* 7. 29); Martial also mentions the white-clad audience at the games (*Epigrams* 4.2, 14.137). The sea of white garments in the front tiers would have presented a blank canvas on which golden *sparsiones* would stand out vividly.

Figure 12.3 View of the tiers of seating in the Colosseum, assigned hierarchically
Source: Photo: Conor Trainor

But were *sparsiones* deliberately sprinkled on the crowd? There are only two references to people getting sprayed, both in Martial. Implicit in 'drenched with a shower of saffron-water' (*Epigrams* 5.25) is that the spectators did get wet, while the Cilicians were 'sprayed with their own mist' (*On the Spectacles* 3.8) – in other words, with the famed saffron of their homeland. Less directly, when Seneca states that the jet of water goes from the centre of the arena to the top of the building (*Natural Questions* 2.9) we can assume some of the audience would have been in the line of fire. The majority of authors, however, mention the stage being sprinkled (Martial *Epigrams* 5.25, 8.33, 9.38; Lucretius 2.416; Ovid *The Art of Love* 1.104; Propertius 4.1.15–16). Two describe saffron sprays as special effects within the arena (Lucan 9.808; Apuleius *Metamorphoses* 10.34) and three refer more generally to the theatre or seats receiving the sprinkles (*Historia Augusta, Hadrian* 19.5; Pliny *Natural History* 21.17; Fronto 1.12).

This breakdown suggests that not everybody in a theatre or amphitheatre was affected (which is also a reason why I believe cooling the crowd was not a key function), and that it was those nearest the stage or arena who were the most likely to be sprinkled. Based on the hierarchical seating mentioned above, and excluding performers, these people would have belonged to the senatorial and equestrian classes, as well as perhaps the imperial family and the Vestals. Yellow splashes on their white clothing would have served as sensory reinforcements of the hierarchy of Roman society, evidence to all of a prominent position at the games or theatre (Colour Plate 4c).[14] Perhaps the scent of saffron lingered on the cloth afterwards, mingling with the other smells of the spectacle and transforming invisible scents into visible marks. That the colour would have been yellowish-orange, akin to gold, is important too. Gold was the colour of ostentation and wealth (see also Marshman, this volume). We only need recall Nero's *Domus Aurea*, with its lavish gilded decoration, and Caligula serving food modelled from gold to his guests, to grasp the links to high social status.

Memories

If *sparsiones* were not primarily sprayed on people but on a stage or within the building generally, we can widen the focus to think more broadly about the function of scent. At some level the saffron aroma probably did temporarily alleviate the smells accumulating from the Roman crowd and the human or animal performers. This colourful contribution to the overall 'smellscape' (Porteous, 2006) of the event affected emotions, made a statement about the donor's access to expensive spices and underlined social hierarchies. The link between smell and memory is worth pursuing (Sutton, 2001; Ben Ze'ev, 2004; Waskul, Vannini and Wilson, 2009). The rather magical power of recall triggered by scents results from direct physiological causes as the olfactory bulbs connect to the part of the brain concerned with memory (Murphy, 2013, p. 246). It can be suggested that the complex layers of smell created embodied memories in the audiences of *munera* and *ludi*, to be triggered at a later date by similar aromas. In a sense, putting on a show involved the crafting of prospective memories

(Sutton, 2001, pp. 28–9; Hamilakis, 2014, pp. 84–5) for people, the deliberate provision of memories through multisensory stimulation for future recollection. On encountering a similar aroma one could be instantly reminded of a visit to the games or theatre and, in an indirect manner, of the generosity of the sponsor and the magnificence of the Roman empire, as well as of one's status within it. Bergmann has also explored this concept, suggesting that mosaics of the circus might have led to recollections of 'the electrifying thrill of a mass victory' (Bergmann, 2008, p. 369), a concept that surely applies to mosaics of *munera* and *venationes* too.

This position can be reversed by concentrating not on memories of the event once it has ended but on memories that were recalled during the event. What might the smell of saffron have reminded an audience of whilst in the theatre or amphitheatre? To answer this, other instances of saffron's use by Romans for its aromatic powers needs to be considered. Its role in perfume has already been mentioned, but of great importance too was its use at funerals. For example, Statius (*Silvae* 2.1.157–62) tells of funerary pyres burning with Cilician saffron along with other sweet-smelling spices and incense (compare Hope, this volume). Saffron was also linked with deities and religious ritual. Macrobius cites Sallust on preparations for a banquet marking Metellus' triumph: the floor was sprinkled with saffron and other preparations were carried out to 'suggest a temple of great renown' (*Saturnalia* 3.13.8). Plutarch describes a temple of Diana whose columns sent forth the smell and colour of saffron when rubbed with a hand (*Themistocles* 8.2).[15] Similarly, streets were strewn with saffron when Nero returned from Greece (Suetonius *Nero* 25), and when saffron spouted from the cakes at Trimalchio's *cena* the guests stood up and gave thanks to the emperor because they thought it was a sacred dish (Petronius *Satyricon* 60). It should not be a surprise that saffron is an appropriate offering to a divinity or (divine) emperor. Gods in the ancient Mediterranean thrived on smells, receiving their nourishment primarily from burnt sacrifices and incense (Weddle, 2013, p. 138, and this volume). The transitional nature of the spice, moving from solid to smoke and able to permeate the boundaries of bodies, structures and human–divine worlds also make it suitable for funerary use (see also Hope, this volume).[16] In the light of these two associations, saffron *sparsiones* achieve a whole new level of mnemonics and meanings. Considering that *munera* had their origin in funeral games in the third century BCE, the scent of saffron is a particularly appropriate complement to gladiatorial combat. Moreover, the close links between religion and *ludi*, which were usually held as part of religious festivals (Beacham, 1991, pp. 20–1), again make the use of saffron in theatres especially apt.

Conclusion

Whether distributed by hand or mechanical means, and whether liquid or powder, coloured and fragrant *sparsiones* were an integral part of Roman public and (elite) private entertainment from the first century BCE into the second century CE. The archaeological evidence is, to date, inconclusive but the variety of literary sources referring to this practice suggests we should think closely about its functions. The assumption that cooling the audience was of primary importance has been shown to be inaccurate, even if this could have been a welcome side-effect on occasion. At one level, *sparsiones* were simply gifts from the sponsor of the games to the crowd, multisensory evidence of their wealth, status and munificence. The rich synaesthetic experience of the ancient spectacles that is conveyed to us in the words of Martial, Statius and other authors can be termed a 'sensorial assemblage' (Hamilakis, 2014, pp. 126–8). In amphitheatres, for example, colours, light and shadow, sparkles and gleams, smells, sounds and tastes, the press of bodies, the heat of the sun or feel of the wind on skin, the marble seating and the tiers of stairs, the excitement and expectation – all combined to create a unique bodily experience. According to Potter (2006, p. 386), it was precisely to get lost in the emotions of the moment that people attended such entertainment, and *sparsiones* undoubtedly contributed to creating this heightened emotion.

A costly spice, saffron, was the additive of choice to these sprinklings, and to profligately spray it on a large scale was something only the wealthy could have afforded. It was an expense that the sponsor had to bear, along with exotic animals, pairs of gladiators and elaborate scenery. The saffron liquids are said to have been sprinkled on the stage or the seats, or used as special effects, rather than raining directly on the crowd, but, depending on one's seating place, temporary staining of clothes, skin or hair may have occurred too. The visual link between the reddish-yellow sprays and gold may have further underlined the association with wealth implicit in using a rare product.

Olfactory stimulation is the other aspect of *sparsiones* that the ancient sources repeatedly stress. The attributes of smell make it a powerful, albeit often unconscious, link to memory and we should think beyond merely masking the scent of crowds and death to what the mnemonic role of sprinklings could have been. Certainly the peculiar aroma of the spectacle would lodge in people's memories and later smelling of similar stimuli could trigger recall of a certain event and, by association, the sponsor's generosity. Similarly, the smell of saffron inside a theatre or amphitheatre may have triggered mnemonic links to funerals and worship, the other contexts in which the spice was utilised.

Of course, there was no one common experience of *munera* or *ludi*; it was determined by a range of factors such as seating position, by being in the sun or under the *velarium*, by the surrounding people, and by each individual's physical capacities and sensory acuity. Literary sources provide an elite view of the events, but sensory archaeology can help to rebalance this. Through considering the range of potential bodily experiences, for example according to seating hierarchy, we can arrive at a more inclusive history of ancient spectacle. Power inequalities were always a factor at these events, however, and if we agree with Hamilakis that power derives its authority in part from the ability to regulate sensorial memories (Hamilakis, 2014, p. 126), the elaborate multisensory experiences crafted by sponsors were another form of political control. Ultimately, the colourful scent of saffron, with its associations with wealth, divinities and death, should be understood as key in making sense of place.[17]

Notes

1 Many thanks to Eleanor Betts and Emma-Jayne Graham for affording me the opportunity to speak at their conference, and to Eleanor for her editorial guidance. Thanks also to the other conference participants for the stimulating discussions and helpful comments on my paper. I am very grateful to Hazel Dodge for her useful suggestions on a draft of this paper, as well as for introducing me to Roman archaeology, and to Penny Day and Conor Trainor for their valuable input.

2 A number of other sources, including Hero of Alexandria and Philo of Byzantium, also refer to this type of pump; see Oleson, 1984, pp. 301–24, for references.

3 See Gleason, 1994 for a discussion of the visual affordances of the Porticus Pompeiana.

4 The terms *global touch* and *reach-touch* come from Rodaway (1994), who also identified two further types of tactile interaction: extended touch and imagined touch.

5 Lilja suggests that saffron was used because its fragrance was linked to a medicinal use as a disinfectant (Lilja, 1972, p. 92).

6 The speed of odour dispersion into the atmosphere depends on a number of factors including wind direction, wind speed, sunlight and topography, and no precise modelling has yet been attempted for *sparsiones* (see, for example, Capelli, Sironi, Del Rosso and Guillot, 2013).

7 On these other aspects of colour, see Saunders, 1999; Jones and McGregor, 2002 (especially papers by Keates and Saunders); also Marshman, this volume.

8 See Bradley, 2009, pp. 74–86 for more about Lucretius on colour.

9 See McMahon, 2013 for an example of elite control of light in buildings as controlling experience, and therefore an expression of power.

10 Martial's *Epigrams* are a particularly rich source on the uses and abuses of perfumes in Rome. Other useful sources include Pliny the Elder (*Natural History* 13.1–5) and the fourth-century BCE Theophrastus (*On Odours*).

11 To make saffron-dyed cloth water-fast, a mordant such as alum must be used to 'fix' the dye.

12 Stein (2004) estimated that force pumps could expel between 24.6 and 28.9 litres a minute, so frequent sprinklings over the course of a day at the games would have required hundreds of litres of saffron-dyed liquid.

13 Inomata and Coben (2006) discuss the role of performance and spectacle in community power relations.

14 One could also wonder whether getting splashed with saffron liquid would have been an annoyance leading to extra washing of togas, rather than something to flaunt. Thanks to Valerie Hope for raising this point.

15 There is a long tradition of linking saffron with women and gynaecology. See Day, 2011 and Hornblower and Spawforth, 1996, p. 463 for further discussion.

16 Howes (1987) has commented at length upon the links between olfaction, transition and rituals.

17 Feld (2005, p. 179) first suggested that as places make sense, so senses make place.

Afterword: Towards a methodology for Roman sensory studies[1]

Eleanor Betts

Each of the contributors to this book has developed a new approach for research of the Roman empire by focusing on the sensory properties and affectiveness of its material culture and generated by its written sources. Topics have centred on people, places, buildings and artefacts, and on specific aspects of behaviour ranging from performance and ritual to everyday life. Several authors have emphasised the experiences of different groups in Roman society, considering their physiological, and sometimes emotional, responses to particular events and activities. Each chapter illustrates how taking a sensory approach to specific aspects of Roman society and culture enriches and increases our understanding of their significance and brings new perspectives to our interpretation of the Roman world. In so doing, they reveal the unlimited potential of sensory studies to further the disciplines of ancient history and classical archaeology, and they demonstrate the value of taking an interdisciplinary approach to the study of past senses.

The underlying themes of the volume demonstrate this unlimited potential. For example, the extent to which both new and existing sensory approaches can be applied to discrete monuments, buildings, locales and landscapes in the Roman world; or to which the senses played a central role within distinctive socio-cultural activities or locales, such as the domestic, political, commercial, religious, funerary and leisure spheres; or to which sensory experiences were instrumental in reinforcing the meaning of particular cultural activities or in undermining traditional expectations. If we return to the theory of embodiment and consider the senses and the self, the role of sensory perception in the construction and maintenance of personal or communal identities (whether fixed or transitory), or in processes connected with memory and the perpetuation of cultural ideologies, are also rich areas for exploration. The contributors have also considered some of the challenges in approaching the past from a multisensory perspective, and have begun to develop methodologies for Roman sensory studies. Some have explored the possibilities for reconstructing sensory experiences of objects, environments and events, whilst others have developed our understanding of the construction and character of particular spaces, through analysis of their sensory properties.

Sensorial assemblages

With sensory responses to – and more importantly, interpretation of – a situation being fundamentally tied to an individual's physiology, life experience, memories and cultural background, it is impossible to reconstruct human experience of past events or practices in their entirety, but the contributors have shown that there are elements which it is possible to access. A wealth of evidence for the Roman empire enables sensory studies to present a more embodied understanding of Roman society and culture. Sensorial assemblages (Hamilakis, 2014, pp. 127–8, p. 201) can be reconstructed from a combination of material and written sources, and this volume has illustrated the potential for such an approach, one which combines all the available types of evidence and which often crosses boundaries between disciplines. When undertaking sensory studies and reconstructing sensory artefacts and sensorial assemblages, we take a holistic approach to the human body and mind, and to the multiple interrelationships of person, artefact and place. This attention to physical sensory properties and their affectiveness enables comparative studies to be used more effectively, whether those studies are taking a text out of its temporal or geographical context, using visual representations to add detail, or exploring ethnographic parallels. It is vital to be clear about the degree to which comparative evidence has been used, and ensure that we use it to both inform and test our hypotheses. Candace Weddle demonstrated that stylised depictions of the *suovetaurilia* sacrifice and ritual banquets tell us something of the participants and performance of the rituals, but their qualities as visual, artistic representations must be disentangled from the realities of sacrifice, which can only be discerned by identifying the sensory properties of the participants and spaces involved. Similarly, Valerie Hope argued that the Amiternum relief presents postures of mourning which can be played out in order to understand better how people *may* have experienced an elite funeral in Rome.

Embodied and imagined sensation

Placing ourselves physically in ancient spaces enables us to experience them, and this is at the heart of a phenomenological approach. As Helen Slaney demonstrated with her exercises relating to the Roman pantomime, it is also possible to use our bodies to increase our understanding of how kinaesthesia and interoception effect emotion (on emotion see Insoll, 2007, pp. 56–9; Scarantino, 2010). Merleau-Ponty's term 'the universal measurement' (1968, p. 268) provides us with a clear reference point for understanding ancient spaces and behaviours, and we should not dismiss the usefulness of biological similarities as a tool for accessing the past. Equally, we must acknowledge differences, and seek to incorporate them in our analyses. Research into mirror neurons indicates that it may be possible to establish 'empathic' ways to better evaluate and understand the social functions of artefacts and places, something which has already been used in archaeological virtual simulations (see for example Forte and Gallese,

2014, pp. 8–12; on mirror neurons and actions see Spaulding, 2013). As with our use of comparative evidence within the discipline, we must be both cautious and open when using these methods, acknowledging that whilst striving for understanding cultural dissonance makes it impossible to reconstruct absolutely any Roman situation or experience. Whether or not we include emotion and empathy, the relationship between biological similarity and dissonance is one of the elements which makes a multisensory approach interesting, as demonstrated by Emma-Jayne Graham in her consideration of the extent to which swaddled baby votives were alike to and different from real babies.

There is a place for imaginative reconstruction in sensory archaeologies and histories, described by Ruth Van Dyke as 'creative nonfiction – the use of archaeological information to construct imagined lives' (2013, p. 395; compare Skeates, 2010, pp. 6–8). Interpretation (itself a 'creative nonfiction') begins during archaeological fieldwork, and partial evidence in any area of classical studies makes the search for Truth redundant. Instead, sensory studies enable us to extract new meaning from our evidence as we strive for better understandings of human individuals and societies. As the chapters in this volume have demonstrated, sensory studies add a new, and nuanced, contribution whether the perspective taken is that of the human perceiver, the objects they used or the places and spaces in which they interacted.

Artists (whatever their medium: whether literary, oral, visual, aural or material) have an enriched vocabulary for describing the multisensory nature of human physical and emotional experience. Part of their skill (and *raison d'être*) is to evoke sensations, emotions, images, sounds, odours and so on; to provoke the imagination. As academics we tend to shy away from the subjective and to focus on the all-important objectivity which gives us credibility in our fields of expertise. If we are to fully explore the possibilities of incorporating sensory studies within our existing frameworks and areas of expertise we need to equip ourselves with the skills and the vocabulary with which to interpret the full range of sensory experiences, to ensure objectivity, but also clarity. 'Close reading' is familiar, but 'agile listening' or sensitivity to touch may be less so, and the English language is biased towards the visual (Day, 2013a, pp. 4–5).

Whether or not we call it creative nonfiction, interpretation of the available evidence is at the core of our work and including sensory studies extends the possibilities of interpretation. Phenomenology, which is at the root of many sensory studies, has the capacity to acknowledge the inevitability of subjectivity whilst aiming to record sensations, emotions and experiences objectively within that caveat. For this reason, sensory archaeologies often begin with, or incorporate, thick description (see for example Betts, 2003; Skeates, 2010; Hamilakis, 2014). This is one area of archaeology where the personal voice of the academic comes through the page. As objective authors and readers we may feel uncomfortable with this approach, and this in part explains why phenomenology and sensory studies have traditionally been so peripheral within archaeology. However, human geographers, sociologists, social anthropologists and ethnographers have used this approach for many years and have established several methods which can be adopted by classical archaeologists and ancient historians. The crux of the problem is that archaeology deals with the human *past*. It is not possible to interview the people we study and we are dependent on the traces they leave behind to piece together an understanding of how they lived.

Sensory responses are in part culturally constructed. It may be possible to record physiological responses to a sensory phenomenon, and to feel empathy, but those responses must be interpreted through a cultural lens. Biological differences combined with cultural specificity mean that our multisensory interpretations can only ever be hypothetical; but that hypothetical interpretation brings with it new and interesting research questions. A significant point of separation between ourselves and those living in the past is memory. Some memories are culturally specific, but all are personal to an individual, which is something that can never be recaptured when our subjects of study belong to an ancient past. Literary and epigraphic sources may provide an insight into the mind of the author, and if we can recognise something of the author's biases, as well as the conventions of the genre in which they were working, we can perhaps come close to extracting particular aspects of a memory. Nevertheless, we can never reconstruct a Roman memory, even one belonging to a writer who commentates on details of daily life in a personalised, albeit contrived, way, such as Seneca, Martial or Juvenal.

Taking each of these elements into consideration, a core principle of sensory archaeologies and histories must therefore be to make clear where imagination, simulation or cognitive techniques have been used in order to gain an insight into the subject of study.

Next steps in Roman sensory studies

The contributors to this volume have explored some specific ways in which sensory studies may be applied to particular aspects of the Roman empire. Each has their own methods and approaches, all of which have the potential to be extended and combined in further studies. This final section summarises the methods and approaches used, and considers briefly how they might be developed in the future.

All contributors have used close reading and analysis of classical literature and epigraphy to underpin parts of their argument, though Ian Marshman and Thomas Derrick less so, due to the nature of their case studies (Roman Britain); and all have combined this with analysis of material culture (artefacts, art and architecture). Combining textual and material analysis in this way enables access to the multisensory experience of aspects of the Roman empire and this method is likely to provide the starting point for any future studies.

An essential next step is extensive text mining for sensory affordances, the benefit of which Alexandre Vincent has demonstrated effectively in his chapter. Part of this process is the identification of nuanced and inferred sensory data. If we take Seneca as an example: *omnia genera vocum, quae in odium possunt aures adducere* is translated in the current Loeb digital edition as 'the assortment of

sounds, which are strong enough to make me hate my very powers of hearing'
(*Letters* 56.1). A computerised text mining program would identify *vocum* and
aures as relating to sound, but asking it to capture the context is more difficult.
For example, *omnia genera vocum* provides significantly different data for experimentation and modelling than *vocum* alone. The detail is important when we
are mining texts for sensory and experiential data. To take this example a little
further, we are dependent on the context and the rest of the letter to decide
whether 'sounds', 'voices' or 'calls' best captures the meaning of *vocum* and, more
importantly for us, the actual sounds which were occurring in the built environment of the baths Seneca describes. The majority of sensory data in textual
sources are subject to inference. Take for example Martial's series of epigrams
relating to food. This is the sort of data we must obtain if we are to access taste
and smell from texts.

The sensory properties of material culture are also deserving of more attention than is currently the norm, and are more tangible than those extrapolated
from texts, with the caveat that function does not necessarily follow form.
There is already a move to incorporate recording of sensory data within
archaeological fieldwork methods, enabling material culture from artefacts
and assemblages to places and landscapes to be recorded in situ with their sensory properties (Hamilton and Whitehouse, 2006; Till, 2015). Nevertheless,
imagination – or the creative nonfiction of archaeological interpretation – is
likely to retain a role in post-excavation analysis. This is not always the case,
however, as demonstrated by the reconstruction of a Roman *tuba* (Vincent,
this volume), which has allowed the evidence of material culture and text to
be combined and tested against each other. There are a number of other ways
in which material culture may be relocated in context with a view to exploring the sensorial assemblage. One is to take a site, whether a building, street,
settlement or landscape, such as the *fullonica* of Stephanus, the Vicus Tuscus
or Vindolanda, and place the material within its spaces and places. This can
be done via desktop survey and (ideally) followed by experimentation on the
ground or by the application of known formulae to architectural remains (see
Betts, Veitch, Derrick, this volume).

The limitations of textual and material evidence can be addressed in several
ways, three of which are demonstrated in this volume. One is to apply theoretical approaches such as phenomenology, embodiment and agency to the places,
people and artefacts which are the subjects of study. Theory presents frameworks
in which to analyse our case studies, drawing us in to explore the properties of
our subjects, the sensory artefacts of, for example, a sacrificial meal, swaddled
baby votives, signet rings and consumer goods in Rome. Archaeological theory
tends to keep the subject and object at a distance from one another, since objectivity is key; but this is less the case with sensory archaeologies and other forms
of sensory studies. More subjective still are the two other approaches taken
in this volume: autoethnographical and empathic. A willingness to note the
subjective elements in an interpretation or analysis should be a tenet of Roman
sensory studies, and is illustrated well in the volume. Ray Laurence, Emma-Jayne

Graham and Jo Day weave personal responses and autoethnograpic observations into their analyses, whilst Helen Slaney's empathic experiments take our study of Graeco-Roman performance in an entirely new direction.

Each of the authors' sensory histories and archaeologies presented in this volume raise new questions and highlight the possibilities (and arguably, the need) for empirical studies, experimentation and collaboration. For example, hypotheses such as those put forward by Ray Laurence, Miko Flohr, Thomas Derrick, Candace Weddle, Valerie Hope and Jo Day have the potential to be tested on the ground via experimentation in spaces and places in which the sounds, smells and other sensory data they describe may be measured and reconstructed. Jeffrey Veitch puts forward a clear methodology for quantitative analysis of the acoustic properties of Roman architectural spaces, into which framework the sounds of everyday life can be reassessed. Miko Flohr and Jeffrey Veitch describe the relative noise of different sounds on the streets of Pompeii and Ostia. Empirical studies, ideally carried out on site, are essential if Roman sensescapes are to be explored fully, and an element of quantitative research and experimentation must be used at some stage to test hypotheses about the multisensory experiences of a particular building, street, city, event or artefact. Such studies can be combined with approaches which extrapolate from the written and material evidence and use these to imagine how that place, object or event may have affected human experience or behaviour. Emitters of sensory data have fewer variables in terms of their sensory properties than the human perceiver, and are consequently more easily quantifiable (see for example Betts, Veitch, Marshman, Vincent, Slaney, this volume). Collaboration and a multisensory approach are essential if we are to see the full potential of sensory studies. Focusing on sight, sound, taste, smell or touch in a vacuum will only ever tell part of the story, whereas investigating the full panoply of sensory experience, and establishing the methodologies necessary to achieve this, will potentially create a 'paradigmatic shift' (Hamilakis, 2014, p. 203) in the way that we approach research into the Roman empire. Sensory studies invite us to collaborate and to cross disciplinary boundaries, making full use of the gamut of qualitative and quantitative analytical tools available.

The 'sensual revolution' has at last come to studies of the Roman world. I leave you with David Howes:

> this 'empire of the senses' is very much a political empire. Rich and rare sensations have been brought together from all over the world. . . . We see here that everything has been displaced from its original setting and brought together to form a new world order.
>
> (Howes, 2005b, p. 13)

The Roman empire is often characterised by its politics and government, the mobility of its people, trade in the 'rich and rare', and the longevity of its 'new world order'. By including sensory studies in our exploration of the Roman world, we will enrich our understanding of that world and gain a more nuanced appreciation of the affectiveness of the senses of the empire.

Note

1 Hamilakis' eleven theses on the archaeology of the senses (2013, pp. 409–19) may be applied to Roman archaeology and ancient history and are recommended as reading alongside this Afterword.

Bibliography

Adams, C., 2012. Transport. In: W. Scheidel, ed. *The Cambridge Companion to the Roman Economy*. Cambridge: Cambridge University Press. pp. 218–40.

Aglioti, S., Smania, N., Manfredi, M. and Berlucchi, G., 1996. Disownership of left hand and objects related to it in a patient with right brain damage. *NeuroReport* 8(1), pp. 293–6.

Aldrete, G., 2014. Urban sensations: opulence and ordure. In: J. Toner, ed. *A Cultural History of the Senses in Antiquity*. London: Bloomsbury. pp. 45–67.

Alexandrescu, C.G., 2010. *Blasmusiker und Standartenträger im Römischen Heer: Untersuchungen zur Benennung, Funktion und Ikonographie*. Cluj-Napoca: Mega Verlag.

Allison, P.M., 2002. Colour and light in a Pompeian house: modern impressions or ancient perceptions. In: A. Jones and G. MacGregor, eds. *Colouring the Past: The Significance of Colour in Archaeological Research*. Oxford: Berg. pp. 195–207.

Allison, P.M., 2013. *People and Spaces in Roman Military Bases*. Cambridge: Cambridge University Press.

Almagor, U., 1987. The cycle and stagnation of smells: pastoralists–fishermen relationships in an East African society. *RES: Anthropology and Aesthetics* 13, pp. 106–21.

Amphoux, P., 2001. L'observation récurrente. In: M. Grosjean and J.-P. Thibaud, eds. *L'espace urbain en méthodes*. Marseilles: Éditions Parenthèses. pp. 153–169.

André, J.-M., 1994. Sénèque et les problèmes de la ville. *Ktéma* 19, pp. 145–54.

Arnaud, P., 2005. *Les routes de la navigation antique: itinéraires en Méditerranée*. Paris: Éditions Errance.

Astolfi, F., 1996. Horrea Agrippiana. In: M. Steinby, ed. *Lexicon Topographicum Urbis Romae III (H–O)*. Rome: Edizioni Quasar. pp. 37–8, p. 394.

Astolfi, F., Guidobaldi, F. and Pronti, A., 1978. Horrea Agrippiana. *Archeologia Classica* 30, pp. 31–106.

Auguet, R., 1972. *Cruelty and Civilization: The Roman Games*. London: Allen and Unwin.

Avery, E., 2013. A whiff of mortality: the smells of death in Roman and Byzantine Beth She'an–Scythopolis. In: J. Day, ed. *Making Senses of the Past: Toward a Sensory Archaeology*. Center for Archaeological Investigations, Occasional Paper No. 40. Carbondale, IL: Southern Illinois University Press. pp. 266–85.

Baggieri, G., Margariti, P.A. and di Giacomo, M., 1996. Fertilità, virilità, maternità. In: G. Baggieri, ed. *L'Antica Anatomia nell'Arte dei Donaria. I Parte: "Speranza e Sofferenza" nei Votivi Anatomici dell'Antichità*. Rome: Ministero per i Beni e le Attività Culturali. pp. 22–7.

Baglione, M.P., 1976. *Il territorio di Bomarzo*. Rome: Giorgio Bretschneider Editore.

Basker, D. and Negbi, M., 1983. Uses of saffron. *Economic Botany* 37(2), pp. 228–36.

Beacham, R., 1991. *The Roman Theatre and Its Audience*. London: Routledge.

Beard, M., 2007. *The Roman Triumph*. London: Belknap Press.

Beard, M., North, J.A. and Price, S.R.F., 1998a. *Religions of Rome, Volume 1: A History*. Cambridge: Cambridge University Press.

Beard, M., North, J.A. and Price, S.R.F., 1998b. *Religions of Rome, Volume 2: A Sourcebook*. Cambridge: Cambridge University Press.

Beck, R., Krampl, U. and Retaillaud-Bajac, E., 2013. *Les cinq sens de la ville du Moyen Âge à nos jours*. Tours: Université François Rabelais.

Bélis, A. and Homo-Lechner, C., eds, 1994. *La pluridisciplinarité en archéologie musicale*. Paris: Maison des Sciences de L'homme.

Bender-Weber, I., 2014. Krokotos and crocota vestis: saffron-coloured clothes and muliebrity. In: C. Alfaro Giner, M. Tellenbach and J. Ortiz, eds. *Production and Trade of Textiles and Dyes in the Roman Empire and Neighbouring Regions. Actas del IV Symposium Internacional sobre Textiles y Tintes del Mediterráneo en el mundo antiguo (València, 5 al 6 de noviembre, 2010), Purpurae Vestes IV (València 2014)*. Valencia: Universitat de València. pp. 129–42.

Bennett, D., 2014. Faunal remains from third-century contexts at Vindolanda. In: J. Blake, ed. *Vindolanda Research: The Excavations of 2007–2013 in the Vicus or Extramural Settlement ('Area B')*. Brampton: Roman Army Museum Publications. pp. 197–216.

Ben Ze'ev, E., 2004. The politics of taste and smell: Palestinian rites of return. In: M. Lien and B. Nerlich, eds. *The Politics of Food*. Oxford: Berg. pp. 141–60.

Bergmann, B., 2008. Pictorial narratives of the Roman circus. In: J. Nelis–Clément and J.-M. Roddaz, eds. *Le cirque romain et son image: actes du colloque tenu á l'Institut Ausonius, Bordeaux, 2006*. Bordeaux: Ausonius. pp. 361–92.

Berkeley, G., 1710. *A Treatise Concerning the Principle of Human Knowledge*. Dublin: Jeremy Pepyat.

Berthoz, A., 2000. *The Brain's Sense of Movement*. Trans. G. Weiss. Cambridge, MA: Harvard University Press.

Berthoz, A. and Petit, J.-L., 2008. *The Philosophy and Phenomenology of Action*. Oxford: Oxford University Press.

Bettini, M., 2008. *Voci. Antropologia Sonora del Mondo Antico*. Turin: Einaudi.

Betts, E., 2003. The sacred landscape of Picenum (900–100 BC): towards a phenomenology of cult places. In: J.B. Wilkins and E. Herring, eds. *Inhabiting Symbols: Symbol and Image in the Ancient Mediterranean*. London: Accordia. pp. 101–20.

Betts, E., 2011. Towards a multisensory experience of movement in the city of Rome. In: R. Laurence and D.J. Newsome, eds. *Rome, Ostia, Pompeii: Movement and Space*. Oxford: Oxford University Press. pp. 118–32.

Bidwell, P., 1985. *The Roman Fort of Vindolanda at Chesterholm, Northumberland*. London: Historic Buildings and Monuments Commission for England.

Bijsterveld, K., 2003. The diabolical symphony of the mechanical age. In: M. Bull and L. Back, eds. *The Auditory Culture Reader*. Oxford: Berg. pp. 165–89.

Bille, M. and Sørensen, T.F., 2007. An anthropology of luminosity: the agency of light. *Journal of Material Culture* 12(3), pp. 263–84.

Birley, A., 2010. *The Nature and Significance of Extramural Settlement at Vindolanda and Other Selected Sites on the Northern Frontier of Roman Britain*. Unpublished PhD thesis. University of Leicester.

Birley, A., 2013. *The Vindolanda Granary Excavations*. Brampton: Roman Army Museum Publications.

Birley, A. and Blake, J., 2005. *Vindolanda: The Excavations of 2003/4*. Bardon Mill: The Vindolanda Trust.

Birley, A. and Blake, J., 2007. *Vindolanda: The Excavations of 2005–2006*. Bardon Mill: The Vindolanda Trust.

Birley, A.R. and Birley, A., 2012. A new Dolichenum, inside the third-century fort at Vindolanda. In: M. Blömer and E. Winter, eds. *Juppiter Dolichenus. Orientalische Religionen in der Antike 8*. Tübingen: Mohr Siebeck. pp. 231–58.

Birley, R., 1977. *The 1976 Excavations at Vindolanda Interim Report*. Bardon Mill: The Vindolanda Trust.

Birley, R., 2009. *Vindolanda: A Roman Frontier Fort on Hadrian's Wall*. Stroud: Amberley.

Birley, R., Blake, J. and Birley, A.R., 1998. *The 1997 Excavations at Vindolanda the Praetorium Site Interim Report*. Bardon Mill: The Vindolanda Trust.

Blake, J., ed, 2014. *Vindolanda Research: The Excavations of 2007–2012 in the Vicus or Extramural Settlement ('Area B')*. Brampton: Roman Army Museum Publications.

Blesser, B. and Salter, L.-R., 2007. *Spaces Speak, Are You Listening? Experiencing Aural Architecture*. Cambridge, MA: The MIT Press.

Bodel, J., 1999. Death on display: looking at Roman funerals. In: B. Bergmann and C. Kondoleon, eds. *The Art of Ancient Spectacle*. New Haven and London: Yale University Press. pp. 259–81.

Bodel, J., 2000. Dealing with the dead: undertakers, executioners and potter's fields in ancient Rome. In: V. Hope and E. Marshall, eds. *Death and Disease in the Ancient City*. London: Routledge. pp. 128–51.

Bodel, J., 2004. The organisation of the funerary trade at Puteoli and Cumae. In: S. Panciera, ed. *Libitina e Dintorni: Atti dell' XI Rencontre franco-italienne sur l'épigraphie. Libitina 3*. Rome: Quasar. pp. 149–70.

Boivin, N., 2009. Grasping the elusive and unknowable: material culture in ritual practice. *Material Religion* 5(3), pp. 266–87.

Bomgardner, D., 2000. *The Story of the Roman Amphitheatre*. London: Routledge.

Bookidis, N., 1997. *The Sanctuary of Demeter and Kore: Topography and Architecture*. Princeton, NJ: American School of Classical Studies at Athens.

Boquet, D. and Nagy, P., 2011. Une histoire des émotions incarnées. *Médiévales* 61, pp. 5–24.

Borić, D. and Robb, J., 2008. *Past Bodies: Body-Centred Research in Archaeology*. Oxford: Oxbow Books.

Bos, J., 2009. The rise and decline of character: humoral psychology in ancient and early modern medical theory. *History of the Human Sciences* 22(3), pp. 29–50.

Bowen, J., 2002. *Religion in Practice*. Needham Heights, MA: Allyn and Bacon.

Bowman, A.K., 1994. *Life and Letters on the Roman Frontier: Vindolanda and Its People*. London: British Museum Press.

Bradley, M., 2002. 'It all comes out in the wash': looking harder at the Roman *fullonica. Journal of Roman Archaeology* 15, pp. 21–44.

Bradley, M., 2009. *Colour and Meaning in Ancient Rome*. Cambridge: Cambridge University Press.

Bradley, M., 2013. Colour as synaesthetic experience in antiquity. In: S. Butler and A. Purves, eds. *Synaesthesia and the Ancient Senses*. Durham: Acumen. pp. 127–40.

Bradley, M., 2015a. Introduction: smell and the ancient senses. In: M. Bradley, ed. *Smell and the Ancient Senses*. Abingdon: Routledge. pp. 1–16.

Bradley, M., 2015b. Foul bodies in ancient Rome. In: M. Bradley, ed. *Smell and the Ancient Senses*. Abingdon: Routledge. pp. 133–45.

Brandt, E., 1968. *Antike Gemmen in Deutschen Sammlungen. Band I, Staatliche Münzsammlung München*. Munich: Prestel.

Bremer, J.M., 1981. Greek hymns. In: H.S. Versnel, ed. *Faith, Hope and Worship: Aspects of Religious Mentality in the Ancient World*. Leiden: Brill. pp. 193–215.

Brück, J., 1998. In the footsteps of the ancestors: a review of Christopher Tilley's *A Phenomenology of Landscape: Places, Paths and Monuments. Archaeological Review from Cambridge* 15(1), pp. 23–36.

Bruun, C., 2009. Civic rituals in imperial Ostia. In: O. Hekster, S. Schmidt-Hofner and C. Witschel, eds. *Ritual Dynamics and Religious Change in the Roman Empire* (Impact of Empire 9). Leiden: Brill. pp. 123–41.

Bruun, C., 2015. Civic identity in Roman Ostia: some evidence from dedications (inaugurations). In: A. Kemezis, ed. *Urban Dreams and Realities in Antiquity: Remains and Representations of the Ancient City.* Leiden: Brill. pp. 347–69.

Buckley, A., ed, 1998. *Hearing the Past: Essays in Historical Ethnomusicology and the Archaeology of Sound.* Liège: Études et Recherches Archéologiques de l'Université de Liège.

Bull, M. and Back, L., 2003. Introduction: into sound. In: M. Bull and L. Back, eds. *The Auditory Culture Reader.* Oxford: Berg. pp. 1–18.

Butler, J., 1997. *Excitable Speech: A Politics of the Performative.* New York: Routledge.

Butler, S. and Purves, A., eds, 2013. *Synaesthesia and the Ancient Senses.* Durham: Acumen.

Calvo-Merino, B., Glaser, D.E., Grèzes, J., Passingham, R.E. and Haggard, P., 2005. Action observation and acquired motor skills: an fMRI study with expert dancers. *Cerebral Cortex* 15, pp. 1243–9.

Calza, G., Becatti, G. and Bloch, H., 1953. *Scavi di Ostia I: Topografia Generale.* Roma: Libreria Dello Stato.

Capelli, L., Sironi, S., Del Rosso, R. and Guillot, J.-M., 2013. Measuring odours in the environment vs. dispersion modelling: a review. *Atmospheric Environment* 79, pp. 731–43.

Carroll, M., 2011. "The mourning was very good": liberation and liberality in Roman funerary commemoration. In: V.M. Hope and J. Huskinson, eds. *Memory and Mourning: Studies on Roman Death.* Oxford: Oxbow. pp. 125–49.

Chidester, D., 2005. The American touch: tactile imagery in American religion and politics. In: C. Classen, ed. *The Book of Touch.* Oxford and New York: Berg. pp. 49–65.

Christensen, P. and Kyle, D., eds, 2013. *A Companion to Sport and Spectacle in Greek and Roman Antiquity.* Malden, MA: Wiley–Blackwell.

Classen, C., 1993. *Worlds of Sense: Exploring the Senses in History and Across Cultures.* London: Routledge.

Classen, C., ed, 2005. *The Book of Touch.* Oxford: Berg.

Classen, C., 2012. *The Deepest Sense: A Cultural History of Touch.* Champaign, IL: University of Illinois.

Classen, C., 2014. *A Cultural History of the Senses.* London: Bloomsbury.

Classen, C., Howes, D. and Synnott, A., 1994. *Aroma: The Cultural History of Smell.* London: Routledge.

Coates, P., 2005. The strange stillness of the past: toward an environmental history of sound and noise. *Environmental History* 10(4), pp. 636–65.

Cockayne, E., 2007. *Hubbub: Filth, Noise and Stench in England, 1600–1770.* London: Yale University Press.

Coleman, K., 1990. Fatal charades: Roman executions staged as mythological enactments. *Journal of Roman Studies* 80, pp. 44–73.

Coleman, K., 1993. Launching into history: aquatic displays in the early Empire. *Journal of Roman Studies* 83, pp. 48–74.

Coleman, K., ed, 2006. *M. Valerii Martialis Liber Spectaculorum.* Oxford: Oxford University Press.

Collon, D., 1997. Ancient Near Eastern seals. In: D. Collon, ed. *7000 Years of Seals.* London: British Museum Press. pp. 11–30.

Connolly, P., 2003. *Colosseum: Rome's Arena of Death*. London: BBC Books.

Corbeill, A., 2004. *Nature Embodied: Gesture in Ancient Rome*. Princeton and Oxford: Princeton University Press.

Corbin, A., 1994. *Les Cloches de la terre. Paysage sonore et culture sensible dans les campagnes au XIXe Siècle*. Paris: Albin Michel.

Corbin, A., 1998. *Village Bells: Sound and Meaning in the Nineteenth Century French Countryside*. New York: Macmillan.

Croom, A., 2000. *Roman Clothing and Fashion*. Stroud: Tempus.

Crowder, R.G. and Schab, F.R., 1995. Introduction. In: R.G. Crowder and F.R. Schab, eds. *Memory for Odors*. Mahwah, NJ: Lawrence Erlbaum. pp. 1–7.

Dalby, A., 2000. *Empire of Pleasures: Luxury and Indulgence in the Roman World*. London: Routledge.

Damasio, A., 1999. *The Feeling of What Happens: Body, Emotion and the Making of Consciousness*. London: William Heinemann.

D'Ambra, E., 2007. Racing with death: circus sarcophagi and the commemoration of children in Roman Italy. In: A. Cohen and J. Rutter, eds. *Constructions of Childhood in Ancient Greece and Italy: Hesperia Supplement 41*. Princeton, NJ: American School of Classical Studies at Athens. pp. 339–51.

Daremberg, C. and Saglio, E., 1873–1919. *Dictionnaire des Antiquités Grecques et Romaines: d'Aprés les Textes et les Monuments*. Vol. IV.2. Paris: Hachette.

Darrigol, O., 2012. *A History of Optics from Greek Antiquity to the Nineteenth Century*. Oxford: Oxford University Press.

Davies, G., 2005. On being seated: gender and body language in Hellenistic and Roman art. In: D. Cairns, ed. *Body Language in the Greek and Roman Worlds*. Swansea: Classical Press of Wales. pp. 213–38.

Day, J., 2005. Adventures in fields of flowers: research on contemporary saffron cultivation and its application to the Bronze Age Aegean. In: C. Briault, J. Green, A. Kaldelis and A. Stellatou, eds. *SOMA 2003: Symposium on Mediterranean Archaeology. British Archaeological Reports International Series 1391*. Oxford: Archaeopress. pp. 49–52.

Day, J., 2007. *An Exploration of the Social Roles of Plants in the Bronze Age Aegean*. Unpublished PhD thesis. Trinity College Dublin.

Day, J., 2011. Crocuses in context: a diachronic survey of the crocus motif in the Aegean Bronze Age. *Hesperia* 80(3), pp. 337–79.

Day, J., ed, 2013a. *Making Senses of the Past: Toward a Sensory Archaeology*. Center for Archaeological Investigations, Occasional Paper No. 40. Carbondale, IL: Southern Illinois University Press.

Day, J., 2013b. Introduction: making senses of the past. In: J. Day, ed. *Making Senses of the Past: Toward a Sensory Archaeology*. Center for Archaeological Investigations, Occasional Paper No. 40. Carbondale, IL: Southern Illinois University Press. pp. 1–31.

Day, J., 2013c. Imagined aromas and artificial flowers in Minoan society. In: J. Day, ed. *Making Senses of the Past: Toward a Sensory Archaeology*. Center for Archaeological Investigations, Occasional Paper No. 40. Carbondale, IL: Southern Illinois University Press. pp. 286–309.

Daybell, J., 2009. Material meanings and the social signs of manuscript letters in early modern England. *Literature Compass* 6(3), pp. 647–67.

De Cazanove, O., 2008. Enfants en langes, pour quels voeux? In: G. Greco and B. Ferrara, eds. *Doni agli dei. Il sistema dei doni votivi nei santuari. Atti del seminario di studi. Napoli 21 aprile 2006*. Naples: Naus. pp. 271–84.

DeLaine, J., 2002. Building activity in Ostia in the second century AD. In: C. Bruun and A. Gallina Zevi, eds. *Ostia e Portus nelle loro relazioni con Roma. Acta Instituti Romani Finlandiea 27*. Roma: Acta Instituti Romani Finlandiea. pp. 41–102.

DeLaine, J., 2005. The commercial landscape of Ostia. In: A. Macmahon and J. Price, eds. *Roman Working Lives and Urban Living*. Oxford: Oxbow Books. pp. 29–47.

Della Corte, M., 1912. Continuazione dello scavo di via dell'Abbondanza durante il mese di luglio 1912. *Notizie degli Scavi di Antichità* 9, pp. 246–59.

Dembski, G., 2005. *Die Antiken Gemmen und Kameen aus Carnuntum*. Vienna: Phoibos.

De Montfort University, 2013. *Leicester Virtual Romans Project* [Online]. Available at http://www.romanleicester.dmu.ac.uk/objects.html (Accessed 30 September 2015).

D'Ercole, M.C., 1990. *La stipe votiva del Belvedere a Lucera. Corpus delle stipe votive in Italia III. Regio II.2*. Rome: Giorgio Bretschneider Editore.

Derks, T., 2014. Seeking divine protection against untimely death: infant votives from Roman Gaul and Germany. In: M. Carroll and E.-J. Graham, eds. *Infant Health and Death in Roman Italy and Beyond: Journal of Roman Archaeology Supplementary Series* 96. Ann Arbor, MI: University of Michigan Press. pp. 47–68.

Detienne, M., 1977. *The Gardens of Adonis: Spices in Greek Mythology*. Atlantic Highlands, NJ: Humanities Press.

De Witte, M., 2011. Touch. *Material Religion* 7(1), pp. 148–55.

Dittenberger, W., 1915–24. *Sylloge Inscriptionum Graecarum*. Leipzig: apud S. Hirzelium.

Dodge, H., 2011. *Spectacle in the Roman World*. London: Bristol Classical Press.

Dodson-Robinson, E., 2011. Performing the 'unperformable' extispicy scene in Seneca's *Oedipus Rex. Didaskalia* 8, pp. 179–84.

Draycott, J., 2015. Trees, flowers and herbs in the ancient world. In: M. Bradley, ed. *Smell and the Ancient Senses*. Abingdon: Routledge. pp. 60–73.

Draycott, J. and Graham, E.-J., eds, 2017. *Bodies of Evidence: Ancient Anatomical Votives Past, Present and Future*. Abingdon: Routledge.

Drobnick, J., 2005. Volatile effects: olfactory dimensions of art and architecture. In: D. Howes, ed. *Empire of the Senses: The Sensual Culture Reader*. Oxford: Berg. pp. 265–80.

Dunbabin, K., 1978. *The Mosaics of Roman North Africa: Studies in Iconography and Patronage*. Oxford: Clarendon Press.

Dutsch, D., 2008. *Nenia*: gender, genre and lament in ancient Rome. In: A. Suter, ed. *Lament: Studies in the Ancient Mediterranean and beyond*. Oxford: Oxford University Press. pp. 258–79.

Dyson, S.L., 2010. *Rome: A Living Portrait of an Ancient City*. Baltimore: The John Hopkins University Press.

Edwards, C., 1997. Unspeakable professions: public performance and prostitution in ancient Rome. In: J. Hallett and M. Skinner, eds. *Roman Sexualities*. Princeton, NJ: Princeton University Press. pp. 66–95.

Elkins, J., 1997. *The Object Stares Back: On the Nature of Seeing*. San Diago: Harcourt Brace.

Ellis, S., 2004. The distribution of bars at Pompeii: archaeological, spatial and viewshed analyses. *Journal of Roman Archaeology* 17, pp. 371–84.

Ellis, S., 2011. *Pes dexter*: superstition and the state in the shaping of shopfronts and street activity in the Roman world. In: R. Laurence and D. Newsome, eds. *Rome, Ostia, Pompeii: Movement and Space*. Oxford: Oxford University Press. pp. 160–73.

Eniex, L., 2014. *Archaeoacoustics: The Archaeology of Sound, Publication of the Proceedings from the 2014 Conference in Malta*. Myakka City: The OTS Foundation.

Epplett, C., 2013. Roman beast hunts. In: P. Christesen and D. Kyle, eds. *A Companion to Sport and Spectacle in Greek and Roman Antiquity*. Malden, MA: Wiley–Blackwell. pp. 520–32.

Everest, F.A. and Pohlmann, K., 2009. *Master Handbook of Acoustics*, 5th edn. London: Mcgraw-Hill.

Fagan, G., 2011. *The Lure of the Arena: Social Psychology and the Crowd at the Roman Games*. Cambridge: Cambridge University Press.

Fahlander, F. and Kjellström, A., eds, 2010a. *Making Sense of Things: Archaeologies of Sensory Perception*. Postdoctoral Archaeological Group, Stockholm Studies in Archaeology 53. Stockholm: Department of Archaeology and Classical Studies, Stockholm University.

Fahlander, F. and Kjellström, A., 2010b. Beyond sight: archaeologies of sensory perception. In: F. Fahlander and A. Kjellström, eds. *Making Sense of Things: Archaeologies of Sensory Perception*. Postdoctoral Archaeological Group, Stockholm Studies in Archaeology 53. Stockholm: Department of Archaeology and Classical Studies, Stockholm University. pp. 1–14.

Fantham, E., 2002. Orator and/et actor. In: P. Easterling and E. Hall, eds. *Greek and Roman Actors: Aspects of an Ancient Profession*. Cambridge: Cambridge University Press. pp. 362–76.

Faraone, C.A. and Naiden, F.S., 2012. Introduction. In: C.A. Faraone and F.S. Naiden, eds. *Greek and Roman Animal Sacrifice*. Cambridge: Cambridge University Press. pp. 1–10.

Favret, M.A., 1993. *Romantic Correspondence*. Cambridge: Cambridge University Press.

Favro, D., 1994. The street triumphant: the urban impact of Roman triumphal parades. In: Z. Çelik, D. Favro and R. Ingersoll, eds. *Streets: Critical Perspectives on Public Space*. Berkeley: University of California Press. pp. 151–64.

Favro, D., 1996. *The Urban Image of Augustan Rome*. Cambridge: Cambridge University Press.

Favro, D., 2011. Construction traffic in imperial Rome: building the Arch of Septimius Severus. In: R. Laurence and D. J. Newsome, eds. *Rome, Ostia, Pompeii: Movement and Space*. Oxford: Oxford University Press. pp. 332–60.

Favro, D., 2014. Moving events: curating the memory of the Roman triumph. In: K. Galinsky, ed. *Memoria Romana: Memory in Rome and Rome in Memory*. Memoirs of the American Academy in Rome Supplement 10. Ann Arbor, MI: University of Michigan Press. pp. 85–101.

Favro, D. and Johanson, C., 2010. Death in motion: funeral processions in the Roman forum. *Journal of the Society of Architectural Historians* 69(1), pp. 12–37.

Febvre, L., 1942. *Le Problème de l'incroyance au XVIe siècle. La religion de Rabelais*. Paris: Albin Michel.

Feld, S., 1982. *Sound and Sentiment: Birds, Weeping, Poetics and Song in Kaluli Expression*. Philadelphia: University of Pennsylvania Press.

Feld, S., 2005. Places sensed, senses placed: toward a sensuous epistemology of environments. In: D. Howes, ed. *Empire of the Senses: The Sensual Culture Reader*. Oxford: Berg. pp. 179–91.

Filmer, P., 2003. Songtime: sound culture, rhythm and sociality. In: M. Bull and L. Back, eds. *The Auditory Culture Reader*. Oxford: Berg. pp. 91–115.

Finlay, R., 2007. Weaving the rainbow: visions of colour in world history. *Journal of World History* 18(4), pp. 383–431.

Fless, F., 1995. *Opferdiener und Kultmusiker auf stadtrömischen historischen Reliefs: Untersuchungen zur Ikonographie, Funktion und Benennung*. Mainz: Philipp von Zabern.

Fless, F. and Moede, K., 2007. Music and dance: forms of representation in pictorial and written sources. In: J. Rüpke, ed. *A Companion to Roman Religion*. Oxford: Blackwell. pp. 249–62.

Fleury, P., 2008. Les *sparsiones* liquides dans les spectacles romains. *Revue des Études Latines* 86, pp. 97–112.

Fleury, P. and Madeleine, S., 2010. An interactive visit to the city of Rome in the fourth century AD. In: B. Frischer, J. Webb Crawford and D. Koller, eds. *Making History Interactive: Computer Applications and Quantitative Methods in Archaeology (CAA). Proceedings of the 37th International Conference, Williamsburg, Virginia, United States of America, March 22–26, 2009. British Archaeological Reports International Series* S2079. Oxford: Archaeopress. pp. 67–75.

Flohr, M., 2011. Reconsidering the *atrium* house: domestic *fullonicae* at Pompeii. In: E. Poehler, M. Flohr and K. Cole, eds. *Pompeii: Art, Industry, Infrastructure*. Oxford: Oxbow. pp. 88–102.

Flohr, M., 2013a. *The World of the Fullo: Work, Economy and Society in Roman Italy*. Oxford: Oxford University Press.

Flohr, M., 2013b. The textile economy of Pompeii. *Journal of Roman Archaeology* 26, pp. 53–78.

Flohr, M. and Wilson, A., 2011. The economy of ordure. In: G. Jansen, A.-O. Koloski-Ostrow and E. Moormann, eds. *Roman Toilets. Their Archaeology and Cultural History*. Leuven: Peeters. pp. 127–36.

Flouda, G., 2010. Agency matters: seal-users in Pylian administration. *Oxford Journal of Archaeology* 29(1), pp. 57–88.

Forte, M. and Gallese, V., 2014. *Embodiment and 3D Archaeology: A Neolithic House at Çatalhöyük*. Unpublished conference paper: Breaking Barriers Chacmool Conference, Calgary 2014.

Foster, C.P., 2013. Beyond the display case: creating a multisensory museum experience. In: J. Day, ed. *Making Senses of the Past: Toward a Sensory Archaeology*. Center for Archaeological Investigations, Occasional Paper No. 40. Carbondale, IL: Southern Illinois University Press. pp. 371–89.

Foster, S.L., 1997. Dancing bodies. In: J.C. Desmond, ed. *Meaning in Motion: New Cultural Studies of Dance*. Durham, NC: Duke University Press. pp. 235–57.

Foster, S.L., 2008. Movement's contagion: the kinesthetic impact of performance. In: T.C. Davis, ed. *The Cambridge Companion to Performance Studies*. Cambridge: Cambridge University Press. pp. 46–59.

Foxhall, L. and Stears, K., 2000. Redressing the balance: dedications of clothing to Artemis and the order of life stages. In: M. Donald and L. Hurcombe, eds. *Gender and Material Culture in Historical Perspective*. Basingstoke: MacMillan. pp. 3–16.

Frayn, J.M., 1993. *Markets and Fairs in Roman Italy: Their Social and Economic Importance from the Second Century BC to the Third Century AD*. Oxford: Clarendon Press.

Freestone, I., Meeks, N., Sax, M. and Higgitt, C., 2007. The Lycurgus Cup: a Roman nano-technology. *Gold Bulletin* 40(4), pp. 270–7.

Freud, S., 1990. Civilization and its discontents. In: J. Strachey, ed. *The Standard Edition of the Complete Psychological Works of Sigmund Freud Vol. XXI (1827–1931)*. London: Vintage. pp. 59–145.

Frischer, B., 2013. *Rome Reborn* [Online]. Available at: http://romereborn.frischerconsulting.com (Accessed 30 September 2015).

Furger, A.R., 2009. Die Siegelstoffe. In: A.R. Furger, A.R.M. Wartmann and E. Riha, eds. *Die römischen Siegelkapseln aus Augusta Raurica*. Augst: Augusta Raurica, Forschungen in Augst Band 44. pp. 29–32.

Furley, W.D. and Bremer, J.M., 2001. *Greek Hymns: Selected Cult Songs from the Archaic to the Hellenistic Period. The Texts in Translation*. Vol. 1. Tübingen: Mohr Siebeck.

Futrell, A., 2006. *The Roman Games: A Sourcebook*. Oxford: Blackwell.

Gallese, V. and Lakoff, G., 2005. The brain's concepts: the role of the sensory-motor system in conceptual knowledge. *Cognitive Neuropsychology* 22(3–4), pp. 455–79.

Gardner, A., 2002. Social identity and the duality of structure in late Roman-period Britain. *Journal of Social Archaeology* 2, pp. 323–51.

Garelli, M.-H., 2007. *Danser le Mythe: la Pantomime et sa Réception dans la Culture Antique*. Louvain: Peeters.

Garrison, D.H., ed, 2010. *A Cultural History of the Human Body in Antiquity*. Oxford: Berg.

Gesztelyi, T., 2000. *Antike Gemmen im Ungrarischen Nationalmuseum. Catalogi Musei Nationalis Hungarici. Seria archaeologica* 4. Budapest: Ungrarischen Nationalmuseum.

Gibson, B., 2006. *Statius Silvae 5*. Oxford: Oxford University Press.

Gibson, J.J., 1986. *The Ecological Approach to Visual Perception*. Hillsdale, NJ: Lawrence Erlbaum Associates.

Gilbert, A., 2008. *What the Nose Knows: The Science of Scent in Everyday Life*. New York: Crown.

Giroire, C. and Roger, D., 2007. *Roman Art from the Louvre*. New York: American Federation of Arts.

Gleason, K., 1994. Porticus Pompeiana: a new perspective on the first public park of ancient Rome. *The Journal of Garden History* 14(1), pp. 13–27.

Gleason, M., 1995. *Making Men: Sophists and Self-presentation in Ancient Rome*. Princeton, NJ: Princeton University Press.

Glinister, F., 2017. Ritual and meaning: contextualising votive terracotta infants in Hellenistic Italy. In: J. Draycott and E.-J. Graham, eds. *Bodies of Evidence: Ancient Anatomical Votives Past, Present and Future*. Abingdon: Routledge, pp. 131–46.

Gliozzo, E., Grassi, N., Bonanni, P., Meneghini, C. and Tomei, M.A., 2010. Gemstones from Vigna Barberini at the Palatine Hill (Rome, Italy). *Archaeometry* 53(3), pp. 469–89.

Goffmann, E., 1963. *Stigma: Notes on the Management of Spoiled Identity*. New York: Simon and Schuster.

Golvin, J.-C., 1988. *L'amphithéâtre romain: essai sur la théorisation de sa forme et de ses fonctions*. Paris: Diffusion de Boccard.

Gorget, C., ed, 2007. *Le Cheval et la Danseuse. À la redécouverte du trésor de Neuvy-en-Sullias*. Orléans: Somogy Éditions d'Art.

Gosden, C., 2001. Making sense: archaeology and aesthetics. *World Archaeology* 33(2), pp. 163–7.

Gosden, C., 2005. What do objects want? *Journal of Archaeological Method and Theory* 12(3), pp. 193–211.

Graham, E.-J., 2005. The quick and the dead in the extra-urban landscape: the Roman cemetery at Ostia/Portus as a lived environment. In: J. Bruhn, B. Croxford and D. Grigoropoulos, eds. *TRAC 2004: Proceedings of the Fourteenth Roman Archaeology Conference, Durham 2004*. Oxford: Oxbow Books. pp. 133–43.

Graham, E.-J., 2011a. Memory and materiality: re-embodying the Roman funeral. In: V.M. Hope and J. Huskinson, eds. *Memory and Mourning: Studies on Roman Death*. Oxford: Oxbow Books. pp. 21–39.

Graham, E.-J., 2011b. From fragments to ancestors: re-defining the role of *os resectum* in rituals of purification and commemoration in Republican Rome. In: M. Carroll and J. Rempel, eds. *Living through the Dead: Burial and Commemoration in the Classical World*. Oxford: Oxbow. pp. 91–109.

Graham, E.-J., 2013. The making of infants in Hellenistic and early Roman Italy: a votive perspective. *World Archaeology* 45(2), pp. 215–31.

Graham, E.-J., 2014. Infant votives and swaddling in Hellenistic Italy. In: M. Carroll and E.-J. Graham, eds. *Infant Health and Death in Roman Italy and Beyond: Journal of Roman Archaeology Supplementary Series 96*. Ann Arbor, MI: University of Michigan Press. pp. 23–46.

Graham, E.-J., 2017. Partible humans and permeable gods: anatomical votives and personhood in the sanctuaries of central Italy. In: J. Draycott and E.-J. Graham, eds. *Bodies of Evidence: Ancient Anatomical Votives Past, Present and Future*. Abingdon: Routledge. pp. 45–62.

Greene, E., 2006. The intaglios. In: B. Birley and E. Greene, eds. *The Roman Jewellery from Vindolanda: Beads, Intaglios, Finger Rings, Bracelets and Ear-Rings. Vindolanda Research Reports. Vol. IV, Fascicule V*. Greenhead: The Vindolanda Trust. pp. 53–116.

Guiraud, H., 2008. *Intailles et camées du l'époque romaine en Gaule (territoire français). Vol. II. Editions du Centre National de la Recherche Scientifique, Supplément à Galia 48*. Paris: Editions du Centre National de la Recherche Scientifique.

Gunderson, E., 2000. *Staging Masculinity: The Rhetoric of Performance in the Roman World.* Ann Arbor, MI: University of Michigan Press.

Hall, E.T., 1966. *The Hidden Dimension: Man's Use of Space in Public and Private.* London: The Bodley Head.

Hall, E., 2008. Is the 'Barcelona Alcestis' a Latin pantomime libretto? In: E. Hall and R. Wyles, eds. *New Directions in Ancient Pantomime.* Oxford: Oxford University Press. pp. 258–82.

Hall, E. and Wyles, R., eds, 2008. *New Directions in Ancient Pantomime.* Oxford: Oxford University Press.

Hamilakis, Y., 2011. Archaeologies of the senses. In: T. Insoll, ed. *The Oxford Handbook of the Archaeology of Ritual and Religion.* Oxford: Oxford University Press. pp. 208–25.

Hamilakis, Y., 2013. Eleven theses on the archaeology of the senses. In: J. Day, ed. *Making Senses of the Past: Toward a Sensory Archaeology.* Center for Archaeological Investigations, Occasional Paper No. 40. Carbondale, IL: Southern Illinois University Press. pp. 409–19.

Hamilakis, Y., 2014. *Archaeology and the Senses: Human Experience, Memory, and Affect.* Cambridge: Cambridge University Press.

Hamilakis, Y., Pluciennik, M. and Tarlow, S., eds, 2002. *Thinking through the Body: Archaeologies of Corporeality.* London and New York: Kluwer Academic/Plenum.

Hamilton, S. and Whitehouse, R., 2006. Three senses of dwelling: beginning to socialise the Neolithic ditched villages of the Tavoliere, southeast Italy. In: V.O. Jorger, J.M. Cardoso, A.M. Vale, G.L. Velho and L.S. Pereira, eds. *Approaching 'Prehistoric and Protohistoric Architectures' of Europe from a 'Dwelling Perspective': Journal of Iberian Archaeology* 8. Porto: Adecap. pp. 159–84.

Hamilton, S. and Whitehouse, R., forthcoming. *Sensual and Social Landscapes of the Prehistory of Northern Puglia, S. Italy.* London: Accordia.

Hammer, D., 2010. Roman spectacle entertainments and the technology of reality. *Arethusa* 43(1), pp. 63–86.

Harlow, M., 2013. Toys, dolls, and the material culture of childhood. In: J.E. Grubbs and T. Parkin, eds. *The Oxford Handbook of Childhood and Education in the Classical World.* Oxford: Oxford University Press. pp. 322–40.

Harris, H., 1974. Lubrication in antiquity. *Greece and Rome* 21(1), pp. 32–6.

Harrop, S., 2010. Physical performance and the languages of translation. In: E. Hall and S. Harrop, eds. *Theorising Performance: Greek Drama, Cultural History, and Critical Practice.* London: Duckworth. pp. 232–40.

Harvey, S.A., 2006. *Scenting Salvation: Ancient Christianity and the Olfactory Imagination.* Berkeley: University of California Press.

Harvey, S.A., 2014. The senses in religion: piety, critique, competition. In: J. Toner, ed. *A Cultural History of the Senses in Antiquity.* London: Bloomsbury. pp. 91–113.

Hatipoğlu, M. and Güney, H., 2013. Archaeo-gemmological investigation of gemstone glyptics (seal stones and ceremonial stones) and ancient jewelleries mounted gemstones in Izmir Archaeological Museum (Turkey). *Journal of Cultural Heritage* 13(3), pp. 165–8.

Hayne, M., Taylor, J., Rumble, R. and Mee, D., 2011. Prediction of noise from small to medium size crowds. *Proceedings of Acoustics 2011,* pp. 1–7.

Hekster, O., 2005. Captured in the gaze of power: visibility, games and Roman imperial representation. In: O. Hekster and R. Fowler, eds. *Imaginary Kings: Royal Images in the Ancient Near East, Greece and Rome.* Oriens et Occidens 11. Stuttgart: Franz Steiner Verlag. pp. 157–76.

Henig, M., 1994. *Classical Gems: Ancient and Modern Intaglios and Cameos in the Fitzwilliam Museum, Cambridge.* Cambridge: Cambridge University Press.

Henig, M., 2007. *A Corpus of Roman Engraved Gemstones from British Sites,* 3rd edn. *British Archaeological Reports British Series* 8. Oxford: Archaeopress.

Henig, M., 2008. The re-use and copying of ancient intaglios set in medieval personal seals mainly found in England: an aspect of the Renaissance of the 12th century. In: N. Adams, J. Cherry and J. Robinson, eds. *Good Impressions: Image and Authority in Medieval Seals: British Museum Research Publication* 168. London: British Museum Press. pp. 25–34.

Henshaw, V., 2014. *Urban Smellscape: Understanding and Designing City Smell Environments.* London: Routledge.

Hickman, M., 2011. Something smells odd in the lucrative world of saffron. *The Independent,* 10 January 2011 [Online]. Available at http://www.independent.co.uk/Life-style/food-and-drink/news/something-smells-odd-in-the-lucrative-world-of-saffron-2180285.html (Accessed 30 September 2015).

Hodder, I., 2012. *Entangled: An Archaeology of the Relationships between Humans and Things.* Chichester: Wiley-Blackwell.

Holleran, C., 2011. The street life of ancient Rome. In: R. Laurence and D.J. Newsome, eds. *Rome, Ostia, Pompeii: Movement and Space.* Oxford: Oxford University Press. pp. 245–61.

Holleran, C., 2012. *Shopping in Ancient Rome: The Retail Trade in the Late Republic and the Principate.* Oxford: Oxford University Press.

Holmes, B., 2010. Medical knowledge and technology. In: D.H. Garrison, ed. *A Cultural History of the Human Body in Antiquity.* Oxford: Berg. pp. 83–105.

Holtorf, C. and Williams, H., 2006. Landscapes and memories. In: D. Hicks and M.C. Beaudry, eds. *The Cambridge Companion to Historical Archaeology.* Cambridge: Cambridge University Press. pp. 235–54.

Homo-Lechner, C. and Vendries, C., 1999. *Le Carnyx et la lyre: archéologie musicale en Gaule celtique et romaine.* Besançon: Musée des Beaux-Arts et d'Archéologie de Besançon.

Hope, V.M., 2007. *Death in Ancient Rome: A Sourcebook.* London: Routledge.

Hope, V.M., 2009. *Roman Death: The Dying and the Dead in Ancient Rome.* London: Continuum.

Hope, V.M., 2010. "The end is to the beginning as the beginning is to the end": birth, death and the classical body. In: D.H. Garrison, ed. *A Cultural History of the Human Body in Antiquity.* Oxford and New York: Berg. pp. 25–44.

Hope, V.M., 2011a. Livia's tears: the presentation of Roman mourning. In: H. Whittaker, ed. *In Memoriam: Commemoration, Communal Memory and Gender Values in the Ancient Graeco-Roman World.* Newcastle upon Tyne: Cambridge Scholars Press. pp. 91–125.

Hope, V.M., 2011b. Remembering to mourn: personal mementos to the dead in ancient Rome. In: V.M. Hope and J. Huskinson, eds. *Memory and Mourning: Studies on Roman Death.* Oxford: Oxbow Books. pp. 176–95.

Hornblower, S. and Spawforth, A., eds, 1996. *Oxford Classical Dictionary,* 3rd edn. Oxford: Oxford University Press.

Horsfall, N., 2003. *The Culture of the Roman Plebs.* London: Bloomsbury.

Hoskins, J., 2006. Agency, biography and objects. In: C. Tilley, W. Keane, S. Küchler, M. Rowlands and P. Spyer, eds. *Handbook of Material Culture.* London: Sage Publications. pp. 74–84.

Howes, D., 1987. Olfaction and transition: an essay on the ritual uses of smell. *Canadian Review of Sociology and Anthropology* 24(3), pp. 398–416.

Howes, D., 2003. *Sensual Relations: Engaging the Senses in Culture and Society.* Ann Arbor, MI: University of Michigan Press.

Howes, D., ed, 2005a. *Empire of the Senses: The Sensual Culture Reader.* Oxford: Berg.

Howes, D., 2005b. Introduction: empires of the senses. In: D. Howes, ed. *Empire of the Senses: The Sensual Cultural Reader.* Oxford: Berg. pp. 1–17.

Howes, D., 2006. Scent, sound and synaesthesia: intersensoriality and material culture theory. In: C. Tilley, W. Keane, S. Küchler, M. Rowlands and P. Spyer, eds. *Handbook of Material Culture.* London: Sage Publications. pp. 161–72.

Howes, D., 2011. Sensation. *Material Religion* 7(1), pp. 92–9.

Howes, D., 2013. *The Expanding Field of Sensory Studies* [Online]. Available at http://www. sensorystudies.org/sensorial-investigations/the-expanding-field-of-sensory-studies/ (Accessed 30 September 2015).

Howes, D. and Classen, C., 2014. *Ways of Sensing: Understanding the Senses in Society*. London and New York: Routledge.

Hughes, E., 1958. *Men and Their Work*. Glencoe: Free Press.

Hughes, E., 1962. Good people and dirty work. *Social Problems* 10(1), pp. 3–11.

Hughes, J., 2017. *Votive Body Parts in Greek and Roman Religion*. Cambridge: Cambridge University Press.

Hughes, L., 2007. Dyeing in Ancient Italy? Evidence for the *purpurarii*. In: C. Gillis, M.L. Nosch, eds. *Ancient Textiles: Production, Craft and Society, Proceedings of the First International Conference on Ancient Textiles, Held at Lund, Sweden, and Copenhagen, Denmark, on March 19–23, 2003*. Oxford: Oxbow. pp. 87–93.

Hughes, L.A., 2005. Centurions at Amiternum: notes on the Apisius family. *Phoenix* 59, pp. 77–91.

Humphrey, J.H., 1986. *Roman Circuses: Arenas for Chariot Racing*. Berkeley and Los Angeles: University of California Press.

Humphrey, J., Oleson, J. and Sherwood, A., 1998. *Greek and Roman Technology: A Sourcebook*. London: Routledge.

Humphries, J., 1996. *The Essential Saffron Companion*. London: Grub Street.

Hunter-Crawley, H., 2013a. Embodying the divine: the sensational experience of the sixth-century Eucharist. In: J. Day, ed. *Making Senses of the Past: Toward a Sensory Archaeology*. Center for Archaeological Investigations, Occasional Paper No. 40. Carbondale, IL: Southern Illinois University Press. pp. 160–76.

Hunter-Crawley, H., 2013b. The cross of light: experiencing divine presence in Byzantine Syria. In: C. Nesbitt and M. Jackson, eds. *Experiencing Byzantium: Papers of the Forty Fourth Spring Symposium of Byzantine Studies*. Farnham: Ashgate. pp. 175–93.

Hurcombe, L., 2007. A sense of materials and sensory perception in concepts of materiality. *World Archaeology* 39(4), pp. 532–45.

Iara, K., 2015. Moving in and moving out: ritual movements between Rome and its *Suburbium*. In: I. Östenberg, S. Malmberg and J. Bjørnebye, eds. *The Moving City: Processions, Passages and Promenades in Ancient Rome*. Bloomsbury: London. pp. 125–32.

Ihde, D., 2003. Auditory imagination. In: M. Bull and L. Back, eds. *The Auditory Culture Reader*. Oxford: Berg. pp. 61–6.

Ihde, D., 2007. *Listening and Voice: Phenomenologies of Sound*, 2nd edn. New York: State University of New York Press.

Ingleheart, J., 2008. *Et mea sunt populo saltata poemata saepe* (*Tristia* 2.519): Ovid and the pantomime. In: E. Hall and R. Wyles, eds. *New Directions in Ancient Pantomime*. Oxford: Oxford University Press. pp. 198–217.

Ingold, T., 2000. *The Perception of the Environment: Essays on Livelihood, Dwelling, and Skill*. London: Routledge.

Inomata, T. and Coben, L., 2006. Overture: an invitation to the archaeological theater. In: T. Inomata and L. Coben, eds. *Archaeology of Performance: Theaters of Power, Community and Politics*. Walnut Creek: Altamira. pp. 11–44.

Insoll, T., 2007. *Archaeology: The Conceptual Challenge*. London: Duckworth.

Insoll, T., Polya, D.A., Bhan, K., Irving, D. and Jarvis, K., 2004. Towards an understanding of the carnelian bead trade from Western India to sub-Saharan Africa: the application of UV-LA-ICP-MS to carnelian from Gujarat, India and West Africa. *Journal of Archaeological Science* 31(8), pp. 1161–73.

Jacobelli, L., 2003. *Gladiators at Pompeii*. Los Angeles: Getty Publications.

James, S., 2002. Writing the legions; the past, present and future of Roman military studies in Britain. *Archaeological Journal* 159, pp. 1–58.

Jashemski, W., 1979. 'The garden of Hercules at Pompeii' (II.viii.6): the discovery of a commercial flower garden. *American Journal of Archaeology* 83, pp. 403–11.

Jeannerod, M., 1994. The representing brain: neural correlates of motor intention and imagery. *Behavioural and Brain Sciences* 17(2), pp. 187–245.

Jeannerod, M., 2001. Neural simulation of action: a unifying mechanism for motor cognition. *NeuroImage* 14, pp. 103–09.

Johanson, C., 2011. A walk with the dead: a funerary cityscape of ancient Rome. In: B. Rawson, ed. *A Companion to Families in the Greek and Roman Worlds*. Chichester: Wiley-Blackwell. pp. 408–30.

Jones, A., 1999. Local colour: megalithic architecture and colour symbolism in Neolithic Arran. *Oxford Journal of Archaeology* 18(4), pp. 339–50.

Jones, A. and MacGregor, G., eds, 2002. *Colouring the Past: The Significance of Colour in Archaeological Research*. Oxford: Berg.

J. Paul Getty Museum, 2004–06. *Thesaurus Cultus et Rituum Antiquorum*. Los Angeles: Getty Publications.

Kahn, D., 2003. The sound of music. In: M. Bull and L. Back, eds. *The Auditory Culture Reader*. Oxford: Berg. pp. 77–90.

Kelman, A., 2010. Rethinking the soundscape: a critical genealogy of a key term in sound studies. *Senses and Society* 5(2), pp. 212–34.

Killeen, J., 1959. What was the *linea dives* (Martial, VIII.78.7)? *The American Journal of Philology* 80(2), pp. 185–8.

Kleiner, D.E.E., 1992. *Roman Sculpture*. New Haven: Yale University Press.

Knappett, C., 2004. The affordances of things: a post-Gibsonian perspective on the relationality of mind and matter. In: E. DeMarrais, C. Gosden and C. Renfrew, eds. *Rethinking Materiality: The Engagement of Mind with the Material World*. Cambridge: McDonald Institute Monographs. pp. 43–51.

Knappett, C., 2005. *Thinking through Material Culture: An Interdisciplinary Perspective*. Philadelphia, PA: University of Pennsylvania Press.

Koloski-Ostrow, A.O., 2015. Roman urban smells: the archaeological evidence. In: M. Bradley, ed. *Smell and the Ancient Senses*. Abingdon: Routledge. pp. 90–109.

Korsmeyer, C., ed, 2005. *The Taste Culture Reader: Experiencing Food and Drink*. Oxford: Berg.

Krampl, U. and Beck, R., 2013. Introduction. Des sens qui font la ville. Pour une histoire sensible du fait urbain. In: R. Beck, U. Krampl and E. Retaillaud-Bajac, eds. *Les cinq sens de la ville du Moyen Âge à nos jours*. Tours: Université François Rabelais. pp. 13–25.

Krug, A., 1981. *Antike Gemmen im Römisch-Germanischen Museum, Köln*. Frankfurt: Zabern.

Kudlien, F., 2002. P. Patulcius L.f., Walker und Probulos um späthellenistischen Magnesia. *Laverna. Beiträge zur Wirtschafts-und Sozialgeschichte der alten Welt* 13, pp. 56–68.

Lada-Richards, I., 2004. Mythōn eikōn: pantomime dancing and the figurative arts. *Arion* 12(2), pp. 111–40.

Lada-Richards, I., 2007. *Silent Eloquence: Lucian and Pantomime Dancing*. London: Duckworth.

Lada-Richards, I., 2013. Mutata corpora: Ovid's changing forms and the metamorphic bodies of pantomime dancing. *Transactions of the American Philological Association* 143(1), pp. 105–52.

Larmour, D.H.J. and Spencer, D., 2007. *The Sites of Rome*. Oxford: Oxford University Press.

Larsson Lovén, L., 2013. Female work and identity in Roman textile production and trade: a methodological discussion. In: M. Gleba and J. Pásztókai-Szeőke, eds. *Making Textiles in pre-Roman and Roman Times: People, Places, Identities*. Oxford: Oxbow. pp. 109–25.

Laurence, R., 2007. *Roman Pompeii: Space and Society*, 2nd edn. London: Routledge.

Laurence, R., 2015. Towards a history of mobility in ancient Rome (300 BCE to 100 CE). In: I. Östenberg, S. Malmberg and J. Bjørnebye, eds. *The Moving City: Processions, Passages and Promenades in Ancient Rome*. Bloomsbury: London. pp. 175–86.

Laurence, R. and Newsome, D., eds, 2011. *Rome, Ostia, Pompeii: Movement and Space*. Oxford: Oxford University Press.

Lavan, L., 2012. Public space in late antique Ostia: excavation and survey in 2008–2011. *American Journal of Archaeology* 116(4), pp. 649–91.

Lawler, L.B., 1964. *The Dance in Ancient Greece*. London: A.C. and Black.

Leach, E., 1983. The gatekeepers of heaven: anthropological aspects of grandiose architecture. *Journal of Anthropological Research* 39, pp. 243–64.

Leach, E.W., 2006. Freedmen and immortality in the tomb of the Haterii. In: E. D'Ambra and G.P.R. Metraux, eds. *The Art of Citizens, Soldiers, and Freedmen in the Roman World*. Oxford: Archaeopress. pp. 1–17.

Lefebvre, H., 1991. *The Production of Space*. Trans. D. Nicholson-Smith. Malden, MA: Blackwell Publishing.

Lefebvre, H., 2004. *Rhythmanalysis: Space, Time and Everyday Life*. London: Continuum.

Lefebvre, H., 2014. *Toward an Architecture of Enjoyment*. Ed. Ł Staneck. Trans. R. Bononno. Minneapolis: University of Minnesota Press.

Leibniz, G.W., 1886. *Nouveaux essais sur l'entendement humain*. Trans. J.-H. Vérin. Paris: Poussielgue Frères.

Lennon, J., 2013. *Pollution and Religion in Ancient Rome*. Cambridge: Cambridge University Press.

Lilja, S., 1972. *The Treatment of Odours in the Poetry of Antiquity*. (Commentationes Humanarum Litterarum 49). Helsinki: Societas Scientiarum Fennica.

Lindsay, H., 2000. Death-pollution and funerals in the city of Rome. In: V.M. Hope and E. Marshall, eds. *Death and Disease in the Ancient City*. London: Routledge. pp. 152–73.

Lindstrøm, T.C., 2010. The animals of the arena: how and why could their destruction and death be endured and enjoyed? *World Archaeology* 42(2), pp. 310–23.

Llewellyn Jones, L., 2005. Body language and the female role-player in Greek tragedy and Japanese Kabuki theatre. In: D. Cairns, ed. *Body Language in the Greek and Roman Worlds*. Swansea: Classical Press of Wales. pp. 73–105.

Lombardi, L., 2001. The water system of the Colosseum. In: A. Gabucci, ed. *The Colosseum*. Trans. M. Becker. Los Angeles: Getty Publications. pp. 229–41.

Lynch, K., 1960. *The Image of the City*. Cambridge, MA: The MIT Press.

Macintosh, F., ed, 2010. *The Ancient Dancer in the Modern World: Responses to Greek and Roman Dance*. Oxford: Oxford University Press.

MacKinnon, M., 2006. Supplying exotic animals for the Roman amphitheatre games: new reconstructions combining archaeological, ancient textual, historical and ethnographic data. *Mouseion* Series III, 6, pp. 137–61.

Madeleine, S., 2007. Le complexe pompéien du Champ de Mars au IVe siècle, témoin de la réappropriation idéologique Julio-Claudienne. *Schedae* 6(1), pp. 81–96.

Mahoney, A., 2001. *Roman Sports and Spectacles: A Sourcebook*. Newburyport, MA: Focus Publishing.

Maiuri, A., 1953. *Roman Painting*. Trans. S. Gilbert. Geneva: Skira.

Malafouris, L., 2008. Between brains, bodies and things: *tectonoetic* awareness and the extended self. *Philosophical Transactions of the Royal Society B* 363, pp. 1993–2002 [Online]. Available at http://www.ncbi.nlm.nih.gov/pmc/articles/PMC2606705/ (Accessed 30 September 2015).

Malmberg, S., 2009. Finding your way in the subura. In: M. Driessen, S. Heeren, J. Hendriks, F. Kemmers and R. Visser, eds. *TRAC 2008: Proceedings of the Eighteenth Annual Theoretical Roman Archaeology Conference Amsterdam 2008*. Oxford: Oxbow Books. pp. 39–52.

Malmberg, S., 2015. 'Ships are seen gliding swiftly along the sacred Tiber': the river as an artery of urban movement and development. In: I. Östenberg, S. Malmberg and J. Bjørnebye, eds. *The Moving City: Processions, Passages and Promenades in Ancient Rome*. London: Bloomsbury. pp. 187–201.

Manning, W.H., 1976. *Romano-British Ironwork in the Museum of Antiquities, Newcastle upon Tyne*. Newcastle: University of Newcastle upon Tyne.

Marcu, F., 2007. Places of worship in forts. *Acta Musei Napocensis* 41–42(1), pp. 75–105.

Marks, L.U., 2002. *Touch: Sensuous Theory and Multisensory Media*. Minneapolis: University of Minnesota Press.

Markus, D., 2004. Grim pleasures: Statius's poetic *consolations*. *Arethusa* 37(1), pp. 105–36.

Mau, A., 1899. *Pompeii: Its Life and Art*. New York: Macmillan.

Maxey, M., 1938. *Occupations of the Lower Classes in Roman Society as Seen in Justinian's Digest*. Chicago: Chicago University Press.

McFarlane, P., 2010. Health and disease. In: D.H. Garrison, ed. *A Cultural History of the Human Body in Antiquity*. Oxford: Berg. pp. 45–66.

McMahon, A., 2013. Space, sound, and light: toward a sensory experience of ancient monumental architecture. *American Journal of Archaeology* 117(2), pp. 163–79.

Meiggs, R., 1973. *Roman Ostia*. 2nd ed. Oxford: Oxford University Press.

Merleau-Ponty, M., 1968 [1964]. *The Visible and the Invisible: Followed by Working Notes: Northwestern University Studies in Phenomenology and Existential Philosophy*. Ed. C. Lefort. Trans. A. Lingis. Evanston: Northwestern University Press.

Meyer, B., Morgan, D., Paine, C. and Plate, S.B., 2010. The origin and mission of 'Material Religion'. *Religion* 40, pp. 207–11.

Meyer, B., Morgan, D., Paine, C. and Plate, S.B., 2011. Introduction: key words in material religion. *Material Religion* 7(1), pp. 4–9.

Millar, S., 2008. *Space and Sense*. Hove: Psychology Press.

Mille, B., 2007. Les trompes gallo-romaines de Neuvy-en Sullias et Saint-Just-sur-Dive, apport d'une étude de laboratoire. In: C. Gorget, ed. *Le Cheval et la Danseuse. À la redécouverte du trésor de Neuvy-en-Sullias*. Orléans: Somogy éditions d'Art. pp. 146–55.

Miller Ammerman, R., 2007. Children at risk: votive terracottas and the welfare of infants at Paestum. In: A. Cohen and J.B. Rutter, eds. *Constructions of Childhood in Ancient Greece and Italy: Hesperia Supplement* 41. Princeton: ASCSA Publications. pp. 131–51.

Molloy, M.E., 1996. *Libanius and the Dancers*. Hildesheim: Olms-Weidmann.

Monteix, N., 2010. *Les lieux de métier: boutiques et ateliers d'Herculanum*. Rome: École Française de Rome.

Monteix, N., 2013. The apple of discord: fleece-washing in Pompeii's textile economy. *Journal of Roman Archaeology* 26, pp. 79–88.

Montgomery Griffiths, J., 2010. Acting perspectives: the phenomenology of performance as a route to reception. In: E. Hall and S. Harrop, eds. *Theorising Performance: Greek Drama, Cultural History, and Critical Practice*. London: Duckworth. pp. 219–31.

Morgan, D., 2009. The look of sympathy: religion, visual culture, and the social life of feeling. *Material Religion* 5(2), pp. 132–55.

Morgan, D., 2010. Introduction: the matter of belief. In: D. Morgan, ed. *Religion and Material Culture: The Matter of Belief*. London and New York: Routledge. pp. 1–17.

Morley, N., 2005. The salubriousness of the Roman city. In: H. King, ed. *Health in Antiquity*. London: Routledge. pp. 192–204.

Morley, N., 2015. Urban smells and Roman noses. In: M. Bradley, ed. *Smell and the Ancient Senses*. Abingdon: Routledge. pp. 110–19.

Murphy, J.M.A., 2013. The scent of status: prestige and perfume at the Bronze Age palace at Pylos, Greece. In: J. Day, ed., *Making Senses of the Past: Toward a Sensory Archaeology*. Center for Archaeological Investigations, Occasional Paper No. 40. Carbondale, IL: Southern Illinois University Press. pp. 243–65.

Murray, P., 1998. Bodies in flux: Ovid's *Metamorphoses*. In: D. Montserrat, ed. *Changing Bodies, Changing Meanings: Studies on the Human Body in Antiquity*. London: Routledge. pp. 80–98.

Mustakallio, K., 2005. Roman funerals: identity, gender and participation. In: K. Mustakallio, J. Hansks, H.-L. Sanio and V. Vuolanto, eds. *Hoping for Continuity: Childhood, Education and Death in Antiquity and the Middle Ages. Acti Instituti Romani Findlandiae* 33. Rome: Instituti Romani Findlandiae. pp. 179–90.

Naerebout, F., 1997. *Attractive Performances. Ancient Greek Dance: Three Preliminary Studies*. Amsterdam: J.C. Gieben.

Nagy, A.M., 2013. *Campbell Bonner Magical Gems Database* [Online]. Available at http://www2.szepmuveszeti.hu/talismans/ (Accessed 16 November 2014).

Nelis-Clément, J., 2002. Les métiers du cirque, de Rome à Byzance: entre texte et image. *Cahiers du Centre Gustave Glotz* 13, pp. 265–309.

Nestorovič, A., 2005. *Images of the World Engraved in Jewels: Roman Gems from Slovenia*. Ljubljana: National Museum of Slovenia.

Newsome, D.J., 2009. Centrality in its place: defining urban space in the city of Rome. In: M. Driessen, S. Heeren, J. Hendriks, F. Kemmers and R. Visser, eds. *TRAC 2008: Proceedings of the Eighteenth Annual Theoretical Roman Archaeology Conference Amsterdam 2008*. Oxford: Oxbow Books. pp. 25–38.

Newsome, D.J., 2011. Introduction: making movement meaningful. In: R. Laurence and D.J. Newsome, eds. *Rome, Ostia, Pompeii: Movement and Space*. Oxford: Oxford University Press. pp. 1–54.

Nibley, H., 1945. Sparsiones. *The Classical Journal* 40(9), pp. 515–43.

Nilson, K.A., Persson, C.B. and Zahle, J., 2008. The foundation and the core of the podium and of the tribunal. In: S. Sande and J. Zahle, eds. *The Temple of Castor and Pollux III: The Augustan Temple*. Roma: "L'Erma" di Bretschneider. pp. 21–74.

Nilsson Stutz, L., 2003. *Embodied Rituals and Ritualized Bodies: Tracing Ritual Practices in Late Mesolithic Burials. Acta Archaeological Lundensia* 46. Lund: Almqvist and Wiksell International.

Norberg-Schulz, C., 1980. *Genius Loci: Towards a Phenomenology of Architecture*. New York: Rizzoli.

Notermans, C. and Jansen, W., 2011. Ex-votos in Lourdes: contested materiality of miraculous healings. *Material Religion* 7(2), pp. 168–93.

Ochs, D.J., 1993. *Consolatory Rhetoric: Grief, Symbol and Ritual in the Greco-Roman Era*. Columbia: University of South Carolina Press.

Oleson, J.-P., 1984. *Greek and Roman Mechanical Water-Lifting Devices: The History of a Technology*. Toronto: University of Toronto Press.

Olsen, W., 1998. Average speech levels and spectra in various speaking/listening conditions: a summary of the Pearson, Bennett and Fidell (1977) Report. *American Journal of Audiology* 7, pp. 1–5.

Olson, K., 2007 [2004–5]. Insignia lugentium: female mourning garments in Roman antiquity. *American Journal of Ancient History* 3–4, pp. 89–130.

Olson, K., 2014. The material world of the Roman *fullo*. Review of Flohr, M.: the World of the *Fullo*. Work, Economy and Society in Roman Italy. *Journal of Roman Archaeology* 27, pp. 596–8.

Packer, J., 1967. Housing and population in imperial Ostia and Rome. *Journal of Roman Studies* 57, pp. 80–95.

Packer, J., 1971. *The Insulae of Imperial Ostia: Memoirs of the American Academy in Rome, Supplement 31.* Rome: American Academy in Rome.

Palazzo, E., 2012. Les cinq sens au Moyen Âge: état de la question et perspectives de recherché. *Cahiers de Civilisation Médiévale* 55, pp. 339–66.

Palazzo, E., 2014. *L'Invention chrétienne des cinq sens dans la liturgie et l'art au Moyen Âge.* Paris: Cerf.

Papi, E., 1999. Vicus Tuscus. In: E.M. Steinby, ed. *Lexicon Topographicum Urbis Romae V (T–Z).* Rome: Edizioni Quasar. pp. 195–7.

Parker, H., 1999. The observed of all observers: spectacle, applause and cultural poetics in the Roman theater audience. In: B. Bergmann and C. Kondoleon, eds. *The Art of Ancient Spectacle.* New Haven: Yale University Press. pp. 163–79.

Paterson, M., 2007. *The Senses of Touch: Haptics, Affects and Technologies.* Oxford: Berg.

Pautasso, A., 1994. *Il deposito votivo presso la Porta Nord a Vulci. Corpus delle stipe votive in Italia VII. Regio VII.3.* Rome: Giorgio Bretschneider Editore.

Péché, V., 1998. *Musiciens et instruments à vent de type tibiae dans le théâtre à Rome du IIIe s. av. J.-C. au IIe s. ap. J.-C.* Unpublished PhD thesis. Paris: École Pratique des Hautes Études.

Pillitteri, A., 2010. *Maternal and Child Health Nursing: Care of the Childbearing Family,* 6th edn. Philadelphia: Wolters Kluwer Linnincott Williams and Wilkins.

Pietrogrande, A.L., 1976. *Le Fulloniche.* Rome: Istituto Poligrafico dello Stato.

Pighi, I.B., 1967. *De Ludis Saecularibus: Populi Romani Quiritium.* Chicago: Argonaut.

Plate, B.S., 2014. *A History of Religion in 5 1/2 Objects: Bringing the Spiritual to its Senses.* Boston: Beacon Press.

Platt, V., 2006. Making an impression: replication and the ontology of the Graeco-Roman seal stone. *Art History* 29(2), pp. 233–57.

Polt, C.B., 2013. Untitled review of Harrison and Liapis, eds, *Performance in Greek and Roman Theatre. Bryn Mawr Classical Review,* 27 November 2013 [Online]. Available at http://bmcr.brynmawr.edu/2013/2013–11–27.html (Accessed 30 September 2015).

Porteous, J.D., 1990. *Landscapes of the Mind: Worlds of Sense and Metaphor.* Toronto: University of Toronto Press.

Porteous, J.D., 2006. Smellscape. In: J. Drobnick, ed. *The Smell Culture Reader.* Oxford: Berg. pp. 89–106.

Porter, J., ed, 1999. *Constructions of the Classical Body.* Ann Arbor, MI: University of Michigan Press.

Potter, D., 2006. Spectacle. In: D. Potter, ed. *A Companion to the Roman Empire.* Malden, MA and Oxford: Blackwell. pp. 385–408.

Potter, D., 2014. The social life of the senses: feasts and funerals. In: J. Toner, ed. *A Cultural History of the Senses in Antiquity.* London: Bloomsbury. pp. 23–44.

Poulsen, B., 2008. Glass. In: K. Slej and M. Culhead, eds. *The Temple of Castor and Pollux II.2★: The Finds and Trenches.* Roma: "L'Erma" di Bretschneider. pp. 253–99.

Prescendi, F., 2008. Le deuil à Rome: mise en scène d'une émotion. *Revue de l'histoire des religions* 225, pp. 297–313.

Ramage, E.S., 1983. Urban problems in ancient Rome. In: R.T. Marchese, ed. *Aspects of Graeco–Roman Urbanism: British Archaeological Reports International Series* 188. Oxford: Archaeopress.

Rapp, G., 2009. *Archaeomineralogy.* Berlin: Springer, Natural Science in Archaeology.

Rasmussen, S.W., 2003. *Public Portents in Republican Rome.* Rome: L'Erma di Bretschneider.

Recke, M., 2013. Science as art: Etruscan anatomical votives. In: J.M. Turfa, ed. *The Etruscan World.* London and New York: Routledge. pp. 1068–85.

Reinarz, J., 2014. *Past Scents: Historical Perspectives on Smell.* DeKalb, IL: University of Illinois Press.

Richlin, A., 2001. Emotional work: lamenting the Roman dead. In: E. Tylawsky and C. Weiss, eds. *Essays in Honor of Gordon Williams: Twenty-Five Years at Yale.* New Haven: Henry R. Schwab. pp. 229–48.

Richter, G.M.A., 1956. *Catalogue of Engraved Gems: Greek, Etruscan, and Roman: The Metropolitan Museum of Art. New York.* Rome: L'Erma di Bretschneider.

Richter, G.M.A., 1971. *Engraved Gems of the Romans.* London: Phaidon.

Riggsby, A., 2003. Pliny in space (and time). *Arethusa* 36(2), pp. 167–86.

Rivet, L., Brentchaloff, D., Roucole, S. and Saulnier, S., 2000. *Atlas topographique des ville de Gaule méridionale. 2. Fréjus. RAN Supplement* 32. Montpellier: Éditions de l'Association de la Revue Archéologique de Narbonnaise.

Robb, J. and Harris, O.J.T., 2013. *The Body in History: Europe from the Palaeolithic to the Future.* Cambridge: Cambridge University Press.

Roberts, M., 1989. *The Jeweled Style: Poetry and Poetics in Late Antiquity.* Ithaca: Cornell University Press.

Robertson, R.H.S., 1986. *Fuller's Earth: A History of Calcium Montmorillonite.* Hythe: Volturna Press.

Rodaway, P., 1994. *Sensuous Geographies: Body, Sense, and Place.* London: Routledge.

Rodríguez Almeida, E., 1985–6. Note di topografia romana: *cosmos myropola,* il *Vicus Unguentarius* e i *"penetralia Pallados nostrae"* (Mart., IV, 53). *Rivista dell'Istituto Nazionale d'Archeologia e Storia dell'Arte* 8–9, pp. 111–17.

Rose, P., 2005. Spectators and spectator comfort in Roman entertainment buildings: a study in functional design. *Papers of the British School at Rome* 73, pp. 99–130.

Rüpke, J., 2007. *Religion of the Romans.* Cambridge: Polity Press.

Saunders, N., 1999. Biographies of brilliance: transformations of matter and being c. AD 1492. *World Archaeology* 31(2), pp. 243–57.

Savay-Guerraz, H. and Sas, K., 2002. Les couleurs du cirque. In: K. Sas and H. Thoen, eds. *Brillance et Prestige: la joaillerie romaine en Europe occidentale.* Leuven: Uitgeverij Peeters. pp. 66–70.

Scarantino, A., 2010. Insights and blindspots of the cognitivist theory of emotions. *The British Journal for the Philosophy of Science* 61(4), pp. 729–68.

Schafer, R., 1977. *The Tuning of the World.* Toronto: McClelland and Stewart.

Scheid, J., 1995. *Graeco Ritu:* a typically Roman way of honoring the gods. *Harvard Studies in Classical Philology* 97, pp. 15–31.

Scheid, J., 2003. *An Introduction to Roman Religion.* Bloomington, IN: Indiana University Press.

Scheid, J., 2007. Sacrifices for gods and ancestors. In: J. Rüpke, ed. *A Companion to Roman Religion.* Oxford: Blackwell. pp. 263–71.

Scheid, J., 2012. Roman animal sacrifice and the system of being. In: C.A. Faraone and F.S. Naiden, eds. *Greek and Roman Animal Sacrifice.* Cambridge: Cambridge University Press. pp. 84–95.

Scheidel, W., 2003. Germs for Rome. In: C. Edwards and G. Woolf, eds. *Rome the Cosmopolis.* Cambridge: Cambridge University Press. pp. 158–76.

Schmidt, W., 1899. *Herons von Alexandria: Druckwerke und Automatentheater,* Leipzig: B.G. Teubner.

Schultz, C.E. and Harvey, P.B., 2006. *Religion in Republican Italy.* Cambridge: Cambridge University Press.

Scobie, A., 1986. Slums, sanitation and mortality in ancient Rome. *Klio* 68(2), pp. 399–433.

Sear, F., 2006. *Roman Theatres: An Architectural Study*. Oxford: Oxford University Press.

Sebesta, J., 2005. The *toga praetexta* of Roman children and praetextate garments. In: L. Cleland, M. Harlow and L. Llewellyn-Jones, eds. *The Clothed Body in the Ancient World*. Oxford: Oxbow Books. pp. 113–19.

Shaw, B., 1996. Seasons of death: aspects of mortality in Imperial Rome. *Journal of Roman Studies* 86, pp. 100–38.

Siegel, R.E., 1970. *Galen on Sense Perception: His Doctrines, Observations and Experiments on Vision, Hearing, Smell, Taste, Touch and Pain, and their Historical Sources*. Basel and New York: Karger.

Sim, D. and Ridge, I., 2002. *Iron for the Eagles: The Iron Industry of Roman Britain*. Stroud: Tempus.

Simon, I., 2008. Un aspect des largesses impériales: les sparsiones de missilia à Rome (Ier siècle avant J.-C. – IIIe siècle aprés J.-C.). *Revue Historique* 648, pp. 763–88.

Skeates, R., 2010. *An Archaeology of the Senses: Prehistoric Malta*. Oxford: Oxford University Press.

Slaney, H., 2013. Seneca's chorus of one. In: F. Budelmann, F. Macintosh and J. Billings, eds. *Choruses: Ancient and Modern*. Oxford: Oxford University Press. pp. 99–116.

Slaney, H., forthcoming. Repetition makes it tragic: emotion in ancient pantomime. In: A. Chaniotis, ed. *Unveiling Emotions IV*. Stuttgart: Steiner Verlag.

Slater, W.J., 1994. Pantomime riots. *Classical Antiquity* 13(1), pp. 120–44.

Smith, B.R., 1999. *The Acoustic World of Early Modern London*. Chicago: University of Chicago Press.

Smith, B.R., 2003. Tuning into London c. 1660. In: M. Bull and L. Back, eds. *The Auditory Culture Reader*. Oxford: Berg. pp. 127–35.

Smith, M.M., 2007. *Sensory History*. Oxford: Berg.

Soranus *Gynaecology*, 1956. Trans. O. Temkin. Baltimore: Johns Hopkins University Press.

Spangenberg, J.E., 2009. Identification of the lipids from the sediments filling the Roman bronze seal boxes in Augusta Raurica, Switzerland. In: A.R. Furger, A.R.M. Wartmann and E. Riha, eds. *Die römischen Siegelkapseln aus Augusta Raurica. Forschungen in Augst Band* 44. Augst: Augusta Raurica. pp. 139–43.

Spaulding, S., 2013. Mirror neurons and social cognition. *Mind and Language* 28(2), pp. 233–57.

Spencer, D., 2010. *Roman Landscape: Culture and Identity. Greece and Rome: New Surveys in the Classics* 39. Cambridge: Cambridge University Press.

Steane, J., 1993. *The Archaeology of the Medieval English Monarchy*. London: Routledge.

Stein, R., 2004. Roman wooden force pumps: a case-study in innovation. *Journal of Roman Archaeology* 17(1), pp. 221–50.

Šterbenc Erker, D., 2011. Gender and Roman funeral ritual. In: V.M. Hope and J. Huskinson, eds. *Memory and Mourning: Studies on Roman Death*. Oxford: Oxbow Books. pp. 40–60.

Stewart, S., 2005. Remembering the senses. In: D. Howes, ed. *Empire of the Senses: The Sensual Culture Reader*. Oxford: Berg. pp. 59–69.

Stillwell, R., 1952. *The Theatre: Corinth*. Vol. 2. Princeton, NJ: American School of Classical Studies at Athens.

Stocking, C.H., 2009. *Bones, Smoke, and Lies: Hellenizing Burnt Sacrifice*. Unpublished PhD thesis. Los Angeles: University of California.

Stoller, P., 1984. Sound in Songhay cultural experience. *American Ethnologist* 11(3), pp. 559–70.

Storey, G., 2003. The 'Skyscrapers' of the ancient Roman world. *Latomus* 62, pp. 3–26.

Sutton, D., 2001. *Remembrance of Repasts: An Anthropology of Food and Memory*. Oxford: Berg.

Synnott, A., 1993. *The Body Social: Symbolism, Self and Society*. London: Routledge.

Thomas, E.V., 2007. *Monumentality and the Roman Empire*. Oxford: Oxford University Press.

Thomas, J., 1996. *Time, Culture and Identity: An Interpretative Archaeology*. London: Routledge.

Thomas, J., 2006. Phenomenology and material culture. In: C. Tilley, W. Keane, S. Küchler, M. Rowlands and P. Spyer, eds. *Handbook of Material Culture*. London: Sage Publications. pp. 43–59.

Thompson, M., 1895. On a Latin deed of sale of a slave; 24th May, AD 166. *Archaeologia* 54, pp. 433–8.

Thuillier, J.-P., 1999. Agitator ou sparsor? A propos d'une célèbre statue de Carthage. *Comptes Rendus des Séances de l'Académie des Inscriptions et Belles-Lettres* 143(4), pp. 1081–106.

Till, R., 2015. *Acoustics and Music of British Prehistory Research Network* [Online]. Available at https://ambpnetwork.wordpress.com/methodologies/ (Accessed 15 February 2015).

Tilley, C., 1994. *The Phenomenology of Landscape: Places, Paths and Monuments*. Oxford: Berg.

Tilley, C., 2010. *Interpreting Landscapes: Geologies, Topographies, Identities. Explorations in Landscape Phenomenology 3*. Walnut Creek, CA: Left Coast Press.

Toner, J., ed, 2014a. *A Cultural History of the Senses in Antiquity*. London: Bloomsbury.

Toner, J., 2014b. Introduction: sensing the ancient past. In: J. Toner, ed. *A Cultural History of the Senses in Antiquity*. London: Bloomsbury. pp. 1–21.

Tonkiss, F., 2003. Aural postcards: sound, memory and the city. In: M. Bull and L. Back, eds. *The Auditory Culture Reader*. Oxford: Berg. pp. 303–9.

Torigoe, K., 2002. A city traced by soundscape. In: H. Järviluoma and G. Wagstaff, eds. *Soundscape Studies and Methods*. Helsinki: the University of Turku, Vaasa. pp. 39–57.

Toynbee, J., 1971. *Death and Burial in the Roman World*. London: Thames and Hudson.

Tringham, R., 2013. A sense of touch – the full-body experience – in the past and present of Çatalhöyük. In: J. Day, ed. *Making Senses of the Past: Toward a Sensory Archaeology*. Center for Archaeological Investigations, Occasional Paper No. 40. Carbondale, IL: Southern Illinois University Press. pp. 177–95.

Tschumi, B., 1996. *Architecture and Disjunction*. Cambridge, MA: The MIT Press.

Tuck, S., 2008–09. Scheduling spectacle: factors contributing to the dates of Pompeian 'munera'. *The Classical Journal* 104(2), pp. 123–43.

Turfa, J.M., 2006. Votive offerings in Etruscan religion. In: N.T. de Grummond and E. Simon, eds. *Religion of the Etruscans*. Austin: University of Texas Press. pp. 90–115.

Turocy, C., 2013. La cosmografia del minor mundo: recovering dance theory to create today's Baroque practice. In: M. Bales and K. Eliot, eds. *Dance on Its Own Terms: Histories and Methodologies*. Oxford: Oxford University Press. pp. 157–74.

Ulrich, R., 2007. *Roman Woodworking*. New Haven: Yale University Press.

Vagnetti, L., 1971. *Il Deposito Votivo di Campetti a Veio (Material Degli Scavi 1937–1938)*. Florence: Sansori Editore.

Van Driel-Murray, C., 1993. The leatherwork. In: A. Iserles, ed. *Vindolanda: Research Reports, New Series Volume III, the Early Wooden Forts*. Bardon Mill: The Vindolanda Trust. pp. 1–75.

Van Driel-Murray, C., 2001. Vindolanda and the dating of Roman footwear. *Britannia* 32, pp. 185–97.

Van Dyke, R.M., 2013. Imagined narratives: sensory lives in the Chacoan southwest. In: J. Day, ed. *Making Senses of the Past: Toward a Sensory Archaeology*. Center for Archaeological Investigations, Occasional Paper No. 40. Carbondale, IL: Southern Illinois University Press. pp. 390–408.

Van Straten, F.T., 1981. Gifts for the gods. In: H.S. Versnel, ed. *Faith Hope and Worship: Aspects of Religious Mentality in the Ancient World*. Leiden, Brill. pp. 65–151.

Vendries, C., 1999. *Instruments à cordes et musiciens dans l'empire romain. Étude historique et archéologique (IIe s. av. J.-C. / Ve s. ap. J.-C.)*. Paris: L'Harmattan.

Vendries, C., 2007. La trompe de Neuvy. Anatomie d'un objet sonore. In: C. Gorget, ed. *Le Cheval et la Danseuse. À la redécouverte du trésor de Neuvy-en-Sullias*. Orléans: Somogy éditions d'Art. pp. 120–44.

Vernant, J.-P., 1989. At man's table: Hesiod's foundation myth of sacrifice. In: M. Detienne and J.-P. Vernant, eds. *The Cuisine of Sacrifice among the Greeks*. Chicago: University of Chicago Press. pp. 21–86.

Veyne, P., 2000. Inviter les dieux, sacrifier, banqueter. Quelques nuances de la religiosité gréco–romaine. *Annales. Économie, sociétés, civilisations* 55, pp. 3–42.

Vincent, A., 2015a. Paysage sonore et sciences sociales: sonorités, sens, histoire. In: S. Emerit, S. Perrot and A. Vincent, eds. *Le paysage sonore de l'Antiquité. Méthodologie, historiographie et perspectives*. Le Caire: Institut Français d'archéologie Orientale. pp. 9–40.

Vincent, A., 2015b. Les silences de Sénèque. *Pallas. Revue d'Études Antiques* 98, pp. 131–43 [Online]. Available at https://pallas.revues.org/2709.

Vincent, A., 2016. *Jouer pour la Cité. Une étude sociale et politique des musiciens professionnels de l'Occident romain*. Rome: École Française de Rome.

Vinge, L., 1975. *The Five Senses: Studies in a Literary Tradition*. Lund: LiberLäromedel.

Vout, C., 2007. Sizing up Rome: or theorizing the overview. In: D.H. J. Larmour and D. Spencer, eds. *The Sites of Rome*. Oxford: Oxford University Press. pp. 295–322.

Wallace-Hadrill, A., 2008. *Rome's Cultural Revolution*. Cambridge: Cambridge University Press.

Wallace-Hadrill, A., 2014. The senses in the marketplace: the luxury market and eastern trade in Imperial Rome. In: J. Toner, ed. *A Cultural History of the Senses in Antiquity*. London: Bloomsbury. pp. 69–89.

Walter, B., 2013. Reading death and the senses in Lucan and Lucretius. In: S. Butler and A. Purves, eds. *Synaesthesia and the Ancient Senses*. Durham: Acumen. pp. 115–25.

Waskul, D., Vannini, P. and Wilson, J., 2009. The aroma of recollection: olfaction, nostalgia and the shaping of the sensuous self. *Senses and Society* 4(1), pp. 5–22.

Webb, R., 2008a. *Demons and Dancers: Performance in Late Antiquity*. Cambridge, MA: Harvard.

Webb, R., 2008b. Inside the mask: pantomime from the performer's perspective. In: E. Hall and R. Wyles, eds. *New Directions in Ancient Pantomime*. Oxford: Oxford University Press. pp. 43–60.

Weddle, C., 2011. *Making Sense of Sacrifice: Sensory Experience in Greco–Roman Cult*. Unpublished PhD thesis. University of Southern California.

Weddle, C., 2013. The sensory experience of blood sacrifice in the Roman imperial cult. In: J. Day, ed. *Making Senses of the Past: Toward a Sensory Archaeology*. Center for Archaeological Investigations, Occasional Paper No. 40. Carbondale, IL: Southern Illinois University Press. pp. 137–59.

Welch, K., 2007. *The Roman Amphitheatre: From Its Origins to the Colosseum*. Cambridge: Cambridge University Press.

Wells, P.S., 2008. *Image and Response in Early Europe*. London: Duckworth.

Whitehouse, R.D., 2001. A tale of two caves: the archaeology of religious experience in Mediterranean Europe. In: P.F. Biehl, F. Bertemes and H. Mellar, eds. *The Archaeology of Cult and Religion*. Budapest: Archaeolingua Alapítvány. pp. 161–7.

Whitmarsh, T., 2005. *The Second Sophistic*. Oxford: Oxford University Press for the Classical Association.

Wiedemann, T., 1992. *Emperors and Gladiators*. London: Routledge.

Williams, H., 2004. Death warmed up: The agency of bodies and bones in early Anglo-Saxon cremation rites. *Journal of Material Culture* 9(3), pp. 263–91.

Wilson, A., 2000. Timgad and textile production. In: D.J. Mattingly and J. Salmon, eds. *Economies beyond Agriculture in the Classical World.* London: Routledge. pp. 271–96.

Wilson, A., 2008. Machines in Greek and Roman technology. In: J.-P. Oleson, ed. *The Oxford Handbook of Engineering and Technology in the Classical World.* Oxford: Oxford University Press. pp. 337–66.

Wilson, P., 2011. Roman Britain in 2010: Vindolanda. *Britannia* 42, pp. 341–3.

Wiseman, T.P., 2014. Popular memory. In: K. Galinsky, ed. *Memoria Romana: Memory in Rome and Rome in Memory. Memoirs of the American Academy in Rome, Supplement* 10. Ann Arbor, MI: University of Michigan Press. pp. 43–62.

Wyles, R., 2008. The symbolism of costume in ancient pantomime. In: E. Hall and R. Wyles, eds. *New Directions in Ancient Pantomime.* Oxford: Oxford University Press. pp. 61–86.

Yegül, F., 2010. *Bathing in the Roman World.* Cambridge: Cambridge University Press.

Yerkes, R.K., 1952. *Sacrifice in Greek and Roman Religions and Early Judaism.* London: Adam and Charles Black.

Young, G.K., 2001. *Rome's Eastern Trade: International Commerce and Imperial Policy, 31 BC–AD 305.* London: Routledge.

Zanker, P., 1988. *The Power of Images in the Age of Augustus.* Ann Arbor, MI: University of Michigan Press.

Zanker, P. and Ewald, B.C., 2012 [2004]. *Living with Myths: The Imagery of Roman Sarcophagi.* Trans. J. Slater. Oxford: Oxford University Press.

Zanobi, A., 2008. The influence of pantomime on Seneca's tragedies. In: E. Hall and R. Wyles, eds. *New Directions in Ancient Pantomime.* Oxford: Oxford University Press. pp. 227–57.

Zardini, M., 2005. Toward a sensorial urbanism. In: M. Zardini, ed. *Sense of the City: An Alternate Approach to Urbanism.* Montréal: Canadian Centre for Architecture and Lars Müller Publishers. pp. 17–27.

Zerouali, B., 2015. "Paysages sonores" au croisement de l'ethnomusicologie et de l'histoire. In: S. Emerit, S. Perrot and A. Vincent, eds. *Le paysage sonore de l'antiquité. Méthodologie, historiographie et perspectives.* Le Caire: Institut Français d'Archéologie Orientale. pp. 41–62.

Zimmermann, B., 2008. Seneca and pantomime. In: E. Hall and R. Wyles, eds. *New Directions in Ancient Pantomime.* Oxford: Oxford University Press. pp. 218–26.

Ziolkowski, A., 1999. Pantheon. In: M. Steinby, ed. *Lexicon Topographicum Urbis Romae IV (P–S).* Rome: Edizioni Quasar. pp. 54–61.

Index

Page numbers in *italics* refer to figures, tables and colour plates.

For Product Safety Concerns and Information please contact our EU representative GPSR@taylorandfrancis.com Taylor & Francis Verlag GmbH, Kaufingerstraße 24, 80331 München, Germany

Printed and bound by CPI Group (UK) Ltd, Croydon, CR0 4YY

02/05/2025

01859320-0001